Hands-On Neural Networks

Learn how to build and train your first neural network model using Python

Leonardo De Marchi
Laura Mitchell

Packt>

BIRMINGHAM - MUMBAI

Hands-On Neural Networks

Copyright © 2019 Packt Publishing

All rights reserved. No part of this book may be reproduced, stored in a retrieval system, or transmitted in any form or by any means, without the prior written permission of the publisher, except in the case of brief quotations embedded in critical articles or reviews.

Every effort has been made in the preparation of this book to ensure the accuracy of the information presented. However, the information contained in this book is sold without warranty, either express or implied. Neither the authors, nor Packt Publishing or its dealers and distributors, will be held liable for any damages caused or alleged to have been caused directly or indirectly by this book.

Packt Publishing has endeavored to provide trademark information about all of the companies and products mentioned in this book by the appropriate use of capitals. However, Packt Publishing cannot guarantee the accuracy of this information.

Commissioning Editor: Sunith Shetty
Acquisition Editor: Devika Battike
Content Development Editor: Manorama Haridas
Technical Editor: Vibhuti Gawde
Copy Editor: Safis Editing
Project Coordinator: Kirti Pisat
Proofreader: Safis Editing
Indexer: Rekha Nair
Graphics: Jisha Chirayil
Production Coordinator: Nilesh Mohite

First published: May 2019

Production reference: 1290519

Published by Packt Publishing Ltd.

Livery Place
35 Livery Street
Birmingham
B3 2PB, UK.

ISBN 978-1-78899-259-6

www.packtpub.com

I would like to dedicate this book to my family, in particular my sister Linda, my grandmother Elda, my uncle Marco and my mum Cristina. A big thank you also to my father, my other uncles and my other grandparents. A special thank you to my wonderful wife Marina and our baby, that she is expecting. Mandi!

--Leonardo De Marchi

I would like to thank all of my friends and family who have supported me throughout my career and the writing of this book. A special thanks to mum, dad, brother Stu, and best friend of 20 years, Gem. They have not tired of listening to my repeatedly saying how excited I am about becoming a published author, something I am very proud of. Kudos to all at Packt Publishing for making this possible!

I am especially grateful to Leo who has fully supported my learning, development and career aspirations. Leo has been a true joy to work for and I am very grateful to him for everything. Last but not least I would like to thank Badoo for all of the opportunities presented to me and for facilitating an environment that has enabled me to flourish as a data scientist; something I will be ever appreciative of.

I would like to dedicate this book to my grandad; a talented engineer and passionate scientist with a curious mind who continued his university studies into his nineties!

--Laura Mitchell

Mapt

mapt.io

Mapt is an online digital library that gives you full access to over 5,000 books and videos, as well as industry leading tools to help you plan your personal development and advance your career. For more information, please visit our website.

Why subscribe?

- Spend less time learning and more time coding with practical eBooks and Videos from over 4,000 industry professionals

- Improve your learning with Skill Plans built especially for you

- Get a free eBook or video every month

- Mapt is fully searchable

- Copy and paste, print, and bookmark content

Packt.com

Did you know that Packt offers eBook versions of every book published, with PDF and ePub files available? You can upgrade to the eBook version at www.packt.com and as a print book customer, you are entitled to a discount on the eBook copy. Get in touch with us at customercare@packtpub.com for more details.

At www.packt.com, you can also read a collection of free technical articles, sign up for a range of free newsletters, and receive exclusive discounts and offers on Packt books and eBooks.

Contributors

About the authors

Leonardo De Marchi is an international speaker, author and consultant. He holds a masters in **Artificial Intelligence** (**AI**) and has worked as a data scientist in the sporting world, with clients such as New York Knicks, Manchester United. He now works as a head of data scientist at Badoo, the largest dating site with over 400 million users. He is also the lead instructor at ideai.io, a company specialized in Machine Learning trainings. With Ideai he provides technical and managerial training to large institutions and dynamic startups. He is also a contractor for the European Commission.

> *First of all, I would like to thank my publisher, Packt, and in particular Devika and Manorama. I would like to thank Badoo, my friends and co-workers for encouraging me, in particular Ed, Candice and my boss Tema. A massive thanks to Laura for agreeing to write this book together and for the amazing path we shared in Badoo. A special thanks to Marina Mattos, for the great images she created for this book.*

Laura Mitchell graduated with a degree in mathematics from the University of Edinburgh and, since then, has gained over 12 years' experience in the tech and data science space. She is currently lead data scientist at Badoo, which is the largest online dating site in the world with over 400 million users worldwide. Laura has hands-on experience in the delivery of projects such as NLP, image classification, and recommender systems, from initial conception through to production. She has a passion for learning new technologies and keeping up to date with industry trends.

About the reviewers

Alan Souza holds a degree in computer engineering from Instituto de Estudos Superiores da Amazônia (IESAM), along with a postgraduate qualification in project management software and a master's degree in industrial processes (applied computing) from Universidade Federal do Pará (UFPA). He has worked with neural networks since 2009, and has already written three books about them. Alan is passionate about programming and applying machine learning techniques to real-world problems. Currently, he is the coordinator of a computer science graduation course, a professor at Universidade da Amazônia (UNAMA), and a PhD candidate at UFPA.

> *I'd like to thank my family members for supporting me throughout my projects. I would also like to thank Packt for inviting me to review this book, which is a significant contribution to the machine learning community. I wish all the readers of this book every success in their individual projects.*

Erhard Dinhobl holds a degree from the Wiener Neustadt higher technical education institute, Austria, as well as two degrees from the Vienna University of Technology. He is self employed and is CEO of a software development company focused on AI, data analysis, and blockchain technologies. He has undertaken projects for telecommunication providers, banks, start-ups, and media companies. Currently, he is working on his PhD thesis about AI applied to graphs in a theoretical and practical way.

Packt is searching for authors like you

If you're interested in becoming an author for Packt, please visit `authors.packtpub.com` and apply today. We have worked with thousands of developers and tech professionals, just like you, to help them share their insight with the global tech community. You can make a general application, apply for a specific hot topic that we are recruiting an author for, or submit your own idea.

Table of Contents

Preface 1

Section 1: Getting Started

Chapter 1: Getting Started with Supervised Learning 9
  History of AI 10
  An overview of machine learning 11
    Supervised learning 12
    Unsupervised learning 12
    Semi-supervised learning 13
    Reinforcement learning 13
  Environment setup 13
    Understanding virtual environments 15
    Anaconda 16
    Docker 17
  Supervised learning in practice with Python 18
    Data cleaning 19
  Feature engineering 20
    How deep learning performs feature engineering 22
      Feature scaling 22
      Feature engineering in Keras 23
  Supervised learning algorithms 24
    Metrics 26
      Regression metrics 26
      Classification metrics 26
    Evaluating the model 27
      TensorBoard 29
  Summary 31

Chapter 2: Neural Network Fundamentals 33
  The perceptron 33
    Implementing a perceptron 35
  Keras 41
    Implementing perceptron in Keras 42
  Feedforward neural networks 44
    Introducing backpropagation 46
    Activation functions 49
      Sigmoid 50
        Softmax 50
        Tanh 50
    ReLU 51

Table of Contents

Keras implementation	52
The chain rule	53
The XOR problem	55
FFNN in Python from scratch	57
FFNN Keras implementation	61
TensorBoard	62
TensorBoard on the XOR problem	63
Summary	66

Section 2: Deep Learning Applications

Chapter 3: Convolutional Neural Networks for Image Processing	69
Understanding CNNs	69
Input data	70
Convolutional layers	71
Pooling layers	75
Stride	75
Max pooling	75
Zero padding	76
Dropout layers	77
Normalization layers	77
Output layers	78
CNNs in Keras	79
Loading the data	79
Creating the model	80
Network configuration	81
Keras for expression recognition	84
Optimizing the network	90
Summary	92
Chapter 4: Exploiting Text Embedding	93
Machine learning for NLP	94
Rule-based methods	94
Understanding word embeddings	95
Applications of words embeddings	96
Word2vec	96
Word embedding in Keras	99
Pre-trained network	104
GloVe	104
Global matrix factorization	104
Using the GloVe model	107
Text classification with GloVe	111
Summary	112
Chapter 5: Working with RNNs	113
Understanding RNNs	114
Theory behind CNNs	116

[ii]

Types of RNNs	117
One-to-one	119
One-to-many	119
Many-to-many	119
The same lag	120
A different lag	120
Loss functions	120
Long Short-Term Memory	**121**
LSTM architecture	122
LSTMs in Keras	**125**
PyTorch basics	129
Time series prediction	130
Summary	**134**
Chapter 6: Reusing Neural Networks with Transfer Learning	**135**
Transfer learning theory	**135**
Introducing multi-task learning	136
Reusing other networks as feature extractors	137
Implementing MTL	**137**
Feature extraction	**139**
Implementing TL in PyTorch	**139**
Summary	**146**

Section 3: Advanced Applications

Chapter 7: Working with Generative Algorithms	**149**
Discriminative versus generative algorithms	**150**
Understanding GANs	**151**
Training GANs	154
GAN challenges	155
GAN variations and timelines	**157**
Conditional GANs	158
DCGAN	158
ReLU versus Leaky ReLU	160
DCGAN – a coded example	161
Pix2Pix GAN	166
StackGAN	167
CycleGAN	168
ProGAN	170
StarGAN	172
StarGAN discriminator objectives	173
StarGAN generator functions	174
BigGAN	**174**
StyleGAN	**175**
Style modules	177
StyleGAN implementation	179
Deepfakes	**180**

Table of Contents

RadialGAN	181
Summary	183
Further reading	183
Chapter 8: Implementing Autoencoders	**185**
Overview of autoencoders	185
Autoencoder applications	186
Bottleneck and loss functions	186
Standard types of autoencoder	187
Undercomplete autoencoders	187
Example	187
Visualizing with TensorBoard	189
Visualizing reconstructed images	190
Multilayer autoencoders	191
Example	191
Convolutional autoencoders	192
Example	192
Sparse autoencoders	195
Example	196
Denoising autoencoders	197
Example	197
Contractive autoencoder	198
Variational Autoencoders	198
Training VAEs	201
Example	203
Summary	207
Further reading	207
Chapter 9: Deep Belief Networks	**209**
Overview of DBNs	209
BBNs	210
Predictive propagation	211
Retrospective propagation	211
RBMs	212
RBM training	214
Example – RBM recommender system	215
Example – RBM recommender system using code	216
DBN architecture	221
Training DBNs	222
Fine-tuning	224
Datasets and libraries	225
Example – supervised DBN classification	226
Example – supervised DBN regression	227
Example – unsupervised DBN classification	228
Summary	229
Further reading	229

Chapter 10: Reinforcement Learning — 231
Basic definitions — 231
Introducing Q-learning — 234
Learning objectives — 235
Policy optimization — 236
Methods of Q-learning — 236
Playing with OpenAI Gym — 237
The frozen lake problem — 239
Summary — 248

Chapter 11: Whats Next? — 249
Summarizing the book — 249
Future of machine learning — 250
Artificial general intelligence — 252
Ethics in AI — 253
Interpretability — 253
Automation — 253
AI safety — 254
AI ethics — 255
Accountability — 255
Conclusions — 255

Other Books You May Enjoy — 257
Index — 261

Preface

Neural Networks (**NNs**) play a very important role in deep learning and **Artificial Intelligence** (**AI**), with applications in a wide variety of domains, from medical diagnosis to financial forecasting, and even machine diagnostics.

Hands-On Neural Networks is designed to guide you through learning about neural networks in a practical way. The book will get you started by giving you a brief introduction to perceptron networks. You will then gain insights into machine learning and also understand what the future of AI could look like. Next, you will study how embeddings can be used to process textual data, and the role of **long short-term memory** (**LSTMs**) networks in helping you to solve common **natural language processing** (**NLP**) problems. The later chapters will demonstrate how you can implement advanced concepts, including transfer learning, **Generative Adversarial Networks** (**GANs**), **autoencoders** (**AEs**), and **reinforcement learning** (**RL**). Finally, you can look forward to further content on the latest advancements in the field of neural networks.

By the end of this book, you will have the skills you need to build, train, and optimize your own neural network model that can be used to provide predictable solutions.

Who this book is for

If you are interested in AI and deep learning and want to further your skills, then this intermediate-level book is for you. Some knowledge of statistics will help you get the most out of this book.

What this book covers

Chapter 1, *Getting Started with Supervised Learning*, covers the big picture of AI and, in particular, deep learning. This chapter introduces the main machine learning concepts, from transforming data to evaluating results. These concepts will be useful in the following chapters, where we will focus only on deep learning applications.

Chapter 2, *Neural Network Fundamentals*, introduces the building blocks of deep learning and the math behind them. We will also explore concepts such as the perceptron and gradient descent, and the math behind them. We will then see how it's possible to use them to build neural networks with an example, to solve a classification task.

Preface

Chapter 3, *Convolutional Neural Networks for Image Processing*, covers more complex network architectures for solving domain-specific problems. In particular, we will look at some techniques for solving some computer vision problems. We will also see how a pre-trained network can reduce the time needed to create and train a neural network.

Chapter 4, *Exploiting Text Embedding*, shows how deep learning can be used for NLP tasks; in particular, how we can use embeddings to process textual data, the theory behind them, and some practical use cases.

Chapter 5, *Working with RNNs*, introduces a more sophisticated type of network, RNNs, and the math and the concepts behind them. In particular, we will focus on LSTM and how it can be used to solve an NLP problem.

Chapter 6, *Reusing Neural Networks with Transfer Learning*, introduces transfer learning, which is the ability of a model to generalize its learning to different tasks than the one it was trained to solve. We will also look at a concrete example of transfer learning using a pre-trained network to solve our particular problem using Keras and the famous VGG network.

Chapter 7, *Working with Generative Algorithms*, introduces one of the most innovative concepts in machine learning in the past decade: GANs. We will see how they work and the math behind them. We will also present an example of how to implement a GAN to generate simple handwritten digits.

Chapter 8, *Implementing Autoencoders*, talks about autoencoders, what they are, the math behind them, and which tasks they can solve. In particular, we will look at improvements to the simple autoencoders algorithm and how it's possible to use autoencoders to generate simple handwritten digits with Keras.

Chapter 9, *Deep Belief Networks*, talks about Deep Belief Networks (DBNs), what they are, the math behind them, and which tasks they can solve.

Chapter 10, *Reinforcement Learning*, introduces RL, starting from the basic concepts, such as the Monte Carlo and Markov chain methods. We will then explain traditional RL methods and how deep learning has improved and revitalized the field.

Chapter 11, *What's Next?*, introduces a quick summary of all the topics that we have covered in the book. We will also provide readers with the details of other titles that could be used as reference materials. Lastly, we will also include the latest advancements that readers can look at in the field of neural networks.

To get the most out of this book

Some knowledge of statistics will help you get the most out of this book.

Download the example code files

You can download the example code files for this book from your account at www.packt.com. If you purchased this book elsewhere, you can visit www.packt.com/support and register to have the files emailed directly to you.

You can download the code files by following these steps:

1. Log in or register at www.packt.com.
2. Select the **SUPPORT** tab.
3. Click on **Code Downloads & Errata**.
4. Enter the name of the book in the **Search** box and follow the onscreen instructions.

Once the file is downloaded, please make sure that you unzip or extract the folder using the latest version of:

- WinRAR/7-Zip for Windows
- Zipeg/iZip/UnRarX for Mac
- 7-Zip/PeaZip for Linux

The code bundle for the book is also hosted on GitHub at https://github.com/PacktPublishing/Hands-On-Neural-Networks. In case there's an update to the code, it will be updated on the existing GitHub repository.

We also have other code bundles from our rich catalog of books and videos available at https://github.com/PacktPublishing/. Check them out!

Download the color images

We also provide a PDF file that has color images of the screenshots/diagrams used in this book. You can download it here: http://www.packtpub.com/sites/default/files/downloads/9781788992596_ColorImages.pdf.

Getting Started with Supervised Learning

Artificial Intelligence (**AI**) is now a buzzword that is added to products and services to make them more appealing, and more often than not, it's a marketing strategy rather than a technical achievement. Most of the time, AI is used as an umbrella term to describe anything from simple analytics to advanced learning algorithms. It's something that sells, as most of the population does not have much knowledge about it, but intuitively everyone now understands that it is something that will change the world we live in.

Luckily, it's not just hype, and we have seen many astonishing achievements made by AI, such as Tesla's self-driving cars. Using recent research into deep neural networks, Tesla managed to create a functionality and made it available to the masses much quicker than most of the experts predicted.

In this book, we will try to steer away from the hype and focus on the actual value that AI can provide, starting from the basics in order to rapidly ramp up to the most recent algorithms.

This chapter will cover the following topics in detail:

- History of AI
- An overview of machine learning
- Environment setup
- Supervised learning in practice with Python
- Feature engineering
- Supervised learning algorithms

History of AI

The idea of AI, entailing machine that can think without human help, is surprisingly old. It can be dated back to the Indian philosophies of Charvaka, from around 1,500 BC.

The basis of AI is the philosophical concept that human reasoning can be mapped into a mechanical process. We can find this process in many civilizations in the first millennium BC, in particular in Greek philosophers such as Aristotle and Euclid.

Philosophers and mathematicians, such as Leibniz and Hobbes, in the 17th century explored the possibility that all of a human being's rational thoughts could be mapped into an algebraic or geometric system.

Only at the beginning of the 20th century was the limits defined of what mathematics and logic can accomplish and how far mathematical reasoning can be abstracted. It was at that time that the mathematician Alan Turing defined the **Turing machine**, a mathematical construct that captures the essence of symbolic manipulation.

Alan Turing, in 1950, published a paper speculating on the possibility of creating a machine that can think. As thinking is a concept difficult to define, he defined a task to determine if a machine was able to achieve a level of reasoning that can be called AI. The task that the machine needs to accomplish consists of engaging in a conversation with a human in a way that the human would not be able to tell if he was talking with a machine or another human.

In the 50's we also see the creation of the first artificial neural network (ANN) that were able to perform simple logical functions. Between the 1950s and the 1970s the world saw the first new big era of discovery in AI, with applications in Algebra, Geometry, language, and robotics. The results were so astonishing that created a big hype around the field, but when these huge expectations were not met, we saw the first AI winter, where research funding were cut off.

The 1950s also saw the creation of the first ANN that was able to perform simple logical functions. Between the 1950s and the 1970s, the world saw the first new big era of discovery in AI, with applications in algebra, geometry, language, and robotics. The results were so astonishing that the field gained a lot of attention, but when these huge expectations were not met, research funding was cut off and interest in AI dwindled.

Fast forwarding to recent years, when we started having access to a huge amount of data and computational power and **Machine Learning** (**ML**) techniques became more and more useful in business. In particular, the advent of the **Graphic Processing Unit** (**GPU**) made it possible to train in an efficient way huge neural networks, usually known as **Deep Neural Networks** (**DNNs**), on very big datasets. The trend seems now that we will collect more and more data, for smart cities, vehicles, portable devices, the **Internet of Things** (**IoT**), and so on. ML can be used to solve a rapidly increasing number of problems. It seems then that we are just at the beginning of this huge revolution, as only very recently compared to human history, we were able to have machines that can take decisions by themselves.

With algorithms, it is possible not only to automate mundane and repetitive tasks but also to improve important fields such as finance and medicines where human biases and limited cognitive power limit the growth of the field.

All this automation can be destabilizing to a large portion of the workforce and can focus more and more wealth and power in the hands of a few select individuals and companies. For this reason, companies such as Google and Facebook are financing long-term research into this project. OpenAI (`https://openai.com/`), in particular, is a company that wants to provide open source research in AI and easy access to its material for everyone.

If it will be proven that we can automatize any task, we might live in a society not bound by resources. Such a society will not need money, as it's just a way to efficiently allocate resources, and we might end up in a utopian society where people can pursue what makes them happy.

At the moment, these are just futurist theories, but ML is becoming more and more advanced by the day. We will now take an overview of the current state of the field.

An overview of machine learning

ML is a variegated field with many different types of algorithms that try to learn in slightly different ways. We can divide them into the following different categories according to the way the algorithm performs the learning:

- Supervised learning
- Unsupervised learning
- Semi-supervised learning
- Reinforcement learning

In this book, we are going to touch on each single category, but the main focus will be supervised learning. We are going to briefly introduce these categories and the type of problems that they help solve.

Supervised learning

Supervised learning is nowadays the most common form of ML applied to business processes. These algorithms try to find a good approximation of the function that is mapping inputs and outputs.

To accomplish that, it is necessary to provide both input values and output values to the algorithm yourself, as the name suggests, and it will try to find a function that minimizes the errors between the predictions and the actual output.

The learning phase is called **training**. After a model is trained, it can be used to predict the output from unseen data. This phase is commonly regarded as **scoring** or **predicting**, which is depicted in the following diagram:

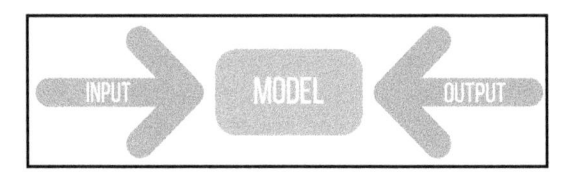

INPUT → MODEL ← OUTPUT

Unsupervised learning

Unsupervised learning works with unlabeled data, so we don't need the actual output, only the input. It tries to find patterns in the data and reacts based on those commonalities, dividing the input into clusters:

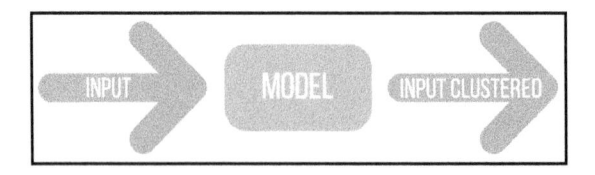

INPUT → MODEL → INPUT CLUSTERED

Usually, unsupervised learning is often used in conjunction with supervised learning to reduce the input space and focus the signal in the data on a smaller number of variables, but it has other goals as well. From this point of view, it is more applicable than supervised learning as sometimes tagging the data is expensive or not reliable.

Common unsupervised learning techniques are **clustering** and **principal component analysis** (**PCA**), **independent component analysis** (**ICA**), and some neural networks such as **Generative Adversarial Networks** (**GANs**) and **Autoencoders** (**AEs**). We will explore the last two in more depth later on in this book.

Semi-supervised learning

Semi-supervised learning is a technique in between supervised and unsupervised learning. Arguably, it should not be a category of machine learning but only a generalization of supervised learning, but it's useful to introduce the concept separately.

Its aim is to reduce the cost of gathering labeled data by extending a few labels to similar unlabeled data. Some generative models are classified semi-supervised approaches.

Semi-supervised learning can be divided into **transductive** and **inductive learning**. Transductive learning is when we want to infer the labels for unlabeled data. The goal of inductive learning is to infer the correct mapping from inputs to outputs.

We can see this process as similar to most of the learning we had at school. The teacher shows the students a few examples and gives them some to take home; to solve those, they need to generalize.

Reinforcement learning

Reinforcement learning (**RL**) is the most distinct category, with respect to the one we saw so far. The concept is quite fascinating: the algorithm is trying to find a policy to maximize the sum of rewards.

The policy is learned by an agent who uses it to take actions in an environment. The environment then returns feedback, which the agent uses to improve its policy. The feedback is the reward for the action taken and it can be a positive, null, or negative number, as shown in the following diagram:

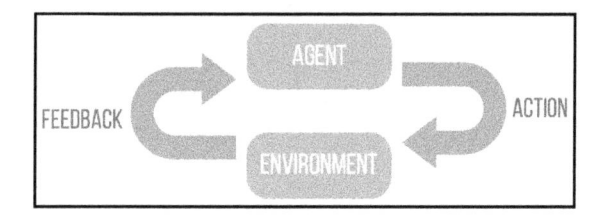

Environment setup

There are only a few viable programming language options when creating ML software. The most popular ones are **Python** and **R**, but Scala is also quite popular. There are other languages, but the better ones in terms of use in ML are Julia, JavaScript, Java, and a few others. In this book, we will be using Python only. The motivation behind this choice is its widespread adoption, its simplicity of use, and the vast ecosystem of libraries that are possible to use.

In particular, we will be using Python 3.7 and a few of its following libraries:

- `numpy`: For fast vectorized numerical computation
- `scipy`: Built on top of `numpy`, with many mathematical functionalities
- `pandas`: For data manipulation
- `scikit-learn`: The main Python library for ML
- `tensorflow`: The engine that powers our deep learning algorithms
- `keras`: The library we are going to use to develop our deep learning algorithms, which sits on top of TensorFlow

Let's focus on the last two libraries for the moment. There are a few libraries that are useful nowadays for **Neural Networks** (**NNs**). The most widespread is TensorFlow. It is a symbolic math library that uses a directed graph to model the dataflow between operations.

It's particularly suitable for matrix multiplications as it can use all the power of the GPU's architecture, composed by many, but not particularly powerful, cores that can execute many operations simultaneously. TensorFlow is also quite versatile as it works on a few different platforms; it's possible to run models on mobile devices using TensorFlow Lite and even on a browser using TensorFlow.js (https://www.tensorflow.org/js).

One of the libraries we are going to use for most of this book will be **Keras**. It is a layer that sits on the top of libraries such as TensorFlow to provide a more abstract interface to the end users. In this regard, Keras is narrower than TensorFlow as it focuses on neural networks, but it's also more generic as it can be used in conjunction with TensorFlow's alternatives such as the **Microsoft Cognitive Toolkit**.

Now, these libraries don't guarantee backward compatibility. Because of this, when working with Python, it's good practice to work in virtual environments. This allows us to isolate the different projects we are working on, but also to distribute our setup to different machines in an easy way and to avoid compatibility issues.

There are a few ways we can create these environments; in this book, we will cover the following:

- Virtual environment
- Anaconda
- Docker

We will go through each one of them to show how they work and explain their advantages and disadvantages.

Understanding virtual environments

While working with Python, you will probably use a multitude of libraries or packages. The virtual environment called **venv** is the first and most immediate way of making a working setup that is easy to reproduce.

From Python 3.3, the `venv` module is Python's built-in module, meaning you don't need to install any external components.

To create an environment in an automated way, it's necessary to create a list with all the libraries you want to install. Pip has a very simple way of defining this list, and it's enough to create a `.txt` file and specify one library per line.

To create the environment, you will need to perform the following steps:

1. Install Python 3.7.
2. Create a new environment called `dl_venv_pip` by using the following command:

    ```
    python3.7 -m venv dl_venv_pip
    ```

3. Specify the required libraries in a file that we will call `requirements.txt`, with the following content:

    ```
    numpy==1.15.4
    scipy==1.1.0
    pandas==0.23.4
    tensorboard==1.12.1
    tensorflow==1.11.0
    scipy==1.1.0
    scikit-learn==0.20.1
    Keras==2.2.4
    ```

Getting Started with Supervised Learning

4. It's possible to now install all the required libraries with this command:

   ```
   pip install -r /path/to/requirements/requirements.txt
   ```

5. Now we can activate our environment by typing in the following command:

   ```
   source dl_venv_pip/bin/activate
   ```

Once the environment is activated, all your calls to the Python interpreter will be redirected to the environment's interpreter. It's a quick and easy way to distribute the requirements, but it's still possible to have compatibility issues due to different operating systems, and also it might require some time to install all libraries as many data science projects rely on many of them.

Anaconda

One of the main drawbacks encountered while using Python for data science is the amount of libraries that are necessary to install. Also, when provisioning instances for deploying your models, you will need to install all the necessary libraries to run your program, which might be problematic if you deploy to different platforms and operating systems.

Luckily, there are few alternatives to venv. One of them is Anaconda: a free and open source Python distribution for data science and machine learning. It aims to simplify package management and deployment. Anaconda's package manager is called `conda` and it installs, runs, and updates packages and their dependencies.

It's possible to have a smaller version of `conda` with a subset of the main libraries, which is called **miniconda**. This version is quite handy when only the main libraries are needed as it reduces the size of the distribution and the time to install it.

To create an environment in an automated way, it's necessary to create a list of dependencies, as we did with venv. Conda is compatible with the pip format, but it also supports the more expressive YAML format. Let's see how this is done by performing the following steps:

1. For example, let's create a `dl.yaml` file with the following content:

   ```
   name: dl_env          # default is root
   channels:
       - conda
   dependencies:         # everything under this, installed by conda
       - numpy
       - scipy
       - pandas
   ```

```
      - Tensorflow
      - matplotlib
      - keras
      - pip:              # everything under this, installed by pip
        - gym
```

2. Place `dl.yaml` in a directory of your choice, and from the terminal in the same location of the file, enter the following command:

   `conda env create python=3.7 --file dl_env.yaml`

3. It's also necessary to activate what. It's possible to do this at any point after installation by typing `activate`:

   `conda activate dl_env`

Now all the Python calls will be directed to the Python's in the `conda` environment that we created.

Docker

Docker is something in between a virtual environment and a virtual machine. It performs operating system-level virtualization, also known as **containerization**, that isolates applications from the operating system to reduce compatibility problems because of libraries or system versions.

As the name suggests, a good analogy for Docker is shipping containers. They solve the following two problems:

- Transporting different goods, that are sometimes incompatible with each other—for example, food and chemicals
- Standardizing the dimension of packages of different sizes

Docker works in a similar way by isolating applications from each other and makes use of a standard layer to allow the spinning up of containers rapidly without much overhead.

One of the main advantages of data science is that it will (almost) solve the **it was working on my machine** problem and will make it easier and faster to distribute the environment to other people or to production systems.

> To install Docker, please visit `https://www.docker.com/get-started`, where you can find the appropriate installer for your system. Then it's possible to install the libraries we installed before.

Supervised learning in practice with Python

As we said earlier, supervised learning algorithms learn to approximate a function by mapping inputs and outputs to create a model that is able to predict future outputs given unseen inputs.

It's conventional to denote inputs as x and outputs as y; both can be numerical or categorical.

We can distinguish them as two different types of supervised learning:

- **Classification**
- **Regression**

Classification is a task where the output variable can assume a finite amount of elements, called **categories**. An example of classification would be classifying different types of flowers (output) given the sepal length (input). Classification can be further categorized in more sub types:

- **Binary classification**: The task of predicting whether an instance belongs either to one class or the other
- **Multiclass classification**: The task (also known as **multinomial**) of predicting the most probable label (class) for each single instance
- **Multilabel classification**: When multiple labels can be assigned to each input

Regression is a task where the output variable is continuous. Here are some common regression algorithms:

- **Linear regression**: This finds linear relationships between inputs and outputs
- **Logistic regression**: This finds the probability of a binary output

In general, the supervised learning problem is solved in a standard way by performing the following steps:

1. Performing data cleaning to make sure the data we are using is as accurate and descriptive as possible.
2. Executing the feature engineering process, which involves the creation of new features out of the existing ones for improving the algorithm's performance.
3. Transforming input data into something that our algorithm can understand, which is known as data transformation. Some algorithms, such as neural networks, don't work well with data that is not scaled as they would naturally give more importance to inputs with a larger magnitude.
4. Choosing an appropriate model (or a few of them) for the problem.
5. Choosing an appropriate metric to measure the effectiveness of our algorithm.
6. Train the model using a subset of the available data, called the **training set**. On this training set, we calibrate the data transformations.
7. Testing the model.

Data cleaning

Data cleaning is a fundamental process to make sure we are able to produce good results at the end. It is task-specific, as in the cleaning you will have to perform on audio data will be different for images, text, or a time series data.

We will need to make sure there is no missing data, and if that's the case we can decide how to deal with it. In the case of missing data—for example, an instance missing a few variables, it's possible to fill them with the average for that variable, fill it with a value that the input cannot assume, such as -1 if the variable is between 0 and 1 or disregard the instance if we have a lot of data.

Also, it's good to check whether the data respects the limitations of the values we are measuring. For example, a temperature in Celsius cannot be lower than 273.15 degrees, if that's the case, we know straight away that the data point is unreliable.

Other checks include the format, the data types, and the variance in the dataset.

Getting Started with Supervised Learning

It's possible to load some clean data directly from `scikit-learn`. There are a lot of datasets for all sort of tasks—for example, if we want to load some image data, we can use the following Python code:

```
from sklearn.datasets import fetch_lfw_people
lfw_people = fetch_lfw_people(min_faces_per_person=70, resize=0.4)
```

This data is known as `Labeled Faces in the Wild`, a dataset for face recognition.

Feature engineering

Feature engineering is the process of creating new features by transforming existing ones. It is very important in traditional ML but is less important in deep learning.

Traditionally, the data scientists or the researchers would apply their domain knowledge and come up with a smart representation of the input that would highlight the relevant feature and make the prediction task more accurate.

For example, before the advent of deep learning, traditional computer vision required custom algorithms that were extracting the most relevant features, such as edge detection or **Scale-Invariant Feature Transform** (**SIFT**).

To understand this concept, let's look at an example. Here, we see an original photo:

And, after some feature engineering—in particular, after running an edge detection algorithm, we get the following result:

One of the great advantages of using deep learning is that is not necessary to hand craft these features, but the network will do the job:

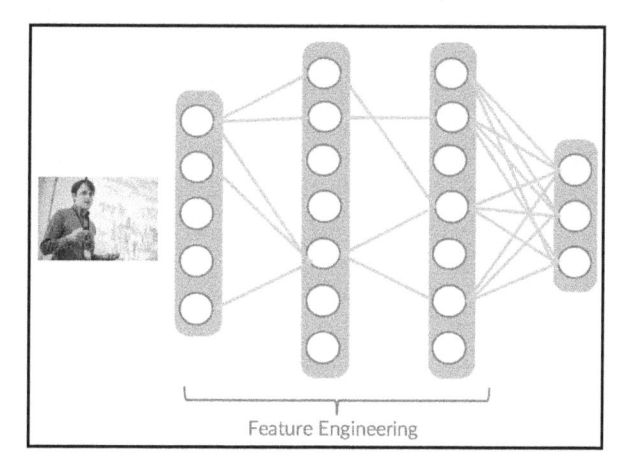

How deep learning performs feature engineering

The theoretical advantage of neural networks is that they are universal approximators. The **Universal Approximation Theorem** states that a feed-forward network with a single hidden layer, a finite number of neurons, and some assumptions regarding the activation function can approximate any continuous functions. However, this theorem does not specify whether the parameters of the network are learnable algorithmically.

In practice, layers are added to the network to increase the non-linearity of the approximated function, and there is a lot of empirical evidence that the deeper the network is and the more the data we feed into the network, the better the results will be. There are some caveats on this statement that we will see later on in this book.

Nevertheless, there are some deep learning tasks that still require feature engineering—for example, **natural Language processing** (NLP). In this case, feature engineering can be anything from dividing the text into small subsets, called **n-grams**, to a vectorized representation using, for example, word embedding.

Feature scaling

A very important engineering technique that is necessary to perform even with neural networks is **feature scaling**. It's necessary to scale the numerical input to have all the features on the same scale; otherwise, the network will give more importance to features with larger numerical values.

A very simple transformation is re-scaling the input between 0 and 1, also known as **MinMax scaling**. Other common operations are standardization and zero-mean translation, which makes sure the standard deviation of the input is 1 and the mean is 0, which in the scikit-learn library are implemented in the **scale** method:

```
from sklearn import preprocessing
import numpy as np
X_train = np.array([[ -3.,  1.,  2.],
                    [  2.,  0.,  0.],
                    [  1.,  2.,  3.]])
X_scaled = preprocessing.scale(X_train)
```

Chapter 1

The preceding command generates the following result:

```
Out[2]:
array([[-1.38873015,  0.        ,  0.26726124],
       [ 0.9258201 , -1.22474487, -1.33630621],
       [ 0.46291005,  1.22474487,  1.06904497]])
```

You can find many other numerical transformations already available in `scikit-learn`. Some other important transformations from its documentation are as follows:

- `PowerTransformer`: This transformation applies a power transformation to each feature in order to transform the data to follow a Gaussian-like distribution. It will find the optimal scaling factor to stabilize the variance and at the same time minimize skewness. The `PowerTransformer` transformation of `scikit-learn` will force the mean to be zero and force the variance to 1.
- `QuantileTransformer`: This transformation has an additional `output_distribution` parameter that allows us to force a Gaussian distribution to the features instead of a uniform distribution. It will introduce saturation for our inputs' extreme values.

Feature engineering in Keras

Keras provides a nice and simple interface to do feature engineering. A task that we will study in particular in this book is **image classification**. For this task, Keras provides the `ImageDataGenerator` class, which allows us to easily pre-process and augment the data.

The augmentation we are going to perform is aimed at generating more images using some random transformations such as zooming, flipping, shearing, and shifting. These transformations help prevent overfitting and make the model more robust to different image conditions, such as brightness.

We will see the code first and then explain what it does. Following Keras' documentation (https://keras.io/), it's possible to create a generator with the mentioned transformations with the code:

```
from keras.preprocessing.image import ImageDataGenerator

datagen = ImageDataGenerator(
        rotation_range=45,
        width_shift_range=0.25,
        height_shift_range=0.25,
        rescale=1./255,
```

[23]

```
    shear_range=0.3,
    zoom_range=0.3,
    horizontal_flip=True,
    fill_mode='nearest')
```

For the generator, it's possible to set a few parameters:

- The `rotation_range` parameter represents value in degrees (0-180), which will be used to randomly find a value to rotate the inputs.
- `width_shift` and `height_shift` are ranges (as a fraction of total width or height) within which it randomly translates pictures vertically or horizontally.
- `Scale` is a common operation used to re-scale a raw image. In this case, we have RGB images, in which each pixel is represented by a value between 0 and 255. Because of this, we use a scaling factor of 1/255 so our values now will be between 0 and 1. We do this as otherwise the numbers would be too high given the typical learning rate, one of the parameters of our network.
- `shear_range` is used for randomly applying shearing transformations.
- `zoom_range` is used to create additional pictures by randomly zooming inside pictures.
- `horizontal_flip` is a Boolean value used to create additional pictures by randomly flipping half of the image horizontally. This is useful when there are no assumptions of horizontal asymmetry.
- `fill_model` is the strategy used for filling in new components

In this way, from one image, we can create many to feed to our model. Notice that we only initialized the object so far, so no instruction has being executed as the generator will perform the action only when it's called; it will be done later on.

Supervised learning algorithms

There are a lot of algorithms at our disposal for supervised learning. We choose the algorithm based on the task and the data we have at our disposal. If we don't have much data and there is already some knowledge around our problem, deep learning is probably not the best approach to start with. We should rather try simpler algorithms and come up with relevant features based on the knowledge we have.

Starting simple is always a good practice; for example, for categorization, a good starting point can be a decision tree. A simple decision tree algorithm that is difficult to overfit is **random forest**. It also gives good results out of the box. For regression problems, linear regression is still very popular, especially in domains, where it's necessary to justify the decision taken. For other problems, such as recommender systems, a good starting point can be Matrix Factorization. Each domain has a standard algorithm that is better to start with.

A simple example of a task could be to predict the price of a house for sale, given the location and some information about the house. This is a regression problem, and there are a set of algorithms in `scikit-learn` that can perform the task. If we want to use a liner regression, we can do the following:

```
from sklearn.datasets.california_housing import fetch_california_housing
from sklearn.linear_model import LinearRegression

# Using a standard dataset that we can find in scikit-learn
cal_house = fetch_california_housing()

cal_house_X_train = cal_house.data[:-20]
cal_house_X_test = cal_house.data[-20:]

# Split the targets into training/testing sets
cal_house_y_train = cal_house.target[:-20]
cal_house_y_test = cal_house.target[-20:]

# Create linear regression object
regr = linear_model.LinearRegression()

# Train the model using the training sets
regr.fit(cal_house_X_train, cal_house_y_train)
# Calculating the predictions
predictions = regr.predict(cal_house_X_test)
# Calculating the loss
print('MSE: {:.2f}'.format(mean_squared_error(cal_house_y_test,
predictions)))
```

It's possible to run the file after activated our virtual environment (or `conda` environment) and saved the code in a file named `house_LR.py`. Then from where you placed your file run the following command line:

```
python house_LR.py
```

The interesting part about NNs is that they can be used instead of any of the tasks mentioned previously, provided that enough data is available. Moreover, when a neural network is trained it means that we have a way to do feature engineering, and part of the network itself can be used to do the feature engineering for similar tasks. This method is called **transfer learning** (TL), and we will dedicate a chapter to it later on.

Metrics

The metric chosen to evaluate the algorithm is another extremely important step in the machine learning process. You can also choose one particular metric as the loss of the algorithm aims to minimize. The loss is a measure of the error that our algorithm produces if we compare its predictions to our ground truth. The loss is very important as it determines how the algorithm will evaluate its mistakes and therefore how it will learn the function that maps the inputs with the outputs.

We can divide again the metrics by the type of problems we have, metrics for classification, or regression.

Regression metrics

In Keras, we can see the following few important metrics:

- **Mean Squared Error**: mean_squared_error, MSE, or mse
- **Mean Absolute Error**: mean_absolute_error, MAE, or mae
- **Mean Absolute Percentage Error**: mean_absolute_percentage_error, MAPE, or mape
- **Cosine Proximity**: cosine_proximity, cosine

In Keras, you can specify the metric you are optimizing for, the loss, only after a model is already instantiated. We will see later in the book how to choose the metrics we are interested in.

Classification metrics

In Keras, we can find the following classification metrics:

- **Binary accuracy**: This measures the accuracy of the result of a binary classification problem. In `keras`, it's possible to use the functions `binary_accuracy` and `acc`.

- **ROC AUC**: It measures the AUC of a binary classification problem. In `keras`, it's possible to use the functions `categorical_accuracy` and `acc`.
- **Categorical accuracy**: It measures the accuracy of the result of a multiclass classification problem. In `keras`, it's possible to use the `categorical_accuracy` and `acc` functions.
- **Sparse categorical accuracy**: It has the same functionality of categorical accuracy but for a sparse problem, `sparse_categorical_accuracy`.
- **Top k categorical accuracy**: It returns the accuracy of the top k elements. In `keras`, it's possible to use the `top_k_categorical_accuracy` functions (this requires you to specify a `k` parameter).
- **Sparse top k categorical accuracy**: It returns the accuracy of the top `k` elements. In `keras`, it's possible to use the `sparse_top_k_categorical_accuracy` function (requires you to specify a `k` parameter).

The first thing we need to determine is whether the dataset in is either balanced or unbalanced, regarding the classes we need to predict. If the dataset is unbalanced (for example, 99% if the instances belong to only one class), metrics such as precision and accuracy can be misleading. In that case, if our system always predicts the most common class, both precision and recall will look very good, but the system will be totally useless. That's why it's important to choose metrics that are useful for the system we are modeling. In this case, for example, ROC AUC will be better as it's looking at the misclassifications our algorithm does and how bad the error is.

Evaluating the model

To evaluate an algorithm, it's necessary to judge the performance of the algorithm on data that was not used to train the model. For this reason, it's common to split the data in the training and test set. The training set is used to train the model, which means that it's used to find the parameters of our algorithm. For example, training a decision tree will determine the values and variables that will create the split of the branches of the tree. The test set must remain totally hidden from the training. That means that all operations such as features engineering or feature scaling must be trained on the training set only and applied to the test set, as in the following example.

Usually, the training set will be 70-80% of the dataset, while the test set will be the rest:

```
from sklearn.model_selection import train_test_split
from sklearn import preprocessing
from sklearn.linear_model import LinearRegression
```

```
from sklearn import datasets

# import some data
iris = datasets.load_iris()

X_train, X_test, y_train, y_test = train_test_split(
    iris.data, iris.target, test_size=0.3, random_state=0)

scaler = preprocessing.StandardScaler().fit(X_train)
X_train_transformed = scaler.transform(X_train)
X_test_transformed = scaler.transform(X_train)

clf = LinearRegression().fit(X_train_transformed, y_train)

predictions = clf.predict(X_test_transformed)

print('Predictions: ', predictions)
```

The most common way to evaluate a supervised learning algorithm offline is **cross-validation**. This technique consists of dividing the dataset into test and training multiple times and use one part for training and one for testing.

This allows to not only check for overfitting but also to evaluate the variance in our loss

For problems where it's not possible to randomly divide the data, such as in a time series, `scikit-learn` has other splitting methods, such as the `TimeSeriesSplit` class.

In Keras, it's possible to specify a simple way to split in train/test directly during `fit`:

```
hist = model.fit(x, y, validation_split=0.2)
```

If the data does not fit in memory, it's also possible to use `train_on_batch` and `test_on_batch`.

For image data, in Keras, it is also possible to use the folder structure to create train and test and specify the labels. To accomplish this, it is important to use the `flow_from_directory` function, which will load the data with the labels and train/test split as specified. We will need to have the following directory structure:

```
data/
    train/
        category1/
            001.jpg
            002.jpg
            ...
        category2/
            003.jpg
```

```
                004.jpg
                ...
        validation/
            category1/
                0011.jpg
                0022.jpg
                ...
            category2/
                0033.jpg
                0044.jpg
                ...
```

Use the following function:

```
flow_from_directory(directory, target_size=(96, 96), color_mode='rgb',
classes=None, class_mode='categorical', batch_size=128, shuffle=True,
seed=11, save_to_dir=None, save_prefix='output', save_format='jpg',
follow_links=False, subset=None, interpolation='nearest')
```

TensorBoard

TensorFlow provides a handy way to visualize a variety of important aspects of our network. To be able to use this useful tool, Keras will need to create some log files that TensorBoard will read.

A way to do this is to use **callbacks**. A callback is a set of functions that is applied at a specified stage during the model's training. It is possible to use these functions to get a view on the internal states and statistics of the model while it's training. Is it possible to pass a list of callbacks to the .fit() method of a Keras model. The relevant methods of the callbacks will then be called at each stage of the training.

Here is an example of callbacks:

```
keras.callbacks.TensorBoard(log_dir='./Graph', histogram_freq=0,
          write_graph=True, write_images=True)
```

Then it's possible to launch the TensorBoard interface to visualize the graph in this case, but it's also possible to visualize the metrics, the loss, or even the words embedding.

To launch TensorBoard from a terminal window, simply type in the following:

```
tensorboard --logdir=path/to/log-directory
```

Getting Started with Supervised Learning

This command will start a server and it will be possible to access it from `http://localhost:6006`. With TensorBoard, it will be possible to easily compare the performances of different network architectures or parameters:

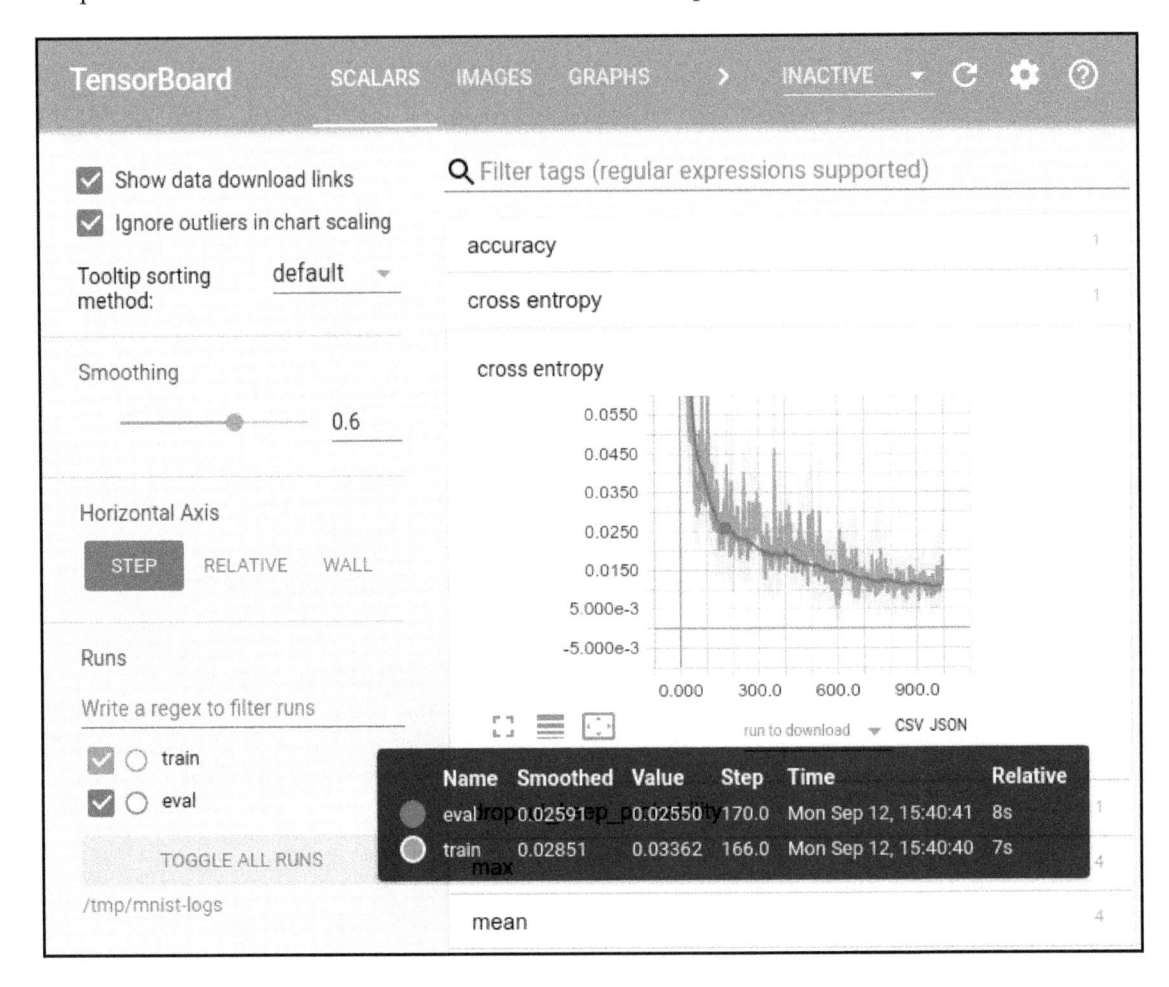

This is the screenshot of a running TensorBoard

Summary

In this chapter, we learned about AI and deep learning. We also dived deep into understanding the various types of machine learning. Then, we learned how to set up our working environment and executed a supervised learning practice in Python. We also looked into feature engineering and supervised learning algorithms and how to use the right metrics to evaluate a model.

In the next chapter, we will learn the building blocks of deep learning and the math behind it.

2
Neural Network Fundamentals

Artificial neural networks (**ANNs**) are a set of bio-inspired algorithms. In particular, they are loosely inspired by biological brains; exactly like animal brains, ANNs consist of simple units (neurons) connected to each other. In biology, these units are called neurons. They receive, process, and transmit a signal to other neurons, acting like a switch.

The elements of a neural network are quite simple on their own; the complexity and the power of these systems come from the interaction between the elements. A human brain has more than 100 billion neurons and 100 trillion connections.

In the previous chapter, we introduced a supervised learning problem. In this chapter, we will cover the main building blocks to create **Neural Networks** (**NNs**) to solve such a problem. We will cover all of the elements to create a feedforward neural network, and we'll explain how to train it, implementing it from scratch and using Keras.

Following are some important topics that we will be covering in this chapter:

- The Perceptron
- A simple Feed forward Neural Network
- FFNN in Python from scratch

The perceptron

As we anticipated before, the concept of the perceptron is inspired by the biological neuron, and its main function is to decide to block or let a signal pass. Neurons receive a set of binary input, created by electrical signals. If the total signal surpasses a certain threshold, the neuron fires an output.

Neural Network Fundamentals

A perceptron does the same, as we can see in the following diagram:

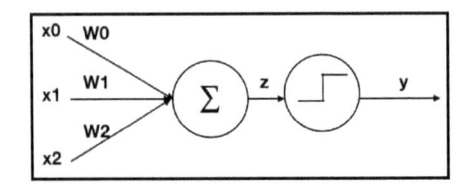

It can receive multiple pieces of input, and this input is then multiplied by a set of weights. The sum of the weighted signal will then pass through an activation function—in this case, a step function. If the total signal is greater than a certain threshold, the perceptron will either let the signal pass, or not. We can represent this mathematically with the following formula:

$$z = \sum_{i=1}^{n} W_i x_i = W^T x$$

This is the mathematical model for a neuron, represented as an explicit sum and as a matrix operation. The term $W^T x$ is the vectorized representation of the formula, where W is the weight matrix that is first transposed and is then multiplied by the vector of inputs, x.

To get a complete mathematical description, we should add a constant term, b, called the bias:

$$z = \sum_{i=1}^{n} W_i x_i + b = W^T x + b$$

Now, we have the generic expression of a linear equation, which is the whole process that happened before the step function.

Next, the linear combination of the input and the weight, z, goes through the activation function, which will determine whether the perceptron will let the signal pass.

The most simple activation function is the step function. The output of the neuron can be approximated by a step function, which can be represented with the following equation:

$$f(x) = \begin{cases} 1 \; if \; W^T x + b > 0 \\ 0 \; otherwise \end{cases}$$

This can be visualized by the following plot:

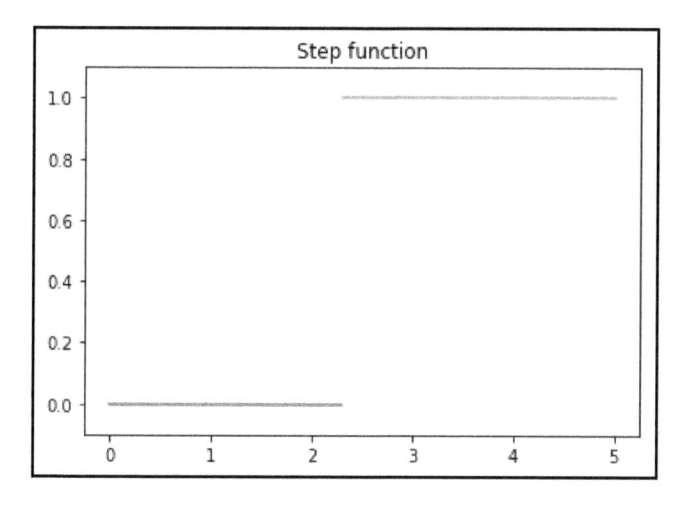

Plot of the step function

There are many types of activation functions; we will describe them later on.

Implementing a perceptron

We will now look at how to build a perceptron from scratch, in order to make sure we understand the concepts as we will use them to build complex networks.

Single-layer perceptrons are only capable of learning patterns that are linearly separable. The learning part is the process of finding the weights that minimize the error of the output.

First of all, let's create a dataset. We will do so by sampling from two distinct normal distributions that we created, labeling the data according to the distribution. After that, we will train our perceptron to distinguish them:

```
import numpy as np
import pandas as pd
import seaborn as sns; sns.set()
from sklearn.metrics import confusion_matrix

# initiating random number
np.random.seed(11)

#### Creating the dataset
```

Neural Network Fundamentals

```
# mean and standard deviation for the x belonging to the first class
mu_x1, sigma_x1 = 0, 0.1

# constat to make the second distribution different from the first
x2_mu_diff = 0.35

# creating the first distribution
d1 = pd.DataFrame({'x1': np.random.normal(mu_x1, sigma_x1 , 1000),
                   'x2': np.random.normal(mu_x1, sigma_x1 , 1000),
                   'type': 0})

# creating the second distribution
d2 = pd.DataFrame({'x1': np.random.normal(mu_x1, sigma_x1 , 1000) + x2_mu_diff,
                   'x2': np.random.normal(mu_x1, sigma_x1 , 1000) + x2_mu_diff,
                   'type': 1})

data = pd.concat([d1, d2], ignore_index=True)


ax = sns.scatterplot(x="x1", y="x2", hue="type",
                     data=data)
```

To visualize the preceding code, we can run it in a Jupyter Notebook with the `%matplotlib inline` option set, obtaining the following plot:

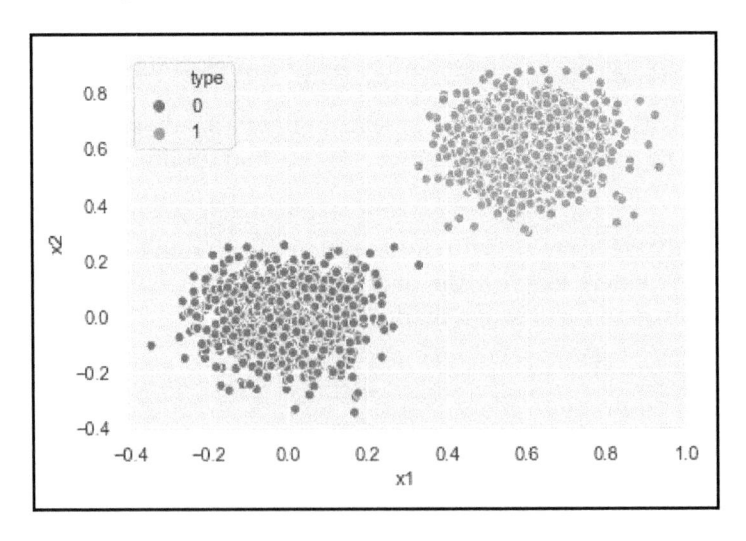

The two distributions, colored according to their type labels

As we can observe, the two distributions are linearly separable, so it's an appropriate task for our model.

Now, let's create a simple class to implement the perceptron. We know that our input data has two pieces of input (the coordinates in our graph) and a binary output (the type of the data point), distinguished by different colors:

```
class Perceptron(object):
    """
    Simple implementation of the perceptron algorithm
    """

    def __init__(self, w0=1, w1=0.1, w2=0.1):
        # weights
        self.w0 = w0 # bias
        self.w1 = w1
        self.w2 = w2
```

We need two weights, one for each input, plus an extra one to represent the bias term of our equation. We will represent the bias as a weight that always receives an input equal to 1. This will make optimization easier.

We now need to add the methods to calculate the prediction to our class, which refers to the part that implements the mathematical formula. Of course, at the beginning, we don't know what the weights are (that's actually why we train the model), but we need some values to start, so we initialize them to an arbitrary value.

We will use the step function as our activation function for the artificial neuron, which will be the filter that decides whether the signal should pass:

```
def step_function(self, z):
    if z >= 0:
        return 1
    else:
        return 0
```

The input will be then summed and multiplied by the weights, so we will need to implement a method that will take two pieces of input and return their weighted sum. The bias term is indicated by the term `self.w0`, which is always multiplied by the unit:

```
def weighted_sum_inputs(self, x1, x2):
    return sum([1 * self.w0, x1 * self.w1, x2 * self.w2])
```

Neural Network Fundamentals

Now, we need to implement the `predict` function, which uses the functions we defined in the preceding code block to calculate the output of the neuron:

```python
def predict(self, x1, x2):
    """
    Uses the step function to determine the output
    """
    z = self.weighted_sum_inputs(x1, x2)
    return self.step_function(z)
```

Later on in this book, you will see that it is better to choose activation functions that are easily derivable, as gradient descent is the more convenient way to train a network.

The training phase, where we calculate the weights, is a simple process that is implemented with the following fit method. We need to provide this method with the input, the output, and two more parameters: the number of epochs and the step size.

An epoch is a single step in training our model, and it ends when all training samples are used to update the weights. For DNNs, it's often required to train with hundreds of epochs, if not more, but in our example, one will be fine.

The step size (or learning rate) is a parameter that helps to control the effect of new updates on the current weights. The **perceptron convergence theorem** states that a perceptron will converge if the classes are linearly separable, regardless of the learning rate. On the other hand, for NNs, the learning rate is quite important. When using gradient descent, it determines the speed of convergence and might determine how close to the minima of the error function you will be able to get. A large step size might make the training jump around the local minima, while a too small step size will make the training too slow.

In the following code block, it's possible to find the code for the method that we need to add to the perceptron's class to do the training:

```python
def predict_boundary(self, x):
    """
    Used to predict the boundaries of our classifier
    """
    return -(self.w1 * x + self.w0) / self.w2

def fit(self, X, y, epochs=1, step=0.1, verbose=True):
    """
    Train the model given the dataset
    """
    errors = []

    for epoch in range(epochs):
```

```python
            error = 0
            for i in range(0, len(X.index)):
                x1, x2, target = X.values[i][0], X.values[i][1],
                y.values[i]
                # The update is proportional to the step size and
                the error
                update = step * (target - self.predict(x1, x2))
                self.w1 += update * x1
                self.w2 += update * x2
                self.w0 += update
                error += int(update != 0.0)
            errors.append(error)
            if verbose:
                print('Epochs: {} - Error: {} - Errors from all epochs:
                {}'\.format(epoch, error, errors))
```

The training process calculates the weight update by multiplying the step size (or learning rate) by the difference between the real output and the prediction. This weighted error is then multiplied by each input and added to the corresponding weight. It's a simple update strategy that will allow us to divide the region in two and classify our data. This learning strategy is known as the **Perceptron Learning Rule**, and it's possible to demonstrate that if the problem is linearly separable, then the Perceptron Learning Rule will find a set of weights that solves the problem in a finite number of iterations.

We also added some error log functionality, so it's possible to test it with more epochs and see how the error is affected by it.

The perceptron class is now complete; we need to create a training and a test set to train the network and validate its results. It's best practice to also use a validation set, but in this example, we will skip it, as we want to focus on the training process. It's also a good practice to use cross-validation, but we will skip that, as well, as we will only use one training and one test set, for simplicity:

```python
# Splitting the dataset in training and test set
msk = np.random.rand(len(data)) < 0.8

# Roughly 80% of data will go in the training set
train_x, train_y = data[['x1','x2']][msk], data.type[msk]
# Everything else will go into the valitation set
test_x, test_y = data[['x1','x2']][~msk], data.type[~msk]
```

Neural Network Fundamentals

Now that we have everything we need for the training, we will initialize the weights to a number close to zero and perform the training:

```
my_perceptron = Perceptron(0.1,0.1)

my_perceptron.fit(train_x, train_y, epochs=1, step=0.005)
```

To check the algorithm's performance, we can use the confusion matrix, which shows all of the correct predictions and the misclassifications. As it's a binary task, we will have three possible options for the result—correct, false positive, or false negative:

```
pred_y = test_x.apply(lambda x: my_perceptron.predict(x.x1, x.x2), axis=1)

cm = confusion_matrix(test_y, pred_y, labels=[0, 1])

print(pd.DataFrame(cm,
            index=['True 0', 'True 1'],
            columns=['Predicted 0', 'Predicted 1']))
```

The preceding code block will produce the following output:

	Predicted 0	Predicted 1
True 0	190	5
True 1	0	201

We can also visualize these results on the input space by drawing the linear decision boundary. To accomplish that, we need to add the following method in our perceptron class:

```
def predict_boundary(self, x):
    """
    Used to predict the boundaries of our classifier
    """
    return -(self.w1 * x + self.w0) / self.w2
```

To find the boundary, we need to find the points that satisfy the equation: $x2*w2 + x1*w1 + w0 = 0$.

Now, we can plot the decision line and the data with the code:

```
# Adds decision boundary line to the scatterplot
ax = sns.scatterplot(x="x1", y="x2", hue="type",
                     data=data[~msk])
ax.autoscale(False)
x_vals = np.array(ax.get_xlim())
y_vals = my_perceptron.predict_boundary(x_vals)
ax.plot(x_vals, y_vals, '--', c="red")
```

Now, you should see the following diagram:

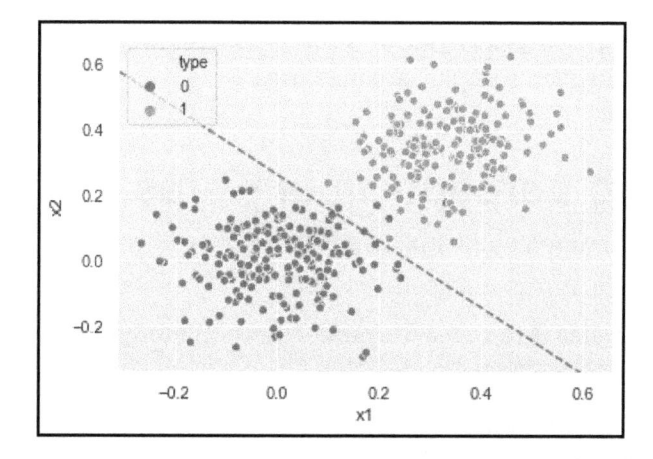

It's also possible to compute continuous output, not just binary; it's sufficient to use a continuous activation function, such as, for example, the logistic function. With this choice, our perceptron becomes a logistic regression model.

Keras

Now that you have seen how to implement a perceptron from scratch in Python and have understood the concept, we can use a library to avoid re-implementing all of these algorithms. Luckily, there are plenty of libraries that make it possible for us to focus on the architecture and the composition of the network without having to lose time in too many implementation issues.

In particular, the main breakthrough of the last decade, and what has made the deep learning evolution so rapid, is the use of graphics cards. In particular, NVIDIA created CUDA, a programming interface that made it possible to use all of the power of modern **Graphical Processing Unit (GPU)** for general programming. A GPU is a piece of hardware primarily designed to render images; it contains a much higher number of cores compared to a CPU, but these cores are only capable of performing simple operations. They are ideal for matrix multiplication, and that's why they are able to speed up the computational time, even by 100, compared to a CPU.

TensorFlow is a library that uses CUDA to interact with the GPU, but it can also run on a normal CPU. Having a GPU is not necessary to run the examples in this book.

We will use Keras on top of TensorFlow, as it provides a high-level, Pythonic API that will allow us to quickly build even complex architectures.

Implementing perceptron in Keras

Let's look at how we can implement a perceptron in Keras, introducing some simple concepts.

The main objective of Keras is to make the model creation more Pythonic and model-centric.

There are two ways to create a model, using either the `Sequential` or `Model` class. The easiest way to create a Keras model is by using the Sequential API. There are some limitations that come with using that class; for example, it is not straightforward to define models that may have multiple different input or output sources, but it fits our purpose.

We can start by initializing the sequential class:

```
my_perceptron = Sequential()
```

Then, we will have to add our input layer and specify the dimensions and a few other parameters. In our case, we will add a `Dense` layer, which means that all of the neurons have a connection with all of the neurons from the next layer.

This `Dense` layer is fully connected, meaning that all of the neurons have one connection with the neurons from the next layer. It performs the product between the input and our set of weights, which is also called the kernel, of course, adding the bias if specified. Then, the result will pass through the activation function.

To initialize it, we need to specify the number of neurons (`1`), the input dimension (`2`, as we have two variables), the activation function (`linear`), and the initial weight value (`zero`). To add the layer to the model, it's possible to use the `add ()` method, like in the in/out example:

```
input_layer = Dense(1, input_dim=2, activation="sigmoid",
kernel_initializer="zero")
my_perceptron.add(input_layer)
```

Now, it's necessary to compile our model. In this phase, we will simply define the loss function and the way we want to explore the gradient, our optimizer. Keras does not supply the step function that we used before, as it's not differentiable and therefore will not work with backpropagation. If we want to use it, it's possible to define custom functions using `keras.backend`, and in this case, we will also have to define the derivative ourselves, but we will leave this as an exercise for the reader.

We will use the MSE instead, for simplicity. Also, as a gradient descent strategy, we are going to use **Stochastic Gradient Descent (SGD)**, which is an iterative method to optimize a differentiable function. When defining the SGD, we can also specify a learning rate, which we will set as `0.01`:

```
my_perceptron.compile(loss="mse", optimizer=SGD(lr=0.01))
```

After this, we only need to train our network with the `fit` method. For this phase, we need to provide the training data and its labels.

We can also provide the number of epochs that we want. An epoch is a pass forward and backward through the network of the entire dataset. In this simple case, one is enough, but for more complex neural networks, we will need many more.

We also specify the batch size, which is the portion of our training set that will be used for one gradient iteration. To make the gradient process less noisy, it's common to batch the data before updating the weights. The size will depend on how much memory is required, but, in general, it will be between 32 and 512 data points. There are a lot of variables that play into that batch size, but in general, a large batch size tends to converse to a pretty sharp minimizer and lose the ability to generalize the learnings outside the training set. To help avoid being stuck in a local minima, we also want to shuffle the data. In this case, every iteration will change the batches, and it will make being stuck in a local minima more difficult:

```
my_perceptron.fit(train_x.values, train_y, nb_epoch=2, batch_size=32,
shuffle=True)
```

Neural Network Fundamentals

Now, we can easily compute the AUC score, as follows:

```
from sklearn.metrics import roc_auc_score

pred_y = my_perceptron.predict(test_x)

print(roc_auc_score(test_y, pred_y))
```

While the model is training, we will see some information printed on the screen. Keras shows the progress of the model, giving us an ETA for each epoch while running. It also has an indication about the loss that we can use to see whether the model is actually improving its performance:

```
Epoch 1/30
1618/1618 [==============================] - 1s 751us/step - loss: 0.1194
Epoch 2/30 1618/1618

[==============================] - 1s 640us/step - loss: 0.0444 Epoch 3/30
1618/1618
```

Feedforward neural networks

One of the main drawbacks of the perceptron algorithm is that it's only able to capture linear relationships. An example of a simple task that it's not able to solve is the logic XOR. The logic XOR is a very simple function in which the output is true only when its two pieces of binary input are different from each other. It can be described with the following table:

	X2 = 0	X2 = 1
X1 = 0	False	True
X1 = 1	True	False

The preceding table can be also represented with the following plot:

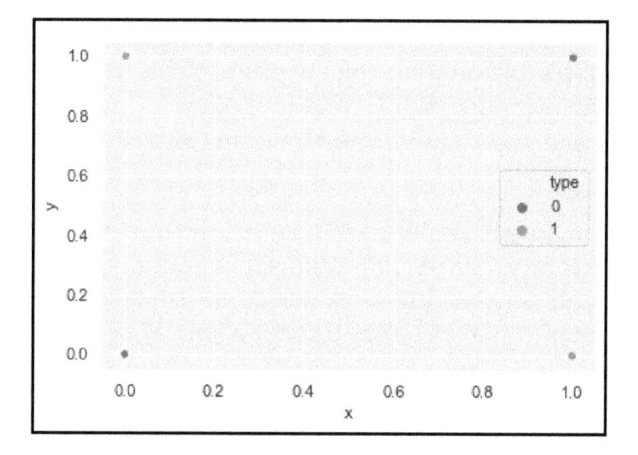

The XOR problem visualized

In the XOR problem, it's not possible to find a line that correctly divides the prediction space in two.

It's not possible to separate this problem using a linear function, so our previous perceptron would not help here. Now, the decision boundary in the previous example was a single line, so it's easy to note that in this case, two lines would be sufficient to classify our input.

But now, we have a problem: if we feed the output of our previous perceptron to another one, we will still only have a linear combination of the input, so in this way, we will not be able to add any non-linearity.

You can easily see that if you add more and more, you will be able to separate the space in a more complex way. That's what we want to achieve with **Multilayer Neural Networks**:

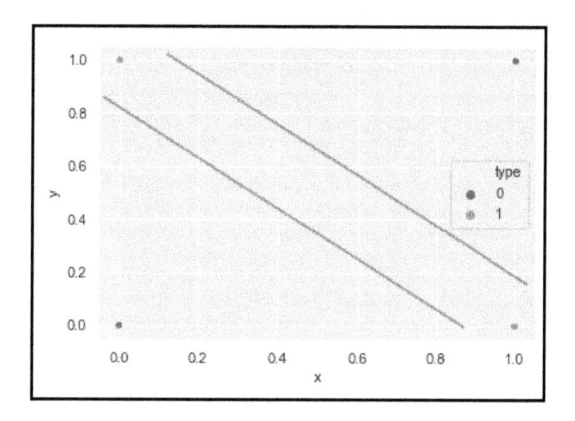

It's possible to correctly separate the space with two distinct linear functions

Another way to introduce non-linearity is by changing the activation function. As we mentioned before, the step function is just one of our options; there are also non-linear ones, such as **Rectified Linear Unit** (**ReLU**) and the `sigmoid`. In this way, it's possible to compute continuous output and combine more neurons into something that divides the solution space.

This intuitive concept is mathematically formulated in the universal approximation theorem, which states that an arbitrary continuous function can be approximated using a multilayer perceptron with only one hidden layer. A hidden layer is a layer of neurons in between the input and output. This result is true for a variety of activation functions, for example, RELU and `sigmoid`.

A Multilayer Neural Network is a particular case of a **feedforward neural network** (**FFNN**), which is a network that has only one direction, from the input to the output.

One of the main differences is how you train an FFNN; the most common way is through backpropagation.

Introducing backpropagation

Before going into the math, it will be useful to develop an intuitive sense of what the training does. If we look back at our perceptron class, we simply measure the error by using the difference between the real output and our prediction. If we wanted to predict a continuous output rather than just a binary one, we would have to use a different way to measure the error, as positive and negative errors might cancel each other out.

A common way to avoid this kind of problem is by measuring the error by using the **root mean square error** (**RMSE**), which is defined as follows:

$$E = (t - y)^2$$

If we plot the square error and we let our prediction vary, we will obtain a parabolic curve:

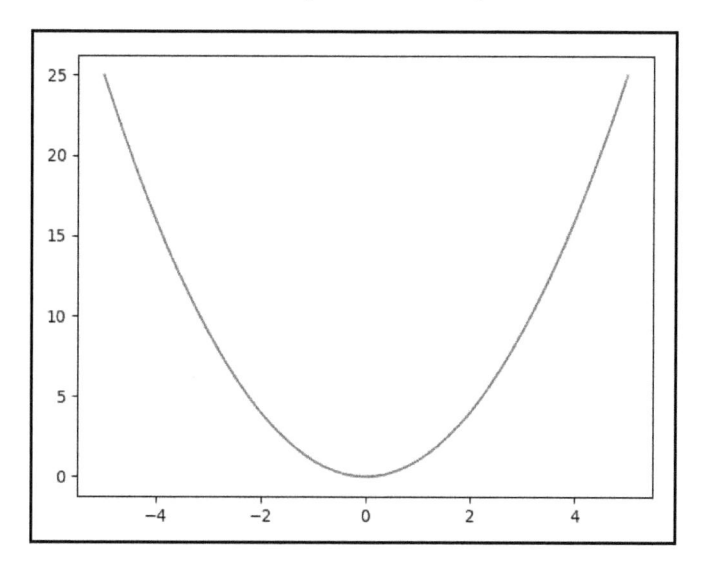

The error surface for a single neuron

In reality, our prediction is controlled by the weights and the bias, which is what we are changing to decrease the error. By varying the weights and the bias, we obtain a more complex curve; its complexity will depend on the number of weights and biases we have. For a generic neuron with n weights, we will have an elliptic paraboloid of an $n+1$ dimension, as we need to vary the bias, as well:

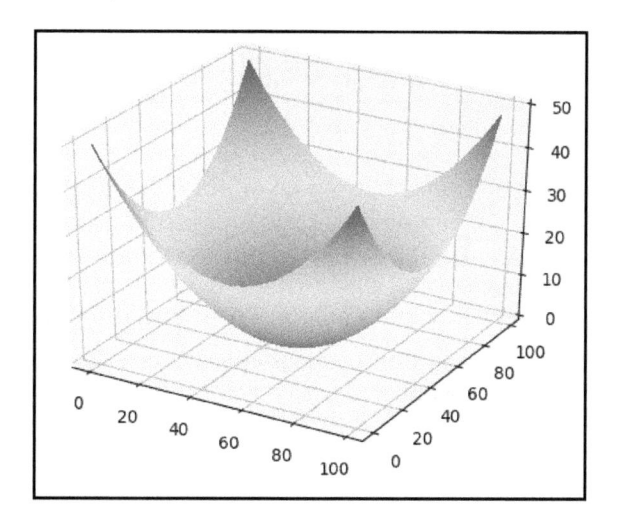

Error surface for a linear perceptron

Neural Network Fundamentals

The lowest point of the curve is known as the global minima, and it's where we have the lowest possible loss, which means that we can't have less of an error than that. In this simple case, the global minima is also the only minima we have, but in complex functions, we can also have a few local minima. A local minima is defined as the lowest point in an arbitrary small interval around, so it's not necessarily the lowest overall.

In this way, we can see the training process as an optimization problem that is looking for the lowest point of the curve in an efficient way. A convenient way to explore the error surface is by using gradient descent. The gradient descent method uses the derivative of the squared error function with respect to the weights of the network, and it follows the downward direction. The direction is given by the gradient. As we will look at the derivative of the function, for convenience, we will consider a slightly different way of measuring the square error, compared to what we saw before:

$$E = \frac{1}{2}(t-y)^2$$

We decided to divide the square error by two, just to cancel out the coefficient that the derivation will add. This will not affect our error surface, even more so because later on, we will multiply the error function by another coefficient called the **learning rate**.

The training of the network is normally done using backpropagation, which is used to calculate the steepest descent direction. If we look at each neuron individually, we can see the same formula that we saw for the perceptron; the only difference is that now, the input of one neuron is the output of an another one. Let's take the neuron j; it will run through its activation function and the result of all of the networks before it:

$$o_j = \phi(\sum_{k=1}^{n} w_{kj} o_k)$$

If the neuron is in the first layer after the input layer, then the input layers are simply the input to the network. With n, we denote the number of input units of the neuron j. With w_{kj}, we denote the weight between the output of the neuron k and our neuron j.

The activation function, which we want to be non-linear and differentiable, is denoted by the Greek letter ϕ. We want it to be non-linear because otherwise, the combination of a series of linear neurons will still be linear, and we want it to be differentiable, because we want to calculate the gradient.

A very common activation function is the logistic function, also known as the `sigmoid` function, defined by the following formula:

$$\phi(z) = \frac{1}{1 + e^{-z}}$$

This has a convenient derivative of the following formula:

$$\frac{d\phi}{dz}\phi(z)(1 - \phi(z))$$

The peculiar part of backpropagation is that not only does the inputs go to the output to adjust the weights, but the output also goes back to the input:

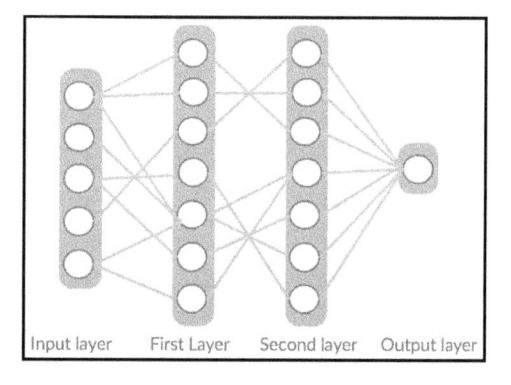

A simple FFNN for binary classification

Activation functions

So far, you have seen two different activation functions: a step function and a `sigmoid`. But there are many others that, depending on the task, can be more or less useful.

Activation functions are usually used to introduce non-linearity. Without it, we will only have a linear combination of input going through another linear function.

We will now look at a few activation functions and their code in Keras, in detail.

Sigmoid

As you have already seen, the `sigmoid` function is a particular case of the logistic function, and it gives us something similar to a step function; therefore, it's useful for binary classifications, indicating a probability as a result. The function is differentiable; therefore, we can run gradient descent for every point. It's also monotonic, which means that it always increases or decreases, but its derivative does not; therefore, it will have a minima. It forces all output values to be between 0 and 1. Because of this, even very high values asymptotically tend to one and very low to 0. One problem that this creates is that the derivative in those points is approximately 0; therefore, the gradient descent process will not find a local minima for very high or very low values, as shown in the following diagram:

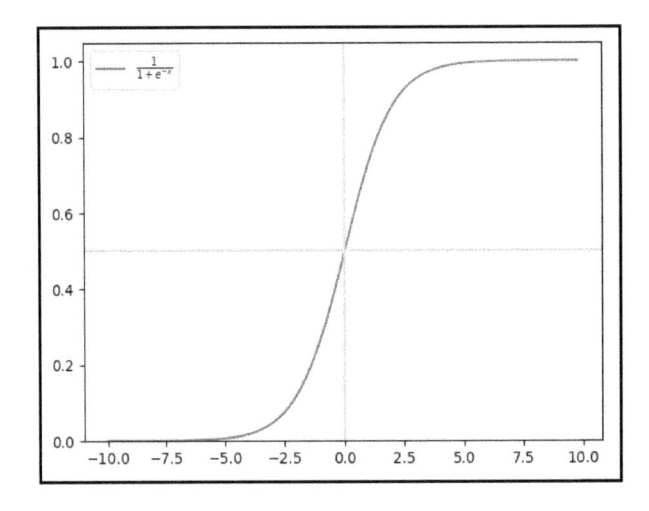

Softmax

The softmax function is a generalization of the `sigmoid` function. While the `sigmoid` gives us the probability for a binary output, softmax allows us to transform an un-normalized vector into a probability distribution. That means that the softmax will output a vector that will sum up to 1, and all of its values will be between 0 and 1.

Tanh

As we said, the logistic sigmoid can cause a neural network to get stuck, as a high or low value input will produce a result very near zero. This will mean that the gradient descent will not update the weights and not train the model.

The hyperbolic tangent, or the `tanh` function, is an alternative to `sigmoid`, and it still has a sigmoidal shape. The difference is that it will output a value between -1 and 1. Hence, strongly negative input to the `tanh` function will map to negative output. Additionally, only zero-valued input is mapped to near-zero output. These properties make the network less likely to get stuck during training:

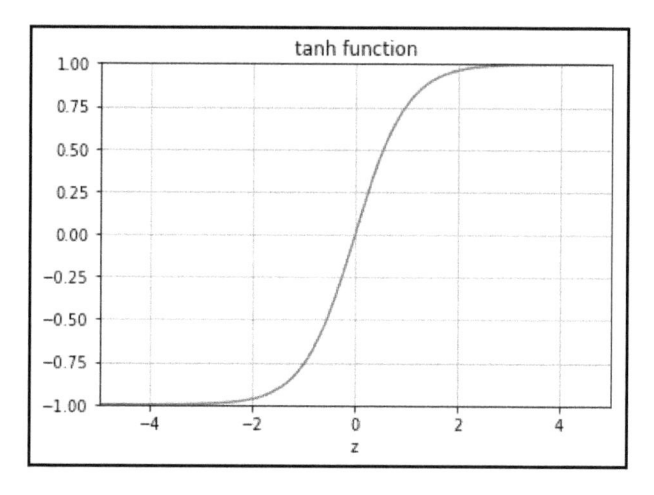

Hyperbolic tangent function

ReLU

ReLU is one of the most commonly used activation functions. It behaves like a linear function when the input is greater than 0; otherwise, it will always be equal to 0. It's the analog of the half-wave rectification in electrical engineering, $f(x) = max(0, x)$:

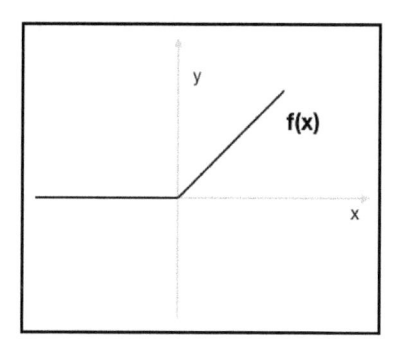

The ReLU function

[51]

Neural Network Fundamentals

The range for this function is from 0 to infinite. The issue is that the negative values become zero; therefore, the derivative will always be constant. This is clearly an issue for backpropagation, but in practical cases, it does not have an effect.

There are a few variants of ReLU; one of the most common ones is Leaky ReLU, which aims to allow a positive small gradient when the function is not active. Its formula is as follows:

$$f(x) = \begin{cases} x & x > 0 \\ ax & x < 0 \end{cases}$$

Here, a is typically 0.01, as shown in the following diagram:

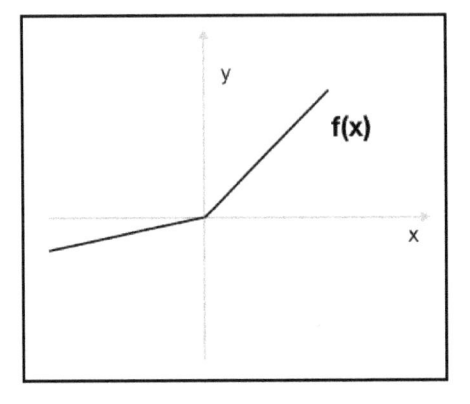

The Leaky ReLU function

Keras implementation

In Keras, it's possible to specify the activations through either an **activation layer** or through the activation argument supported by all forward layers:

```
from keras.layers import Activation, Dense
model.add(Dense(32))
model.add(Activation('tanh'))
```

This is equivalent to the following command:

```
model.add(Dense(32, activation='tanh'))
```

You can also pass an element-wise TensorFlow/Theano/CNTK function as an activation:

```
from keras import backend as K
model.add(Dense(32, activation=K.tanh))
```

The chain rule

One of the fundamental principles to compute backpropagation is the chain rule, which is a more generic form of the delta rule that we saw for the perceptron.

The chain rule uses the property of derivatives to calculate the result of the composition of more functions. By putting neurons in series, we are effectively creating a composition of functions; therefore, we can apply the chain rule formula:

$$\frac{dz}{dx} = \frac{dz}{dy} \cdot \frac{dy}{dx}$$

In this particular case, we want to find the weight that minimizes our error function. To do that, we derive our error function in respect to the weights, and we follow the direction of the descending gradient. So, if we consider the neuron j, we will see that its input comes from the previous part of the network, which we can denote with $network_j$. The output of the neuron will be denoted with o_j; therefore, applying the chain rule, we will obtain the following formula:

$$\frac{\partial E}{\partial w_{ij}} = \frac{\partial E}{\partial o_j} \frac{\partial o_j}{\partial network_j} \frac{\partial network_j}{\partial w_{ij}}$$

Let's focus on every single element of this equation. The first factor is exactly what we had before with the perceptron; therefore, we get the following formula:

$$\frac{\partial E}{\partial o_j} = \frac{\partial}{\partial o_j} \frac{1}{2}(t - o_j)^2 = \frac{\partial}{\partial o_j} \frac{1}{2}(t - y)^2 = y - t$$

This is because in this case, o_j is also the output of the neurons in the next layer that we can denote with L. If we denote the number of neurons in a given layer with l, we will have the following formula:

$$\frac{\partial E}{\partial o_j} = \frac{\partial}{\partial o_j} \frac{1}{2}(t - o_j)^2 = \frac{\partial}{\partial o_j} \frac{1}{2}(t - y)^2 = y - t$$

[53]

Neural Network Fundamentals

That's where the delta rule that we used previously comes from.

When it's not the output neuron that we are deriving, the formula is more complex, as we need to consider each single neuron as it might be connected with a different part of the network. In that case, we have the following formula:

$$\frac{\partial E}{\partial o_j} = \sum_{l \in L} \frac{\partial E}{\partial o_l} \frac{\partial o_l}{\partial network_l} w_{jl}$$

Then, we need to derive the output representation we found in respect to the rest of the network. In this case, the activation function is a `sigmoid`; therefore, the derivative is pretty easy to calculate:

$$\frac{\partial o_j}{\partial network_j} = \frac{\partial \phi(network_j)}{\partial network_j} = \phi(network_j)(1 - \phi(network_j))$$

The derivative of the input of neuron o_j ($network_j$) with respect to the weight that connects the neuron with our neuron j is simply the partial derivative of the activation function. In the last element, only one term depends on w_{ij}; therefore, everything else becomes 0:

$$\frac{\partial network_j}{\partial w_{ij}} = \frac{\partial}{\partial w_{ij}} w o_i = o_i$$

Now, we can see the general case of the delta rule:

$$\frac{\partial E}{\partial w_{ij}} = \delta_j o_i$$

Here, we denote the following formula:

$$\delta_j o_i = \frac{\partial E}{\partial o_j} \frac{\partial o_j}{\partial network_j}$$

Now, the gradient descent technique wants to move our weights one step toward the direction of the gradient. This one step is something it's up to us to define, depending on how fast we want the algorithm to converge and how close we want to go to the local minima. If we take too large of a step, it's unlikely that we will find the minima, and if we take too small of a step, it will take too much time to find it:

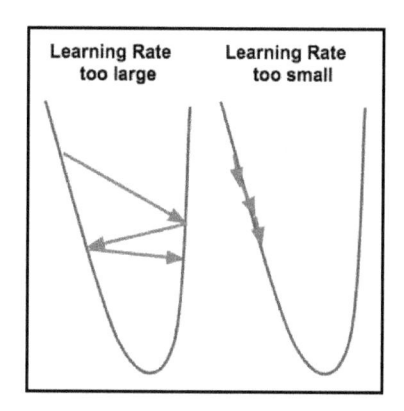

We mentioned that with gradient descent, we are not guaranteed to find a local minima, and this is because of the non-convexity of error functions in neural networks. How well we explore the error space will depend on parameters such as the step size and the learning rate, but also on how well we created the dataset.

Unfortunately, at the moment, there is no formula that guarantees a good way to explore the error function. It's a process that still requires a bit of craftsmanship, and because of that, some theoretical purists look at deep learning as an inferior technique, preferring the more complete statistical formulations. But if we choose to look at the other side of the matter, this can be seen as a great opportunity for researchers to advance the field. The growth of deep learning in practical applications is what has driven the success of the field, demonstrating that the current limitations are not major drawbacks.

The XOR problem

Let's try to solve the XOR problem we presented earlier with a simple FFNN, by performing the following steps:

1. First of all, let's import everything we will need for this task and seed our random function:

    ```
    import numpy as np
    import pandas as pd
    from sklearn.metrics import confusion_matrix
    ```

Neural Network Fundamentals

```
from sklearn.metrics import roc_auc_score
from sklearn.metrics import mean_squared_error
import matplotlib

matplotlib.use("TkAgg")

# initiating random number
np.random.seed(11)
```

2. To make it more similar to a real-word problem, we will add some noise to the XOR input, and we will try to predict a binary task:

```
#### Creating the dataset

# mean and standard deviation for the x belonging to the first
class
mu_x1, sigma_x1 = 0, 0.1

# Constant to make the second distribution different from the first
# x1_mu_diff, x2_mu_diff, x3_mu_diff, x4_mu_diff = 0.5, 0.5, 0.5,
0.5
x1_mu_diff, x2_mu_diff, x3_mu_diff, x4_mu_diff = 0, 1, 0, 1

# creating the first distribution
d1 = pd.DataFrame({'x1': np.random.normal(mu_x1, sigma_x1,
                    1000) + 0,
                   'x2': np.random.normal(mu_x1, sigma_x1,
                    1000) + 0,'type': 0})

d2 = pd.DataFrame({'x1': np.random.normal(mu_x1, sigma_x1,
                    1000) + 1,
                   'x2': np.random.normal(mu_x1, sigma_x1,
                    1000) - 0,'type': 1})

d3 = pd.DataFrame({'x1': np.random.normal(mu_x1, sigma_x1,
                    1000) - 0,
                   'x2': np.random.normal(mu_x1, sigma_x1,
                    1000) - 1,'type': 0})

d4 = pd.DataFrame({'x1': np.random.normal(mu_x1, sigma_x1,
                    1000) - 1,
                   'x2': np.random.normal(mu_x1, sigma_x1,
                    1000) + 1, 'type': 1})

data = pd.concat([d1, d2, d3, d4], ignore_index=True)
```

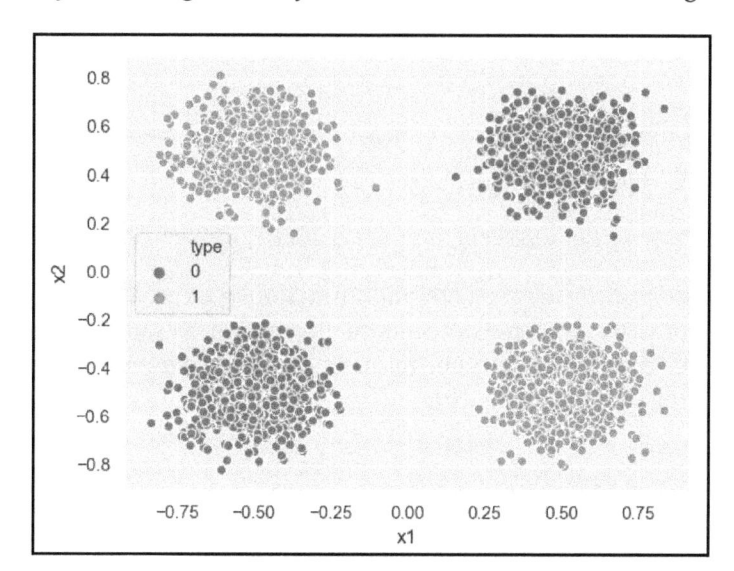

In this way, we will get a noisy XOR, as shown in the following screenshot:

FFNN in Python from scratch

To create our network, we will create a class similar to the one we created in the previous chapter for the perceptron. Contrary to what **object-oriented programming (OOP)** would dictate, we will not take advantage of the perceptron class we previously created, as it's more convenient to work with matrices of weights.

Our goal is to show the code how to understand how to implement the theory we just explained; therefore, our solution will be quite specific for our use case. We know that our network will have three layers, and that the input size will be 2, and we know the number of neurons in the hidden layer:

```
class FFNN(object):

    def __init__(self, input_size=2, hidden_size=2, output_size=1):
        # Adding 1 as it will be our bias
        self.input_size = input_size + 1
        self.hidden_size = hidden_size + 1
        self.output_size = output_size

        self.o_error = 0
        self.o_delta = 0
        self.z1 = 0
```

Neural Network Fundamentals

```
            self.z2 = 0
            self.z3 = 0
            self.z2_error = 0

            # The whole weight matrix, from the inputs till the
            hidden layer
            self.w1 = np.random.randn(self.input_size, self.hidden_size)
            # The final set of weights from the hidden layer till
            the output layer
            self.w2 = np.random.randn(self.hidden_size, self.output_size)
```

As we decided to use `sigmoid` as the activation function, we can add it as an external function. Also, we know we need to compute the derivative, as we are using SGD; therefore, we will implement it as another method. By using the preceding formulas, the implementation is pretty straightforward:

```
def sigmoid(s):
    # Activation function
    return 1 / (1 + np.exp(-s))

def sigmoid_prime(s):
    # Derivative of the sigmoid
    return sigmoid(s) * (1 - sigmoid(s))
```

We will then have one function to calculate the forward pass, and one for the backward pass. We will calculate the output using the `dot` product between the input and the weights and we'll pass everything through the `sigmoid`:

```
def forward(self, X):
    # Forward propagation through our network
    X['bias'] = 1 # Adding 1 to the inputs to include the bias
    in the weight
    self.z1 = np.dot(X, self.w1) # dot product of X (input)
    and first set of 3x2 weights
    self.z2 = sigmoid(self.z1) # activation function
    self.z3 = np.dot(self.z2, self.w2) # dot product of hidden
    layer (z2) and second set of 3x1 weights
    o = sigmoid(self.z3) # final activation function
    return o
```

The forward propagation is also what we will use for predictions, but we will create an alias, as it's most common to use the name `predict` for this task:

```
def predict(self, X):
    return forward(self, X)
```

The most important concept in backpropagation is the backward propagation of the error to adjust the weights and reduce the error. We implement this function in the `backward` method. For this, we start from the output and calculate the error between our prediction and the actual output. This will be used to calculate the delta that is used to update the weights. In all layers, we take the output of the neurons and use it as input, passing it through the derivative of the `sigmoid` and multiplying it by the error and the step, also known as the learning rate:

```
def backward(self, X, y, output, step):
    # Backward propagation of the errors
    X['bias'] = 1 # Adding 1 to the inputs to include the bias
    in the weight
    self.o_error = y - output # error in output
    self.o_delta = self.o_error * sigmoid_prime(output) * step #
    applying derivative of sigmoid to error

    self.z2_error = self.o_delta.dot(
        self.w2.T) # z2 error: how much our hidden layer weights
        contributed to output error
    self.z2_delta = self.z2_error * sigmoid_prime(self.z2) * step #
    applying derivative of sigmoid to z2 error

    self.w1 += X.T.dot(self.z2_delta) # adjusting first of weights
    self.w2 += self.z2.T.dot(self.o_delta) # adjusting second set
    of weights
```

When training the model for each data point, we will do two passes, one forward and one backward. Therefore, our `fit` method will be as follows:

```
def fit(self, X, y, epochs=10, step=0.05):
    for epoch in range(epochs):
        X['bias'] = 1 # Adding 1 to the inputs to include the bias
        in the weight
        output = self.forward(X)
        self.backward(X, y, output, step)
```

Now, our NN is ready, and it can be used for our task. We will need a training and a testing set again:

```
# Splitting the dataset in training and test set
msk = np.random.rand(len(data)) < 0.8

# Roughly 80% of data will go in the training set
train_x, train_y = data[['x1', 'x2']][msk], data[['type']][msk].values

# Everything else will go into the validation set
test_x, test_y = data[['x1', 'x2']][~msk], data[['type']][~msk].values
```

Neural Network Fundamentals

We can now train the network, as follows:

```
my_network = FFNN()

my_network.fit(train_x, train_y, epochs=10000, step=0.001)
```

We'll verify the performance of our algorithm, as follows:

```
pred_y = test_x.apply(my_network.forward, axis=1)

# Reshaping the data
test_y_ = [i[0] for i in test_y]
pred_y_ = [i[0] for i in pred_y]

print('MSE: ', mean_squared_error(test_y_, pred_y_))
print('AUC: ', roc_auc_score(test_y_, pred_y_))
```

The MSE, after 1,000 epochs is less than 0.01—a pretty good result. We measured the performance by using the ROC **Area Under the Curve** (**AUC**), which measures how good we were to order our predictions. With an AUC of over 0.99, we are confident that there are a few mistakes, but the model is still working very well.

It's also possible to verify the performances using a confusion matrix. In this case, we will have to fix a threshold to discriminate between predicting one label or another. As the results are separated by a large gap, a threshold of 0.5 seems appropriate:

```
threshold = 0.5
pred_y_binary = [0 if i > threshold else 1 for i in pred_y_]

cm = confusion_matrix(test_y_, pred_y_binary, labels=[0, 1])

print(pd.DataFrame(cm,
                  index=['True 0', 'True 1'],
                  columns=['Predicted 0', 'Predicted 1']))
```

We will obtain one good result that's possible to check with the following confusion matrix:

	Predicted 0	Predicted 1
True 0	8	417
True 1	392	0

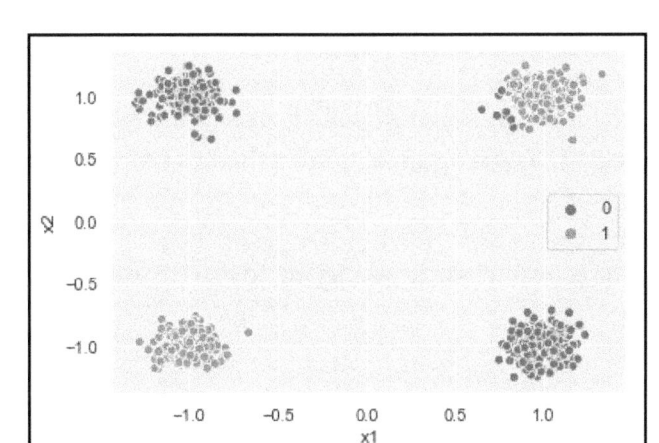

Visualizing the clusters, it's clear where the errors are, as shown in the following diagram:

FFNN Keras implementation

To implement our network in Keras, we will again use the `Sequential` model, but this time with one input neuron, three hidden units, and of course, one output unit, as we are doing a binary prediction:

1. Let's import all of the necessary parts to create our network:

    ```
    from keras.models import Sequential
    from keras.layers.core import Dense, Dropout, Activation
    from keras.optimizers import SGD
    from sklearn.metrics import mean_squared_error
    import os
    from keras.callbacks import ModelCheckpoint, Callback, EarlyStopping, TensorBoard
    ```

2. Now, we need to define the first hidden layer of the network. To accomplish this, it's sufficient to specify the hidden layer's input—two in the XOR case. We can also specify the number of neurons in the hidden layer, which is as follows:

    ```
    model = Sequential()
    model.add(Dense(2, input_dim=2))
    ```

3. As an activation function, we chose to use `tanh`:

    ```
    model.add(Activation('tanh'))
    ```

Neural Network Fundamentals

4. We then add another fully connected layer with one neuron, which, with a `sigmoid` activation function, will give us the output:

   ```
   model.add(Dense(1))
   model.add(Activation('sigmoid'))
   ```

5. We again use SGD as the optimization method to train our neural network:

   ```
   sgd = SGD(lr=0.1)
   ```

6. We then compile our network, specifying that we want to use the MSE as `loss` function:

   ```
   model.compile(loss='mse', optimizer=sgd)
   ```

7. As the last step, we train our network, but this time we don't care about the batch size and we run it for 2 epochs:

   ```
   model.fit(train_x[['x1', 'x2']], train_y,batch_size=1, epochs=2)
   ```

8. As usual, we measure the MSE on the test set as follows:

   ```
   pred = model.predict_proba(test_x)

   print('NSE: ',mean_squared_error(test_y, pred))
   ```

TensorBoard

This was a simple example of how to solve a simple non-linear problem with a neural network; it's really as simple as it gets.

In real life, we will face much bigger challenges; we will have to run multiple experiments and debug our network, and only using the information Keras prints on the screen will not be enough. Luckily, Keras and TensorFlow come with specific tools to help us to visualize and understand our network. We will now see how to use TensorBoard, a suite of visualization tools that we can use to plot quantitative metrics about the neural network. It's also possible to use it to visualize additional data, such as images.

TensorBoard on the XOR problem

TensorBoard comes with TensorFlow by default, so to launch the program, we only need to type in a console that is open where the network code is saved:

```
tensorboard --logdir ../logs
```

And we will see a URL on the screen, which is where the TensorBoard server will be accessible. If you simply follow the preceding instructions, it will be at http://localhost:6006/. It will read the files in the logs folder; as, for the moment, it's empty, we will not be able to see any information.

To start logging, we will have to modify the code we previously wrote. We will use the callbacks function.

A callback is just a set of functions that will be applied at given stages of the training procedure. We can use them to peek into the internal states and statistics of the model during training. To define a callback, we need to run the following command:

```
from keras.callbacks import Tensorboard
```

We can then pass a list of callbacks (as the keyword argument) to the fit methods in both the Sequential and the Model classes. Then, the callbacks will be called at each stage of the training.

We can add a callback that will show us the model of the graph:

```
basedir = '..'
logs = os.path.join(basedir, 'logs')
tbCallBack = TensorBoard(
    log_dir=logs, histogram_freq=0, write_graph=True,
    write_images=True)
callbacks_list = [tbCallBack]
```

The only thing we will need to change on the code we previously wrote will be the training call; it will need a callbacks list so that they can be executed at the end of each epoch:

```
model.fit(train_x[['x1', 'x2']], train_y, batch_size=1, epochs=10,
callbacks=callbacks_list)
```

Neural Network Fundamentals

Note that we increased the number of epochs, just to be able to analyze more data.

Now, if we reload our **TensorBoard** page, we will be able to see the following two things:

- The graph of our network
- How the loss evolved during each epoch

Let's look at the preceding things on the following **TensorBoard** page:

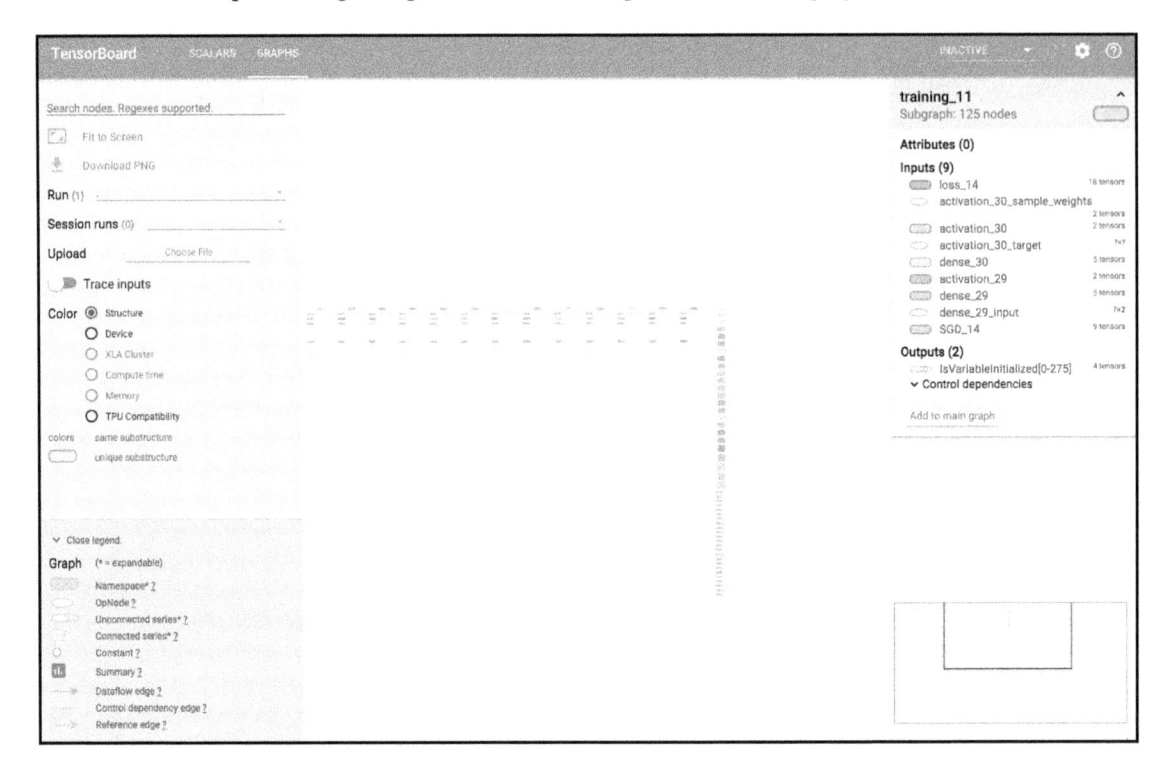

Using TensorBoard, it's possible to visualize the tensors graphs and their computation to see potential bottleneck and optimize performances:

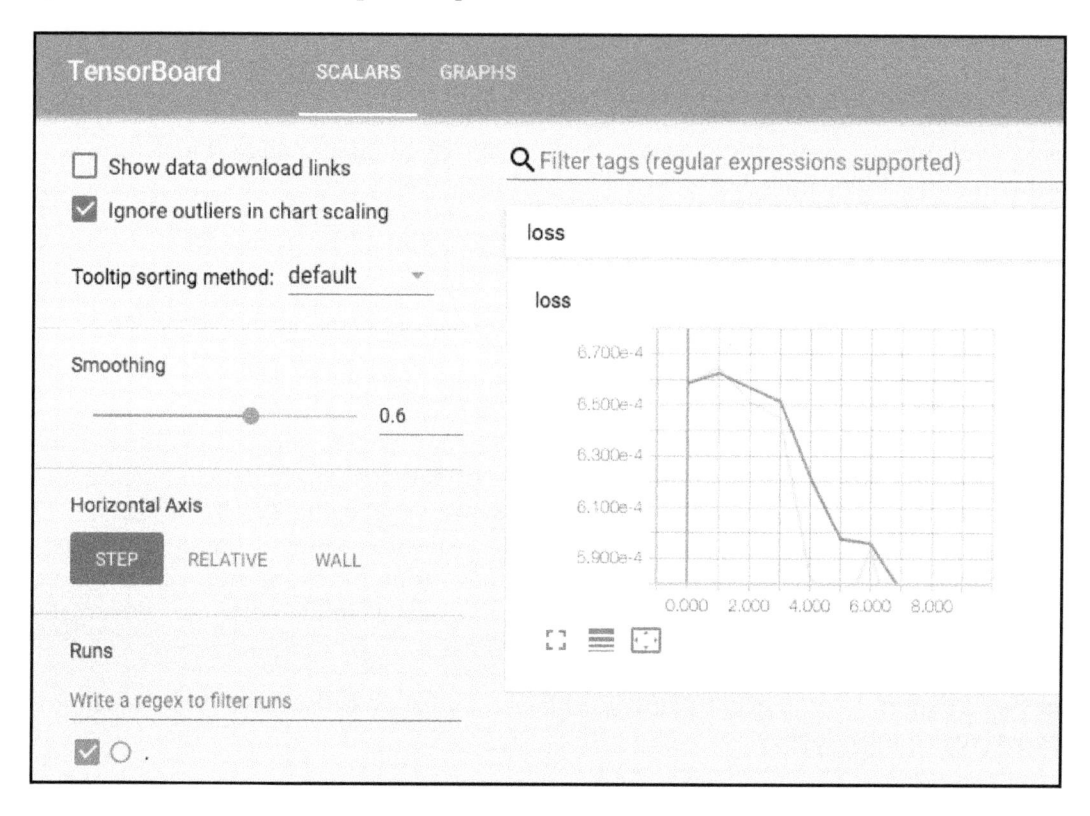

Visualization of our loss function during training

Training a complex network can be a task that could last for days or even weeks. There are multiple things that can go wrong during this time, such as the machine can run out of resources or there can be an hardware or electrical failure. To protect our work, we would like to have a way to save the current state of the training to be able to re-open it at a later time. Luckily, the state of a network is pretty much the weights connecting our neurons; therefore, it's easy to save it. To do this programmatically during training, we will again use our callbacks and, in particular, something called checkpoint:

```
filepath = "checkpoint-{epoch:02d}-{acc:.2f}.hdf5"

checkpoint = ModelCheckpoint(
    filepath, monitor='accuracy', verbose=1, save_best_only=False,
mode='max')
```

Let's add it now to our callbacks, and we can tell Keras to monitor the accuracy. To add accuracy, we will have to add it as a metric:

```
callbacks_list = [tbCallBack, checkpoint]

model.compile(loss='mse', optimizer=sgd, metrics=['accuracy'])
```

Also, after we fit our model, it will return to us an object containing all of the history, a record of training loss values and metrics values for each epoch:

```
history = model.fit(train_x[['x1', 'x2']], train_y, batch_size=1,
epochs=10, callbacks=callbacks_list)
```

Summary

In this chapter, we introduced the perceptron concept and how to solve a linear problem with a perceptron. We discovered different ways to update the parameters of our model, and we saw how to implement a perceptron from scratch and using Keras. We then introduced neural networks as a set of connected neurons that are able, theoretically, to approximate any function. We saw a few different activation functions and we discussed their advantages and disadvantages. We saw how to create a simple network from scratch, and how to do it using Keras.

In the next chapter, we will explain how to solve an image classification problem, using the concepts we just introduced.

Section 2: Deep Learning Applications

In this section, we will look at the concrete application of deep learning methods. In particular, we will focus on computer vision and **natural language processing** (**NLP**).

The following chapters are included in this section:

- Chapter 3, *Convolutional Neural Networks for Image Processing*
- Chapter 4, *Exploiting Text Embedding*
- Chapter 5, *Working with RNNs*
- Chapter 6, *Reusing Neural Networks with Transfer Learning*

3
Convolutional Neural Networks for Image Processing

In the previous chapter, we saw how it's possible to use a fully connected neural network to approximate a nonlinear function. These types of networks suffer from one major problem: they have too many parameters to learn. This will not only increase the computational time, but also the chance of overfitting the data. Overfitting occurs when our model is not able to generalize outside the training data, and results in poor performance on new inputs. This is quite dangerous, because you might realize you are overfitting only after implementing the model in production.

There are many different neural network architectures that can counter this issue. The most common one, especially in computer vision, is the **Convolutional Neural Network** (**CNN**).

The following topics will be covered in this chapter:

- Understanding CNNs
- Convolutional layers
- CNNs in Keras

Understanding CNNs

A problem that arises from using fully connected, feed-forward neural networks in real-life applications is that the inputs of the problems we are trying to solve, for example images, are very large. If we just consider a simple image, 100 x 100 pixels in size, we will have 10,000 weights for each neuron in the first hidden layer alone. It's easy to see how this can rapidly become a huge problem.

CNN is a network architecture that uses some of the properties of the input data to reduce the amount of connections needed to connect different network layers. In particular, CNN relies on the input data having strong spatial correlation, meaning that correlated features will be close together and noncorrelated features further apart. This property is typical of images, where usually your task is to identify and classify subcomponents of a broader image. An example of such a task is to recognize a person in a broad picture: all the features relevant to the task will be in the same area. There are other tasks that can benefit from CNN, such as speech analysis. In general, as we said, if you know that the features of the problem you are working on have high spatial correlation you can consider using CNNs.

CNNs take inspiration from the connectivity pattern between neurons, which resembles the visual cortex. Individual neurons will only react to stimuli in a restricted region of the visual field, known as the **receptive field**. The receptive fields of different neurons partially overlap, such that they cover the entire visual field.

As the name suggests, convolution is the most important operation in CNN, which is a **feed-forward neural network** (**FFNN**) usually composed of the following layers:

- Input layers
- Convolutional layers
- Activation layers
- Pooling layers
- Normalization layers
- Fully connected layers
- Output layers

We will now see the theory behind these concepts and then how to code them in Keras. We have already discussed activation functions, so they will not be covered again.

We will now discuss each layer in detail.

Input data

In a CNN, the input is some data that has a high spatial correlation. Let's take an image as an example; the digital representation of any image is a matrix of pixels. Each pixel represents a point in the image and, for a black and white image, is a single number; for example between 0 and 255 if we use an 8 bit (one byte) representation. This is because our machine will be using a binary representation, so we will have 2^8 possible values:

Chapter 3

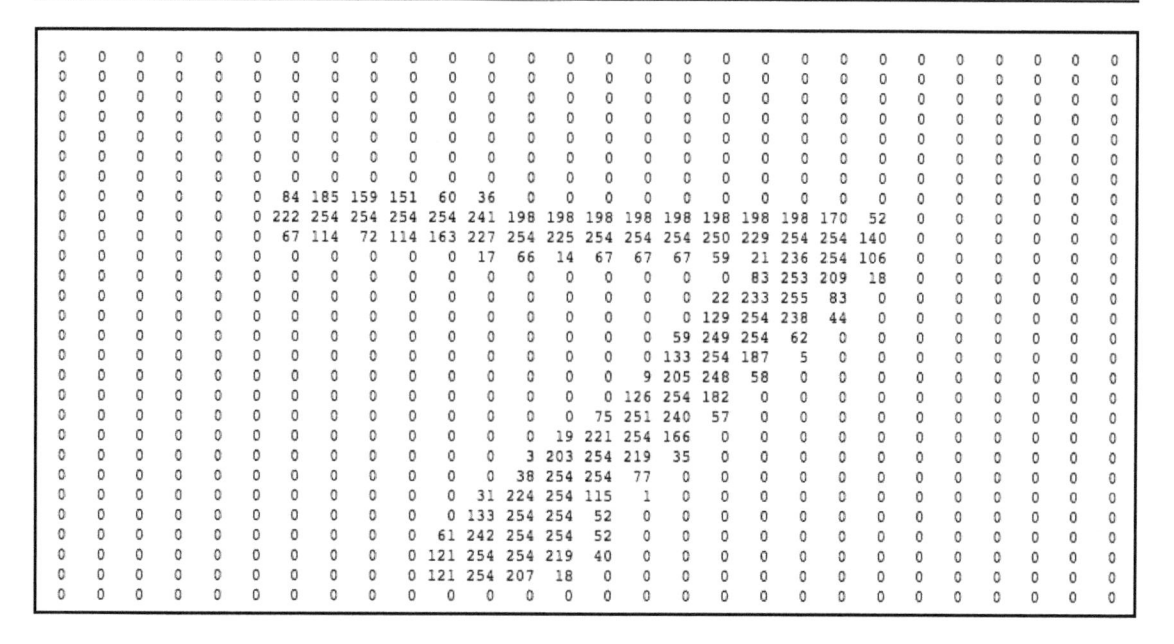

```
0   0   0   0   0   0   0   0   0   0   0   0   0   0   0   0   0   0   0   0   0   0   0   0   0   0   0   0
0   0   0   0   0   0   0   0   0   0   0   0   0   0   0   0   0   0   0   0   0   0   0   0   0   0   0   0
0   0   0   0   0   0   0   0   0   0   0   0   0   0   0   0   0   0   0   0   0   0   0   0   0   0   0   0
0   0   0   0   0   0   0   0   0   0   0   0   0   0   0   0   0   0   0   0   0   0   0   0   0   0   0   0
0   0   0   0   0   0   0   0   0   0   0   0   0   0   0   0   0   0   0   0   0   0   0   0   0   0   0   0
0   0   0   0   0   0   0   0   0   0   0   0   0   0   0   0   0   0   0   0   0   0   0   0   0   0   0   0
0   0   0   0   0   0   0   0   0   0   0   0   0   0   0   0   0   0   0   0   0   0   0   0   0   0   0   0
0   0   0   0   0   0  84 185 159 151  60  36   0   0   0   0   0   0   0   0   0   0   0   0   0   0   0   0
0   0   0   0   0   0 222 254 254 254 254 241 198 198 198 198 198 198 198 198 170  52   0   0   0   0   0   0
0   0   0   0   0   0  67 114  72 114 163 227 254 225 254 254 254 250 229 254 254 140   0   0   0   0   0   0
0   0   0   0   0   0   0   0   0   0   0  17  66  14  67  67  67  59  21 236 254 106   0   0   0   0   0   0
0   0   0   0   0   0   0   0   0   0   0   0   0   0   0   0   0   0  83 253 209  18   0   0   0   0   0   0
0   0   0   0   0   0   0   0   0   0   0   0   0   0   0   0   0  22 233 255  83   0   0   0   0   0   0   0
0   0   0   0   0   0   0   0   0   0   0   0   0   0   0   0 129 254 238  44   0   0   0   0   0   0   0   0
0   0   0   0   0   0   0   0   0   0   0   0   0   0   0  59 249 254  62   0   0   0   0   0   0   0   0   0
0   0   0   0   0   0   0   0   0   0   0   0   0   0 133 254 187   5   0   0   0   0   0   0   0   0   0   0
0   0   0   0   0   0   0   0   0   0   0   0   0   9 205 248  58   0   0   0   0   0   0   0   0   0   0   0
0   0   0   0   0   0   0   0   0   0   0   0 126 254 182   0   0   0   0   0   0   0   0   0   0   0   0   0
0   0   0   0   0   0   0   0   0   0   0  75 251 240  57   0   0   0   0   0   0   0   0   0   0   0   0   0
0   0   0   0   0   0   0   0   0   0  19 221 254 166   0   0   0   0   0   0   0   0   0   0   0   0   0   0
0   0   0   0   0   0   0   0   0   3 203 254 219  35   0   0   0   0   0   0   0   0   0   0   0   0   0   0
0   0   0   0   0   0   0   0   0  38 254 254  77   0   0   0   0   0   0   0   0   0   0   0   0   0   0   0
0   0   0   0   0   0   0   0  31 224 254 115   1   0   0   0   0   0   0   0   0   0   0   0   0   0   0   0
0   0   0   0   0   0   0   0 133 254 254  52   0   0   0   0   0   0   0   0   0   0   0   0   0   0   0   0
0   0   0   0   0   0   0  61 242 254 254  52   0   0   0   0   0   0   0   0   0   0   0   0   0   0   0   0
0   0   0   0   0   0   0 121 254 254 219  40   0   0   0   0   0   0   0   0   0   0   0   0   0   0   0   0
0   0   0   0   0   0   0 121 254 207  18   0   0   0   0   0   0   0   0   0   0   0   0   0   0   0   0   0
0   0   0   0   0   0   0   0   0   0   0   0   0   0   0   0   0   0   0   0   0   0   0   0   0   0   0   0
```

One of the images from the Modified National Institute of Standards and Technology (MNIST) dataset, in which we can recognize an handwritten number seven

As we have mentioned, this is just an example of all the suitable tasks a CNN can solve. In general, they are very good at dealing with input that has a high spatial correlation. These problems must have a grid-like topology. Other examples include videos, recommendation systems, and even time-series because you can see them as a one-dimensional grid.

One of the advantages of a CNN is that it can process all inputs that do not fit the classical tabular form, for example when inputs have different sizes. This is possible because the convolution operation processes only one part of the input at a time. The CNN will repeat the process of applying it to the **kernel** to the image patch; the number of repeats needed is totally dependent on the size of the input. It can be seen as a multiple matrix multiplication between the input and the kernel.

Convolutional layers

Convolution is a typical operation in signal processing that expresses how two functions modify each other and create a third function. Convolution layers are actually implementing an autocorrelation operation, but in practice for our case convolution and autocorrelation are the same, as they can be interchanged with a simple rotation operation.

Let's call our input x, the set of weights it passes through w, the output signal s, and the time t. We want to give more importance to inputs that are more recent, therefore we will use the function w(a) to define the weights, where a is the age of the measurement. The convolutional operation is the process of combining the signal s and the set of weights, which is also called a kernel. As we are dealing with data from real applications and not just match abstractions, the time must be discrete. In mathematical terms the convolution is defined as follows:

$$s(t) = (x * w)(t) = \sum_{a=-\infty}^{\infty} x(a)w(t-a)$$

In deep learning, our input as we said is usually a matrix and also the set of weights, therefore, we only need to compute the summation over a finite set of items. Most implementations do not use the convolution operation, instead cross-correlation is preferred. The two operations for our purpose, just in convolution the kernel needs to be flipped, meaning that you would have to rotate the kernel by 180 degrees:

Input			Kernel			Inverted Kernel		
1	2	3	1	2	1	-1	-2	-1
4	5	6	0	0	0	0	0	0
7	8	9	-1	-2	-1	1	2	1

Kernel rotation

As before, the goal of our training is to find the set of weights, so in this case the kernel. Convolution in CNN is never used alone, but together with other operations:

Input				Kernell		
a	b	c		w11	w12	
d	e	f		w21	w22	
g	h	i				
aw11+bw12+d w21+ew22	bw11+cw12+ew 21+fw22					

Example of correlation calculation

Chapter 3

Typically, CNNs have sparse weights, also known as sparse connectivity, meaning that there are only a few connections between each layer.

There is a way to reduce the number of parameters in the network and reduce the computational load necessary to train and use the network. This goal is achieved by having the size of the kernel much smaller than the inputs, which can be smaller.

The improvement in terms of computation is quite drastic, as you can see by looking at the matrix multiplication operations that we can save:

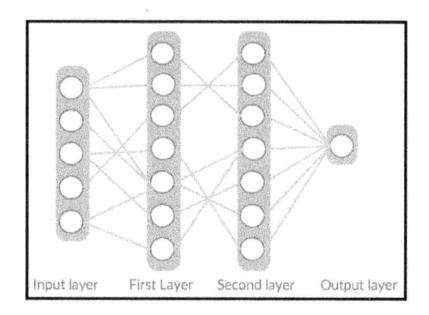

Another advantage is weight sharing. Let's take as an example, an image detection problem. We know that to be able to recognize an object the algorithm should focus on specific traits of the image, such as edges. This property of our data has been exploited for many years, but different algorithms where these features were extracted with different algorithms are explicitly designed to recognize those properties.

To accomplish the same goal, a CNN computes multiple convolution, using separate kernels. These are also called filters and they are typically quite small. For example, a filter for a colored image can be 5 x 5 x 3 pixels in size, and we have many of these in each layer. We will apply our convolution between each filter and the output of the previous layer, forming dot products. What's different from the previously explained FFNN process is the sliding part; the filter is moved around the whole set of inputs whereas, earlier, there was only one set of weights:

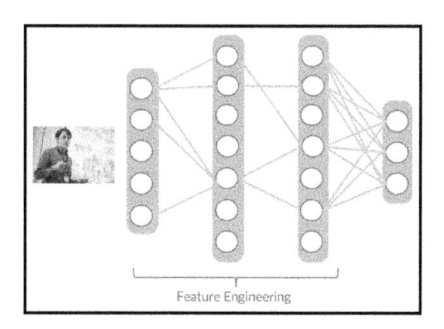

[73]

Convolutional Neural Networks for Image Processing

In this way, every filter will be trained to recognize a specific feature. The closer we are to the inputs, the simpler the features are; for example, orientations and colors. The closer we go to the output, the more complex the feature will become; for example, the filters in the last layers can detect a wheel-like pattern. Each filter will produce a two-dimensional activation map, staking these filters will produce the output volume.

Sometimes sharing weights might not be the best way to achieve good predictive performances. Sharing weights makes sense when we expect features to be a part of our image that can be located anywhere in our inputs, but sometimes there are features that must stay very specific. An example is face recognition, where we want to use some very peculiar shapes, such as the shape of the eyes, to differentiate.

Now that the first stage of the process is done, the convolution has created a set of filters that can be linearly activated. This set of filters will then be the input of a nonlinear function, which is most frequently going to be the **Rectified Linear Unit (ReLU)** function that we saw in the previous chapter. This is when the actual detection appends, and that's why it's also called the **detector stage**.

Let's now have a more visual example. We have two matrices, the first one is a part of a larger image and the second one is the filter that we are convoluting it with. Convolution between the two matrices is shown in the following image:

0	0	0	0	0	40	40
0	0	0	0	80	40	40
0	0	0	90	80	0	0
0	0	90	80	0	0	0
0	0	90	90	0	0	0
0	0	90	80	0	0	0
0	0	90	80	0	0	0

The matrix above is part of a larger image

0	0	0	0	0	10	0
0	0	0	0	30	0	0
0	0	0	30	0	0	0
0	0	0	30	0	0	0
0	0	0	30	0	0	0
0	0	0	30	0	0	0
0	0	0	0	0	0	0

The matrix above is the filter we are using to convolute the other matrix with

In this case, the convolution between these two matrices is going to be a large number as the shapes of the two are quite similar, which means that the filter recognized the image's feature and so, it will let the signal pass.

Pooling layers

It's common to periodically have a pooling layer in between convolutional layers. We can think about the pooling layer as a way to sample our inputs and gradually reduce their dimensionality. This helps with overfitting, as we will have fewer parameters to learn, and reduce the amount of computational power needed. It also helps with invariant to small translations in the inputs.

Stride

Stride is defined as the number of cells that we move our weights after each convolution with the kernel. The stride must be a number greater than one, but usually the choice is between one and two. For our task in particular, we know that the neighboring pixels are highly correlated; therefore, a big stride will lead to high information loss. As we said, the innovative part of the convolution is that we shift our weights over the inputs. To do so we implicitly assumed that we would move the weights by one pixel each time, but nothing guarantees that this is the best way to proceed. That's actually a parameter of our network that is called **stride**. A common choice is a stride 2 with a kernel size 2 x 2 for the pooling layer. It's possible to define different strides for different directions, going left or down the matrix.

Max pooling

Max pooling is a simple operation that takes the kernel and keeps only the maximum value of the input area covered by the kernel. Max pooling is the most popular form of pooling, as it has been shown to work better in practice than other forms of pooling: average and L2-norm pooling. Usually a filter of 2 x 2 is used together with a stride 2, which is represented in the following image:

This operation is effectively downsampling the image and, as we said, helps to control overfitting:

This is a perfect example of downsampling.

Max pooling is effectively downsampling

Zero padding

One of the problems that we face in applying convolution and pooling is that we are shrinking the size of the signal we are working with. This makes it impossible to use deep networks, which are networks that have tens of layers. We know from practical experience that the best results are obtained with very large amounts of data and very deep networks. Therefore, it is very important to find a way to maintain the size of our signal throughout the layers of our network.

Zero padding is a simple operation to artificially increase the size of our signal. It only adds zeros around our signal and will not influence the max pooling operation, as any number in the network must be greater than or equal to zero, but it will increase the size of the output, as it's possible to observe in the following image:

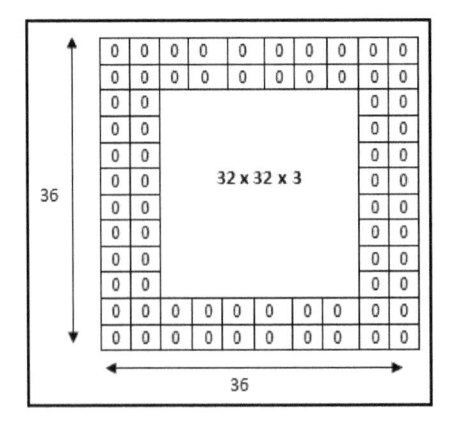

Example of the zero padding process

The size of the padding, together with the kernel size and the stride, will determine the size of the outputs.

If we denote with:

- W and H, respectively, represent the width and the height of the input
- F_w, F_h represents the width and the height of the filter
- P represents the size of the padding
- S_w and S_h represent the stride along the width and the height dimension

What we have is as follows:

Different strides horizontally and vertically. The following equations calculate the exact size of the output of our convolution. We will denote with W the width of the image, with H the height. For the filters, we will use F_h for the filter's height and F_w for the filter's width:

$$outputwidth = \frac{W - F_w + 2P}{S_w} + 1$$

$$outputwidth = \frac{H - F_h + 2P}{S_h} + 1$$

Dropout layers

Dropout layers the function of reducing the effect of overfitting. In networks, because of the very high number of weights and the multiple times that the inputs are used to train the network, it becomes a major problem hence many techniques are used to alleviate it. The idea behind dropout is quite simple and a bit radical. By randomly setting some activation to zero, hence the term **dropout**, we will force the network to create some redundancy, as we train it to classify our inputs correctly. The redundant parts will be on the most important features, leaving less space to the network to feature that are too specific and will make more difficult to generalize. It's important to note that this operation must occur during training only, as when the network is trained we want to use all the information available.

Normalization layers

Normalization layers are used to normalize the activation of the previous batch of data. For example, maintaining the mean activation close to zero and the standard deviation close to one.

In `keras`, normalization layers support multiple arguments, such as momentum and scale if the following layer is not linear.

Output layers

So far, we have only seen simple output: our prediction was either a probability for a set of classes or a value. CNNs can produce more-complex output, for example a high-dimensional object. They can provide a probability of belonging to a specific class for each input pixel. This capability allows CNNs to produce masks around the object they predict, and even map which part of the image is contributing to increase the probability of outputting a certain classification. The problem is that often the output image is much smaller than the input.

The most common output for a CNN has a fixed size, for example a vector of probability. Sometimes, we also allow the output size to vary, as for the input. An example of this is when we want to label each single pixel of the input.

The output depends on the task itself, and CNN can be used for various tasks. We will focus in particular on the image domain. Image classification, or recognition, is a very common task for CNN and it consist on deciding what is contained inside a specific box that contains the object we want to classify.

In the image (of the object) detection problem, we don't know how many objects we have and not only do we need to recognize the object, but also locate it in the image.

Object detection is the task of detecting a predefined object in our image, and the goal is to draw a box around the object we have detected. So it's not just simple object recognition, which might happen by detecting a few features of the object. We also need to identify the boundaries of the object itself. This of course makes the task more complicated. This problem is solved with **Region-CNN (R-CNN)** and **You Only Look Once (YOLO)**. R-CNN at first generates a few thousands bounding box proposals, looking at colors and other visual similarities within regions of the image. Then R-CNN uses CNN for image classification and, finally, refines each bounding box using regression.

The main problem of this approach is the speed and computational cost, as they need to decompose the images into several parts and then analyze them.

Another framework, YOLO, as the name suggests will analyze the image as a whole. It splits the image into a S x S grid, and image classification and localization are applied to each square. Then, YOLO takes the m boxes and a single CNN predicts the bounding of the boxes.

CNNs are also used for object classification, image generation, and visual question answering. Style transfer is another application of CNNs, which will be discussed in detail in Chapter 5, *Working with RNNs*. Style transfer consists of extracting the style of an image and applying it to others.

CNNs in Keras

To showcase the CNN architecture, we will use a classic classification problem: the **Modified National Institute of Standards and Technology (MNIST)** dataset. The MNIST database is a set of handwritten digits composed of 60,000 datapoints for testing and 10,000 for training.

Keras provides ready to use datasets, including the MNIST dataset. The resolution of the images is only 28 x 28 pixels and is black and white, therefore, the computational cost to train the network is relatively low.

We will now illustrate how to create a CNN in Keras to solve a classification task using the MNIST dataset and achieve human-like performance.

Loading the data

First, we need to load the data and the libraries required to build our network. We decided to only train for two epochs, as the performance is already quite good. However, it's possible to increase them by increasing the number of epochs:

```
import keras
from keras.datasets import mnist
from keras.models import Sequential
from keras.layers import Dense, Dropout, Flatten, Conv2D, MaxPooling2D

batch_size = 128
epochs = 2

# We know we have 10 classes
# which are the digits from 0-9
num_classes = 10

# the data, split between train and test sets
(X_train, y_train), (X_test, y_test) = mnist.load_data()
```

Convolutional Neural Networks for Image Processing

We now have to transform the data to make it suitable for our network, and scale the image as we saw previously:

```
# the data, split between train and test sets
(X_train, y_train), (X_test, y_test) = mnist.load_data()

# input image dimensions
img_rows, img_cols = X_train[0].shape

# Reshaping the data to use it in our network
X_train = X_train.reshape(X_train.shape[0], img_rows, img_cols, 1)
X_test = X_test.reshape(X_test.shape[0], img_rows, img_cols, 1)
input_shape = (img_rows, img_cols, 1)

# Scaling the data
X_train = X_train / 255.0
X_test = X_test / 255.0
```

Let's check one of the datapoints:

```
import numpy as np
from matplotlib import pyplot as plt
plt.imshow(X_test[1][..., 0], cmap='Greys')
plt.axis('off')
plt.show()
```

That produces the following image:

Creating the model

Now, let's see how to create a simple model for our image recognition problem. We will still use a sequential model and will add a couple of convolutional layers with a ReLU activation function. We will also use a dropout layer that will randomly delete 25% of connections and a final dropout of 30%:

```
model = Sequential()
model.add(Conv2D(32, kernel_size=(3, 3),
                activation='relu',
                input_shape=input_shape))
model.add(Conv2D(32, (3, 3), activation='relu'))
```

```
model.add(MaxPooling2D(pool_size=(2, 2)))
model.add(Dropout(0.25))
model.add(Flatten())
model.add(Dense(128, activation='relu'))
model.add(Dropout(0.3))
model.add(Dense(num_classes, activation='softmax'))
```

We will use categorical cross entropy, as we are dealing with a multiclass problem:

```
loss = 'categorical_crossentropy'
optimizer = 'adam'

model.compile(
    loss=loss, optimizer=optimizer, metrics=['accuracy'])
```

Then we can finally fit the model and evaluate its performance on our test set:

```
model.fit(X_train, y_train,
          batch_size=batch_size,
          epochs=epochs,
          verbose=1,
          validation_data=(X_test, y_test))
score = model.evaluate(X_test, y_test, verbose=0)

print(f'Test loss: { score[0]} - Test accuracy: {score[1]}')
```

The output is pretty good, with 0.9775 accuracy after only two epochs:

```
60000/60000 [==============================] - 90s 1ms/step - loss: 0.3057 - acc: 0.9082 - val_loss: 0.0688 - val_acc: 0.9775
```

Network configuration

Until now, we have not discussed how to find the best parameter for our network. For simple algorithms, such as decision trees, finding the best parameters is not too difficult. The main strategy in that case is usually the good old **grid search**, which is a very simple technique. The user lies down a set of possible values for each parameter, and the process simply tries every possible combination.

Convolutional Neural Networks for Image Processing

There is no official rule to determine the network configuration, but we know that each additional layer makes the network able to catch a less linear environment.

An important step is to choose the number of filters and their dimensions. we can do that using a grid search approach, let's see how we can approach it in `keras`:

```
import keras
from keras.datasets import mnist
from keras.models import Sequential
from keras.layers import Dense, Dropout, Flatten, Conv2D, MaxPooling2D
import itertools
import os

batch_size = 512
num_classes = 10
epochs = 1
N_SAMPLES = 30_000

model_directory = 'models'

# the data, split between train and test sets
(X_train, y_train), (X_test, y_test) = mnist.load_data()

# input image dimensions
img_rows, img_cols = X_train[0].shape

# Reshaping the data to use it in our network
X_train = X_train.reshape(X_train.shape[0], img_rows, img_cols, 1)
X_test = X_test.reshape(X_test.shape[0], img_rows, img_cols, 1)

input_shape = (img_rows, img_cols, 1)

# Scaling the data
X_train = X_train / 255.0
X_test = X_test / 255.0

# convert class vectors to binary class matrices
y_train = keras.utils.to_categorical(y_train, num_classes)
y_test = keras.utils.to_categorical(y_test, num_classes)
```

We will take a sample of our data, to reduce the computational time, and will test a few different options regarding the numbers of filters and a few kernel sizes:

```
loss = 'categorical_crossentropy'
optimizer = 'adam'

X_train = X_train[:N_SAMPLES]
X_test = X_test[:N_SAMPLES]
```

```
y_train = y_train[:N_SAMPLES]
y_test = y_test[:N_SAMPLES]

filters = [4, 8, 16]
kernal_sizes = [(2, 2), (4, 4), (16, 16)]
```

A simple strategy is to loop through the possible configurations. So that we create all possible configurations we will be using the `itertools` library:

```
config = itertools.product(filters, kernal_sizes)
```

Now, we will just iterate through the configurations, create a very simple network, and see which one is performing best:

```
for n_filters, kernel_size in config:
    model_name = 'single_f_' + str(n_filters) + '_k_' + str(kernel_size)
```

We are still using a sequential model, and we are adding a **Conv2D layer**. This layer calculates the two-dimensional convolution between the inputs and the filters. It accepts the number of filters as first argument of the initialization function, and it's also possible to specify an activation function using the **activation** argument.

The function of the **flatten** layer is to create a one-dimensional vector from whatever the input is, and is needed before a dense layer. The dense layer don't look at local patches, but has all neurons connected to each other, that's why we want to flat the array. This layer also accepts an `argument:data_format`. It's quite simple, reorder the dimension of the input based on the data format you specify. If we specify `channel_first`, the layer will expect the channel to be the first dimension of the past; with `channel_last`, which is the default, it will expect the opposite.

As we said, this last layer is where the real classification happens, while all the other layers are creating the features that the last layer will use.

As we are dealing with multiple classes, we will need to use the softmax `activation` function in the final layer, as it will give us a probability distribution:

```
model = Sequential(name=model_name)
model.add(
    Conv2D(
        n_filters,
        kernel_size=kernel_size,
        activation='relu',
        input_shape=input_shape))
model.add(Flatten())
model.add(Dense(num_classes, activation='softmax'))
```

```
    model.compile(loss=loss, optimizer=optimizer, metrics=['accuracy'])

    model.fit(
        X_train,
        y_train,
        batch_size=batch_size,
        epochs=epochs,
        verbose=1,
        validation_data=(X_test, y_test))
    score = model.evaluate(X_test, y_test, verbose=0)

# print(f'{model_name} Test loss: { score[0]} - Test accuracy: {score[1]}')
    print(model_name, 'Test loss:', score[0], 'Test accuracy:', score[1])

    model_path = os.path.join(model_directory, model_name)
    model.save(model_path)
```

Then, when a network is created, it is possible to reduce the amount of neurons necessary to obtain a similar performance.

Keras for expression recognition

Let's now see a more complex problem—recognize facial expressions from pictures of human faces. For this we will use the **Facial Expression Recognition** (**FER**) 2013 dataset. This is a challenging task, as there are many mislabelled images, some are not centered well, and a few are not even human faces. Currently, in the literature, accuracy is below 75% for CNNs trained from scratch on only the FER 2013 dataset.

The FER 2013 dataset is provided on a comma-separated values (CSV) file, but as we want to demonstrate another way of reading the data we will transform it into a collection of images to make it easier to inspect the dataset:

```
#!/usr/bin/env python
# coding: utf-8

import os
import pandas as pd
from PIL import Image

# Pixel values range from 0 to 255 (0 is normally black and 255 is white)
basedir = os.path.join('..', 'data', 'raw')
file_origin = os.path.join(basedir, 'fer2013.csv')
data_raw = pd.read_csv(file_origin)

data_input = pd.DataFrame(data_raw, columns=['emotion', 'pixels', 'Usage'])
```

```python
data_input.rename({'Usage': 'usage'}, inplace=True)
data_input.head()

label_map = {
    0: '0_Anger',
    1: '1_Disgust',
    2: '2_Fear',
    3: '3_Happy',
    6: '4_Neutral',
    4: '5_Sad',
    5: '6_Surprise'
}

# Creating the folders
output_folders = data_input['Usage'].unique().tolist()
all_folders = []

for folder in output_folders:
    for label in label_map:
        all_folders.append(os.path.join(basedir, folder, label_map[label]))

for folder in all_folders:
    if not os.path.exists(folder):
        os.makedirs(folder)
    else:
        print('Folder {} exists already'.format(folder))

counter_error = 0
counter_correct = 0


def save_image(np_array_flat, file_name):
    try:
        im = Image.fromarray(np_array_flat)
        im.save(file_name)
    except AttributeError as e:
        print(e)
        return

for folder in all_folders:

    emotion = folder.split('/')[-1]
    usage = folder.split('/')[-2]

    for key, value in label_map.items():
        if value == emotion:
            emotion_id = key
```

Convolutional Neural Networks for Image Processing

```
        df_to_save = data_input.reset_index()[data_input.Usage == usage][
            data_input.emotion == emotion_id]
        print('saving in: ', folder, ' size: ', df_to_save.shape)
        df_to_save['image'] = df_to_save.pixels.apply(to_image)
        df_to_save['file_name'] = folder + '/image_' + df_to_save.index.map(
            str) + '_' + df_to_save.emotion.apply(
            str) + '-' + df_to_save.emotion.apply(
            lambda x: label_map[x]) + '.png'
        df_to_save[['image', 'file_name']].apply(
            lambda x: save_image(x.image, x.file_name), axis=1)
        df_to_save.apply(lambda x: save_image(x.pixels, os.path.join(basedir,
    x.file_name)), axis=1)
```

The images are black and white, so we will only have one color channel, and their resolution is 48 x 48 pixels. Therefore, the dimension of the matrix will be 48 x 48 x 1.

We have over 28,000 images in the training set, and over 3,000 in the validation set. These images are classified into seven different and distinct categories: **Angry**, **Disgust**, **Fear**, **Happy**, **Neutral**, **Sad**, and **Surprise**, as shown in the following screenshot:

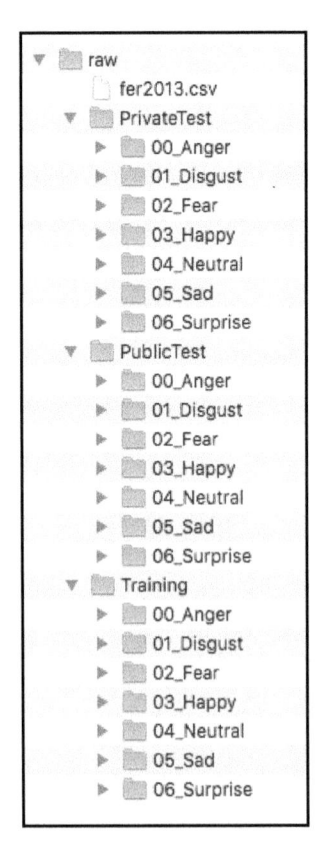

```
▼ 📁 raw
    📄 fer2013.csv
  ▼ 📁 PrivateTest
    ▶ 📁 00_Anger
    ▶ 📁 01_Disgust
    ▶ 📁 02_Fear
    ▶ 📁 03_Happy
    ▶ 📁 04_Neutral
    ▶ 📁 05_Sad
    ▶ 📁 06_Surprise
  ▼ 📁 PublicTest
    ▶ 📁 00_Anger
    ▶ 📁 01_Disgust
    ▶ 📁 02_Fear
    ▶ 📁 03_Happy
    ▶ 📁 04_Neutral
    ▶ 📁 05_Sad
    ▶ 📁 06_Surprise
  ▼ 📁 Training
    ▶ 📁 00_Anger
    ▶ 📁 01_Disgust
    ▶ 📁 02_Fear
    ▶ 📁 03_Happy
    ▶ 📁 04_Neutral
    ▶ 📁 05_Sad
    ▶ 📁 06_Surprise
```

Chapter 3

The folder containing the images must follow a precise structure to be able to be read from disk.

Let's start by importing all the necessary libraries, as follows:

```python
#!/usr/bin/env python
# coding: utf-8
from keras.preprocessing.image import ImageDataGenerator
from keras.models import Sequential
from keras.layers.convolutional import Convolution2D
from keras.layers.convolutional import MaxPooling2D
from keras.layers import Dense, Dropout, Flatten
from keras.callbacks import ModelCheckpoint, TensorBoard
import os

# To solve a macOS specific issue
os.environ['KMP_DUPLICATE_LIB_OK'] = 'True'
```

Now, let's set up the folder structure that we'll need:

```python
basedir = '..'
name = 'layer'
logs = os.path.join(basedir, 'logs')

basedir_data = os.path.join(basedir, 'data', 'espression')
train_feature = os.path.join(basedir, 'data', 'raw', 'Training')
train_target = os.path.join(basedir, 'data', 'raw', 'Training')
test_feature = os.path.join(basedir, 'data', 'raw', 'PrivateTest')

# The following folders need to exist
train_processed_images = os.path.join(basedir, 'data', 'processed', 'Training')
test_processed_images = os.path.join(basedir, 'data', 'processed', 'PrivateTest')
```

Now, we can define all the necessary logs and callback functions. We will also create a checkpoint:

```python
# Logs to track the progress
tbCallBack = TensorBoard(
  log_dir=logs, histogram_freq=0, write_graph=True, write_images=True)

filepath = "weights-improvement-{epoch:02d}-{accuracy:.2f}.hdf5"

checkpoint = ModelCheckpoint(
  filepath, monitor='val_acc', verbose=1, save_best_only=True, mode='max')
callbacks_list = [tbCallBack]
```

[87]

Now, we will define the main variables of our script:

```
_loss = 'categorical_crossentropy'
_optimizer = 'adam'

img_width, img_height = 48, 48
color_channels = 1
img_shape = (img_width, img_height, color_channels)
epochs = 110
batch_size = 512

emotions = {
0: '0_Anger',
1: '1_Disgust',
2: '2_Fear',
3: '3_Happy',
6: '4_Neutral',
4: '5_Sad',
5: '6_Surprise'
}

num_classes = len(emotions)

nb_train_samples = 28698
nb_validation_samples = 3589

n_filters = 32
kernel_size = (5, 5)
pooling_size = (2, 2)

model_name = 'model_nfilters_' + str(n_filters) + '_kernel_size_' +
str(kernel_size)
```

Now, we can define our CNN architecture. We will use a set of convolutional layers, max pooling with padding and finally the dense layer. We will also add a dropout layer, which randomly drops a certain amount of neurons, which is possible to specify as an argument. This will help with overfitting, as the network will have to create redundant features, focusing on the most important ones:

```
model = Sequential(name=model_name)
# Feature maps
model.add(Convolution2D(n_filters, kernel_size, padding='same',
  input_shape=img_shape, activation='relu'))
model.add(MaxPooling2D(pool_size=pooling_size, padding='same'))

model.add(Convolution2D(n_filters, kernel_size, activation='relu',
padding='same'))
model.add(MaxPooling2D(pool_size=pooling_size, padding='same'))
```

```
model.add(Dropout(0.2))
model.add(Flatten())

model.add(Dense(128, activation='relu'))

model.add(Dense(num_classes, activation='softmax', name='preds'))
# Compile model
model.compile(
  loss='categorical_crossentropy',
  optimizer='adam',
  metrics=['accuracy'])
```

Now, we define the data generator. In the generator we can specify some preprocessing steps, for example rescaling, centering, and normalizing the data. It's also possible to define some parameters that will change various aspects of the image. For example, it's possible to change the orientation of the image, shift it in weight and height, and also flip, zoom, and rotate it. These transformations will not only increase the amount of data available for our algorithm, but will also make it more robust to noisy data:

```
train_datagen = ImageDataGenerator(
  rescale=1. / 255,
  shear_range=0.2,
  zoom_range=0.2,
  featurewise_center=True,
  featurewise_std_normalization=True,
  rotation_range=20,
  width_shift_range=0.2,
  height_shift_range=0.2,
  horizontal_flip=True,
)
```

It's not necessary to do these transformations on the test set, except for the rescaling, so we need to define another generator:

```
test_datagen = ImageDataGenerator(rescale=1. / 255)
```

Now, it's possible to use the `flow_from_directory` method to load all the datasets in a predefined structured useful for the deep learning task.

```
# Use folders to get data and labels
# Setting the train_generatorand validation_generator to categorical and it
will one-hot encode your classes.
train_generator = train_datagen.flow_from_directory(
  directory=train_feature,
  color_mode='grayscale',
  target_size=(img_width, img_height),
  batch_size=batch_size,
```

```
    class_mode='categorical'
    # save_to_dir=train_processed_images
)
validation_generator = test_datagen.flow_from_directory(
    directory=test_feature,
    color_mode='grayscale',
    target_size=(img_width, img_height),
    batch_size=batch_size,
    class_mode='categorical'
    # save_to_dir=test_processed_images
)
```

Finally, we can compile our model:

```
model.compile(
  loss=_loss, optimizer=_optimizer, metrics=['accuracy'])

nn_history = model.fit_generator(
  train_generator,
  steps_per_epoch=nb_train_samples // batch_size,
  epochs=epochs,
  validation_data=validation_generator,
  validation_steps=nb_validation_samples // batch_size,
  callbacks=callbacks_list,
  workers=4)

model.save(model.name + ".h5")
```

We can access the while training history by using the variable nn_history and save the train model for future use.

Optimizing the network

It would be great now to identify what we could improve in our network and also how our filters are reacting. It makes intuitive sense that it's possible to map the input pixels and understand which pixel helped determine a certain classification. This can help us understand why our model is not working correctly, as we can see which parts of the image mislead our model, and how it's possible to improve.

We will now see how it's possible to use it to further improve our network. To make it easier to understand and follow we will look at the MNIST dataset.

Chapter 3

Let's start with a saliency map, which highlights the importance of each pixel in a classification context and can be regarded as a type of image segmentation. The map will highlight some specific areas in our image that contributed the most to the classification, as shown in the following image:

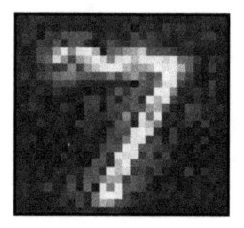

The saliency map of a single digit

Also, as we said previously, the filters learn local patterns, so it's possible to inspect them to find out the best.

We can see if the saliency map is not highlighting the correct parts, it means we will not be able to easily classify our image. In the following images, we can see saliency maps from models with a single convolutional layer and a different number of filters and kernel sizes:

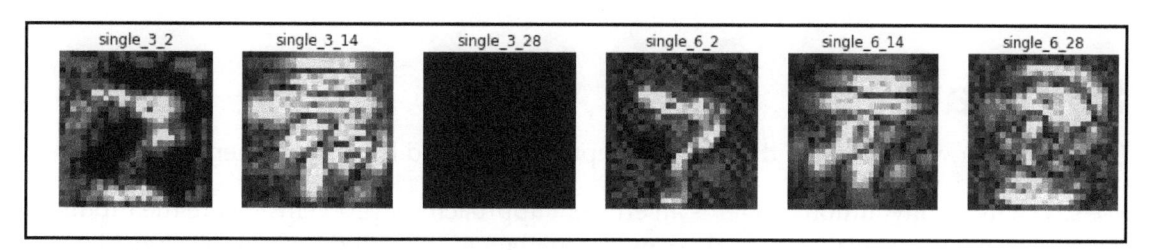

Saliency maps from models working well

Also, as we said, the filters are capturing local features, so visualizing them can help to see if we are capturing useful information such as lines and curves:

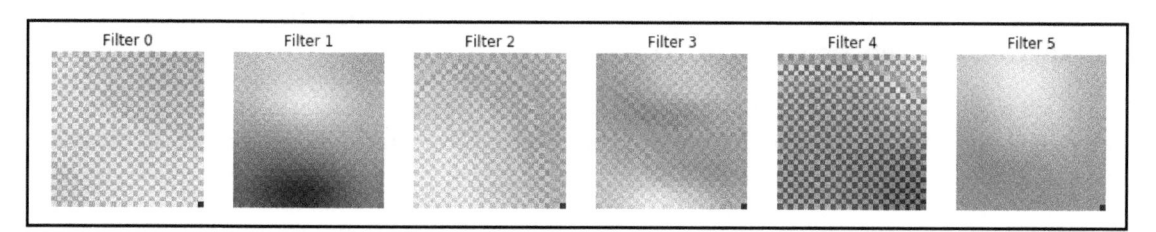

Visualizing the filters of our convolutional layer

[91]

Finally, our network aim is to be able to generalize a concept (for example a particular handwritten digit) and to be able to recognize many of them. It's something our brain does naturally. For example, if we think about the concept 'behind a chair', we might have a specific chair in mind, but we have no problem recognizing a different type of chair if we see one.

Similarly a network must create this concept of the object we are classifying in its weight, and use it to categorize unseen instances. It's possible to visualize this information by plotting the activation map for the dense layer. This will allow us to check whether the essence that our network captured makes intuitive sense, and if our network is looking at the interesting parts:

The activation map of the handwritten eight digit

Summary

In this chapter, we explained the main concept of CNNs and how to use them in Keras.

We saw why a convolutional layer is an efficient approach for problems where the inputs have high spatial correlation. We also saw the mathematics behind the convolutional layer, and how our filters are able to capture the features.

We discussed the need for pooling layers, softmax activation, and zero padding to avoid the shrinking of our images, especially for **deep neural networks** (**DNNs**).

We also saw how it's possible to debug our network to detect problems, checking the activation maps, filters, and saliency maps.

We discussed the various possible uses of CNN-like image classification and image detection, and how they are actually very flexible and can be used to solve many different tasks.

In the next chapter, we will focus on deep learning for natural language processing, but later in this book we will come back to some concepts we have touched on here.

4
Exploiting Text Embedding

Working with text has a varied set of challenges compared to images. One of the major issues with text is that it does not have a standard form. The vast multitude of languages leads to a hoard of valid ways to express the same concept and even these ways are constantly evolving. Texting, emoticons, and abbreviations are relatively recent trends and yet have been institutionalized already, with even world leaders jumping on the bandwagon and using social media to connect with the masses. The machine learning subfield that deals with language related task is known as **natural language processing** (**NLP**).

Deep learning has provided significant help with solving issues revolving around this topic. In recent years, we have seen great improvements in a domain that was a bit stagnant compared to other machine-learning fields.

In this chapter, we will learn some of the classic machine-learning methods used to deal with text. Then we will see how it's possible to take advantage of deep learning and more recent techniques to improve the results obtained using old methods.

In particular, we will see what text embedding is and how it can be used to allow us to take advantage of mathematical models on textual data.

To understand these concepts with clarity, we will look at the following topics:

- Machine learning for NLP
- Understanding word embeddings
- GloVe

Machine learning for NLP

Text has always been a great source of data and information and has historically been a major way to share knowledge and ideas. This rich source of information can be extremely interesting for machine-learning systems. It's a prime example of so-called non-structured data.

Even though it's challenging, the field of machine learning for NLP is very important in that it can unlock major improvements in our lives.

These are some of the major sub-fields of NLP:

- Speech, such as speech recognition and text-to-speech, in which the given text will transform into a spoken representation.
- Automatic summarization, the task of producing a summary of a long text that maintains its meaning and is readable.
- Semantics, the branch that wants to understand the meaning of words in a context. Common examples are machine translation and natural language generation.
- Syntax, for example, **lemmatization,** which is the task of identifying the core of a word, without inflectional endings.

Before the advent of words embeddings, NLP was mainly using the following two methods:

- Rule-based methods
- Statistical methods

The following two sections are dedicated to understanding these methods.

Rule-based methods

Rule-based methods try to exploit common linguistic rules, such as grammar, to infer the function of a word or to perform stemming. Stemming is an important NLP task, very often used as a data pre-processing stage, whose aim is to identify the root of the word.

In the Python ecosystem, there are tools that do these tasks almost automatically. To see an example, we need to install another Python library—**Natural Language Toolkit** (**NLTK**).

Install the NTLK library using `conda`, by executing the following command line:

```
conda install -c anaconda nltk
```

Alternatively, we can also use `pip` as follows:

```
pip install nltk
```

The following is an example of stemming:

```
import nltk
from nltk.stem.porter import *

ps = PorterStemmer()

print(ps.stem('run'))

print(ps.stem('dogs'))

print(ps.stem('mice'))

print(ps.stem('were'))
```

The preceding commands generates the following output:

```
[[('hello', 'NN'), ('world', 'NN')],
 [('this', 'DT'), ('is', 'VBZ'), ('a', 'DT'), ('test', 'NN')]]
```

Part-of-Speech (**PoS**) tagging is another common task that comprises assigning tags, such as verb, adjective, or noun, to part of the sentence.

Understanding word embeddings

Embedding is a mathematical structure contained within another instance. If we are embedding an object X in an object Y, we will be preserving the structure of the objects and so the instance.

Word embedding is a technique to map words to vectors, creating a multidimensional space that will allow the creation of similar representations for similar words. Each word is represented by a single vector with often tens or hundreds of dimensions, in contrast to other representations such as one-hot encoding that can have thousands or even millions of dimensions.

When we have words in the form of vectors, we end up using all mathematical techniques that we would on pure numbers. Also when transformed into vectors, words will keep the same proprieties that numbers have.

It also means that we could start doing operations as follows:

King - man + woman =queen

Being able to treat words as numbers is, surely, very useful and is a great achievement. We will also see how it's possible to deal with sentences and even full paragraphs using word embedding.

This representation is arguably the most significant contribution of deep learning to the field of NLP.

Applications of words embeddings

The problem with old NLP techniques is that they consider single words without taking into consideration the similarity between them.

In generic terms, word embeddings learn a vector representation based on the usage of words. Therefore, based on the words that keep appearing around the words we are considering, we can determine a vectorized representation.

We will see now one of these techniques in more detail, namely Word2vec, which pioneered the field.

The following are two commonly used types of word embeddings:

- Frequency-based embedding
- Prediction-based embedding

Word2vec

Word2vec is a subset of text embedding techniques that map words to a vector space using a neural network. Usually, these networks are shallow: typically two-layer networks. The goal of these networks is to reconstruct the linguistic context that the words are used in.

Each word would then be represented by a single vector formed by hundreds of dimensions. Words that appear in a similar context will be represented by two vectors lying close together in the embedded space.

The initial Word2vec model was designed and patented by Google, but after that, many researchers studied it and came up with different implementations, like for example in the gensim library.

We need to produce a sparse representation. To do that, Word2vec can utilize the following two architectures:

- **Continuous bag-of-words (CBOW)**
- Continuous skip-gram

The **CBOW** method tries to predict the center word based on the source context words:

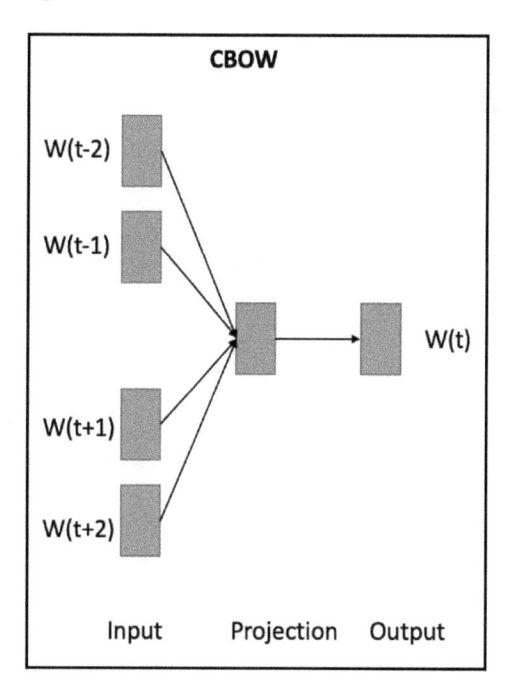

Exploiting Text Embedding

Using this architecture, we make the assumption that the order of the words in the window does not influence the prediction. If this is not the case, we need to use a different architecture, such as continuous skip-gram:

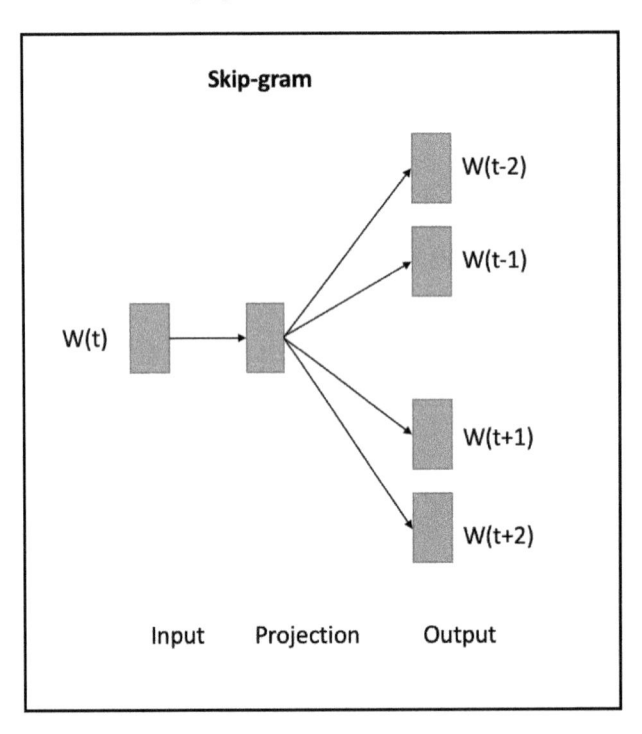

![Skip-gram architecture diagram showing W(t) as input, a projection layer, and outputs W(t-2), W(t-1), W(t+1), W(t+2)]

Continuous skip-gram still uses a window around the word but uses higher weights for words close to the word we are considering. This is usually more precise, especially for infrequent words, but due to the additional weights, this is quite a bit slower than CBOW.

Let's consider skip-gram as an example. The first step of the algorithm is to one-hot encode for each word. Then we feed the whole word as input to the network.

Word2vec is a very simple neural network, completed by a single hidden layer. During training, we find the weight that minimizes the loss of the prediction task, which for skip-gram is to calculate the probability of the words near the input word.

In reality, we don't care about the task itself; we care more about the hidden weights. The weights that connect the hidden layers with the outputs, and during training, so the goal is to adjust those weights and use them as word embedding.

Word2vec's approach is not only applicable to text sets but also to graphs, social media, gene sequences, and many more. The generic approach is called **sequence vectors**, because it can extract information on any sequence data as it models the likelihood of co-occurrence.

These types of models typically require more data than the traditional ones, mostly because traditionally NLP researchers used to create features by themselves, leveraging their domain expertise. This approach started to show limitations when it was applied to different domains. In such cases, the researcher would need to spend a lot of time creating new features.

In contrast, deep learning finds the best feature by itself during training, so we can apply very similar approaches in different domains.

After we train our network, we will use a vector of numbers, called a neural word embedding, to represent each word. In this regard, it's a similar process to autoencoders, for which we also have a vectorized representation of the input. We will talk more about autoencoders in Chapter 5, *Working with RNNs*, but their goal is basically to find a compact way of representing the input so it would be possible to reconstruct it.

On the other side, as we have already mentioned, we want to predict one word, given the context, so our representation will be optimized for that.

These concepts can also be used to help with translating text. When we have two embeddings trained in different languages, we can also map them to each other.

Word embedding in Keras

We will now see how it is possible to create this embedding layer using a binary classification task to train our network and derive the word representation. We will be using Keras and, in particular, the embedding layer, which turns positive integers – the indexes of our vocabulary – into dense vectors of fixed size, for example:

$$[[2], [11]] -> [[0.25, 0.1], [0.6, -0.2]]$$

To accomplish this, we will create a simple classification task. For example, for a simple corpus of sentences about pizza, we want to find out its sentiment. It's a simple binary classification task that is different from the neural networks we use for Word2vec, but we are now only interested in the embedding layer.

Exploiting Text Embedding

To create the embedding layer, follow these steps:

1. Import the libraries we want to use, in particular, some pre-processing that we will need to transform and pre-process the textual data:

   ```
   from numpy import array
   from keras.preprocessing.text import one_hot
   from keras.preprocessing.sequence import pad_sequences
   from keras.models import Sequential
   from keras.layers import Dense
   from keras.layers import Flatten
   from keras.layers.embeddings import Embedding
   import pandas as pd
   ```

2. Define a simple dataset. We define a vector of sentences regarding pizza. Each of these sentences will only have one sentiment, which can be either positive or negative. Provide the class of the sentences in a separate vector:

   ```
   # define the corpus
   corpus = ['This is good pizza',
            'I love Italian pizza',
            'The best pizza',
            'nice pizza',
            'Excellent pizza',
            'I love pizza',
            'The pizza was alright',
            'disgusting pineapple pizza',
            'not good pizza',
            'bad pizza',
            'very bad pizza',
            'I had better pizza']

   # creating class labels for our
   labels = array([1, 1, 1, 1, 1, 1, 0, 0, 0, 0, 0, 0])

   output_dim = 8
   pd.DataFrame({'text': corpus, 'sentiment':labels})
   ```

The preceding commands generate the following output:

	text	sentiment
0	This is good pizza	1
1	I love Italian pizza	1
2	The best pizza	1
3	nice pizza	1
4	Excellent pizza	1
5	I love pizza	1
6	The pizza was alright	0
7	disgusting pineapple pizza	0
8	not good pizza	0
9	bad pizza	0
10	very bad pizza	0
11	I had better pizza	0

3. Transform the words of our corpus using a one-hot encoding representation. This is because the embedding layer requires a unique integer:

```
# we extract the vocabulary from our corpus
sentences = [voc.split() for voc in corpus]
vocabulary = set([word for sentence in sentences for word in
sentence])

vocab_size = len(vocabulary)
encoded_corpus = [one_hot(d, vocab_size) for d in corpus]
encoded_corpus
```

We will obtain the following encoded output:

```
[[15, 18, 19, 2],
 [15, 12, 7, 2],
 [11, 15, 2],
 [4, 2],
 [15, 2],
 [15, 12, 2],
 [11, 2, 2, 11],
 [4, 7, 2],
 [9, 19, 2],
 [19, 2],
 [6, 19, 2],
 [15, 1, 14, 2]]
```

4. Our output is composed by vectors of variable length. To have all of them with the same size, we pick one size for all of them, filling with zero to reach missing value. The extra spaces will not be filled with zeros towards the end of the vector:

```
# we now pad the documents to
# the max length of the longest sentences
# to have an uniform length
max_length = 5
padded_docs = pad_sequences(encoded_corpus, maxlen=max_length, padding='post')
print(padded_docs)
```

The preceding commands will give us the following padded output:

```
[[15 18 19  2  0]
 [15 12  7  2  0]
 [11 15  2  0  0]
 [ 4  2  0  0  0]
 [15  2  0  0  0]
 [15 12  2  0  0]
 [11  2  2 11  0]
 [ 4  7  2  0  0]
 [ 9 19  2  0  0]
 [19  2  0  0  0]
 [ 6 19  2  0  0]
 [15  1 14  2  0]]
```

5. Define the model with only two layers. We will use a sequential model with an embedding layer:

```
# model definition
model = Sequential()
model.add(Embedding(vocab_size, output_dim,
input_length=max_length, name='embedding'))
model.add(Flatten())
model.add(Dense(1, activation='sigmoid'))
# compile the model
model.compile(optimizer='adam', loss='binary_crossentropy',
metrics=['acc'])
# summarize the model
print(model.summary())
# fit the model
model.fit(padded_docs, labels, epochs=50, verbose=0)
# evaluate the model

loss, accuracy = model.evaluate(padded_docs, labels, verbose=0)
print('Accuracy: %f' % (accuracy * 100))
```

> It's possible to specify the maximum length of the sequence by setting the num_timesteps parameter. Shorter sequences are padded with values at the end while longer ones are truncated.

The preceding commands generate the following output:

```
Layer (type)                    Output Shape              Param #
=================================================================
embedding_4 (Embedding)         (None, 5, 8)              160
_____
flatten_4 (Flatten)             (None, 40)                0
_____
dense_4 (Dense)                 (None, 1)                 41
=================================================================
Total params: 201
Trainable params: 201
Non-trainable params: 0
_____
None
Accuracy: 83.333331
```

Exploiting Text Embedding

The model to create the embedding. We printed the accuracy although that is not the goal, especially because we trained and tested on the same dataset. The goal is to create a vectorized representation of our world, which it can now be found in the embedding layer.

Pre-trained network

Embedding usually works well when trained in large datasets. Most of the time, this would mean spending a lot of time and resources training the network and having an infrastructure that allows you to do so.

Luckily, there are many pre-trained models that are available to download and use.

GloVe

GloVe stands for **Global Vectors** and is a model to produce a distributed word representation. It's an unsupervised learning method that finds a useful word representation in a vector space using statistics on the co-occurrence words from a corpus.

It combines two methods: global matrix factorization and local context windows. We will now explain these two models in more detail and show an example of how to use it.

Global matrix factorization

Matrix factorization, also known as matrix decomposition, is the decomposition of a matrix into a product of multiple matrices. There are many ways to decompose a matrix depending on the class of problems we aim to solve.

Matrix factorization is intended as a set of algorithms, commonly used in recommender systems. In this case, the system goal is to represent users and items in a lower-dimensional space. This space is also called **latent** and is where latent features, or variables, lie. A latent variable is a variable that is not observable in the inputs but is inferred using a mathematical model, usually called a **latent variable model**.

The main reason to use latent variables is that it's possible to reduce the dimensionality of the data. In recommender systems, data can be really sparse. For example, Amazon Marketplace recommendations deal with millions of users and objects, most of them with little to no interaction.

These types of problems are quite similar to our text task, for which there are many different words, some of them with more than one meaning, of which most won't interact with each other.

With text, we usually have interchangeable words, and, as we saw before, it's possible to infer this by how many times they co-occur in the same context. Words are also represented as term-document frequency, which gives us the frequency of the word in each document in the corpus. In this case, words represent the columns, while the rows represent the documents.

Latent semantic analysis (**LSA**) is only one of the models that use correlations between words to infer the meaning. Others include the following:

- **Hyperspace Analogue to Language (HAL)**
- Syntax- or dependency-based models
- Semantic folding
- Topic models, such as LDA

The factorization of a generic *m*-by-*n* matrix *M* into a product $U \Sigma V^*$, where *U* is *m*-by-*m* and unitary, Σ is an *m*-by-*n* rectangular diagonal matrix (the non-zero entries of which are known as the **singular values of M**), and *V* is *n*-by-*n* and unitary, which looks like this:

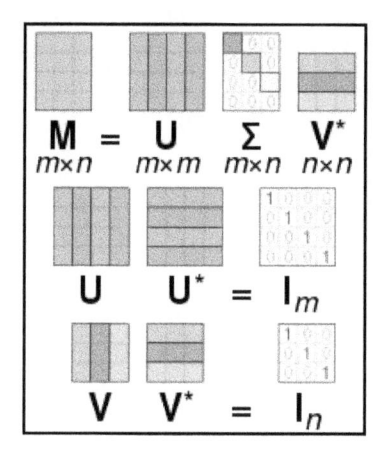

We will now see how it's possible to implement in Python the matrix factorization that we just saw:

```
from numpy import array
from numpy import diag
from numpy import zeros
from numpy import linalg
```

Exploiting Text Embedding

```python
# define a matrix that we want to
A = array([
    [1, 2, 3, 4],
    [5, 6, 7, 8],
    [9, 10, 11, 12]
        ])
print('Initial matrix')
print(A)
# Applying singular-value decomposition
# VT is already the vector we are looking in
# as the formula return it transposed
# while we are interested in the normal form
U, s, VT = linalg.svd(A)
# creating a m x n Sigma matrix
Sigma = zeros((A.shape[0], A.shape[1]))
# populate Sigma with n x n diagonal matrix
Sigma[:A.shape[0], :A.shape[0]] = diag(s)
# select only two elements
n_elements = 2
Sigma = Sigma[:, :n_elements]
VT = VT[:n_elements, :]
# reconstruct
A_reconstructed = U.dot(Sigma.dot(VT))
print(A_reconstructed)
# Calculate the result
# By the dot product
# Between the U and sigma
# In python 3 it's possible to
# calculate the dot product using @
T = U @ Sigma
# for python 2 should be
# T = U.dot(Sigma)
print('dot product between U and Sigma')
print(T)
print('dot product between A and V')
T_ = A @ VT.T
print(T_)

print('Are the dot product similar? ',
      'Yes' if np.isclose(X, X_a).all() else 'no')
```

Using the GloVe model

GloVe computes the probability of the next word given the previous one. In a log-bilinear model, this can be calculated in the following way:

$$P(wi = w|w_i - 1, .., w1) = \frac{\exp(\phi(w)^T c)}{\sum_{w' \in V} \exp(\phi(w')^T c)}$$

Here, let's take a look at the following terms used in the preceding formula:

- $\phi(w)\phi(w)$ is a `word-vector`
- *c* is the context for w_i

c is computed as follows:

$$c = \sum i - 1n = \text{lan}\phi(wn)$$

GloVe is, essentially, a log-bilinear model with a weighted least-squares objective, which means that the overall solution minimizes the sum of the squares of the residuals created in the results of every single equation. The probabilities of the ratios of word-word occurring together, or simultaneously, has the ability to encode some meaning.

We can take an example from the GloVe website (https://nlp.stanford.edu/projects/glove/) and consider the probability that the two words, ice and steam, occur together. This is done by probing with the help of some words from the vocabulary. The following are some probabilities from a word corpus of around 6 billion:

Probability and Ratio	k = solid	k = gas	k = water	k = fashion
P(k|ice)	1.9×10^{-4}	6.6×10^{-5}	3.0×10^{-3}	1.7×10^{-5}
P(k|steam)	2.2×10^{-5}	7.8×10^{-4}	2.2×10^{-3}	1.8×10^{-5}
P(k|ice)/P(k|steam)	8.9	8.5×10^{-2}	1.36	0.96

Looking at these conditional probabilities, we can see that the word *ice* occurs together more frequently near the word *solid* than it does with *gas*, whereas *steam* occurs together less frequently with *solid* compared to *gas*. Steam and gas co-occur with the word *water* frequently, as they are states that water can appear as. On the other hand, they both occur together with the word *fashion* less frequently.

Noise from non-discriminative words, such as water and fashion, cancels out in the ratio of probabilities in a way that any value greater than 1 can correlate with the features specific to that of ice and any value smaller than 1 correlates well with the features that are specific to that of steam. Thus, the ratio of probabilities correlates with the non-realistic concept of thermodynamics.

GloVe's goal is to create vectors that represent words in a way that their dot product will equal the logarithm of the probability words and their co-occurrence. As we know, in the logarithmic scale a ratio is equivalent to the difference of the logarithm of the two elements considered. Because of this, the ratio of the logarithms of the probability of the elements will be translated in the vector space in the difference between two words. Because of this property, it's convenient to use these ratios to encode the meaning in a vector, and this will make it possible to use it for differences and obtain analogies such as the example we saw in Word2vec.

Now let's see how it's possible to run GloVe. First of all, we need to install it using the following commands:

- To compile GloVe we need `gcc`, a c compiler. On macOS, execute the following commands:

    ```
    conda install -c psi4 gcc-6
    pip install glove_python
    ```

- Alternatively, it's possible to execute the following commands:

    ```
    export CC="/usr/local/bin/gcc-6"
    export CFLAGS="-Wa,-q"
    pip install glove_python
    ```

- On macOS using `brew`:

    ```
    brew install gcc
    and then export gcc into CC like:
    export CC=/usr/local/Cellar/gcc/6.3.0_1/bin/g++-6
    ```

Test GloVe with some Python code. We will use an example from https://textminingonline.com:

1. Import the main libraries as follows:

    ```
    import itertools
    from gensim.models.word2vec import Text8Corpus
    from glove import Corpus, Glove
    ```

Chapter 4

2. We need `gensim` just to use their `Text8Corpus`:

   ```
   sentences = list(itertools.islice(Text8Corpus('text8'),None))

   corpus = Corpus()

   corpus.fit(sentences, window=10)
   glove = Glove(no_components=100, learning_rate=0.05)

   glove.fit(corpus.matrix, epochs=30, no_threads=4, verbose=True)
   ```

   Observe the training of the model:

   ```
   Performing 30 training epochs with 4 threads
   Epoch 0
   Epoch 1
   Epoch 2
   ...
   Epoch 27
   Epoch 28
   Epoch 29
   ```

3. Add the dictionary to `glove`:

   ```
   glove.add_dictionary(corpus.dictionary)
   ```

4. Check the similarity among words:

   ```
   glove.most_similar('man')
   Out[10]:
   [(u'terc', 0.82866443231836828),
    (u'woman', 0.81587362007162523),
    (u'girl', 0.79950702967210407),
    (u'young', 0.78944050406331179)]

   glove.most_similar('man', number=10)
   Out[12]:
   [(u'terc', 0.82866443231836828),
    (u'woman', 0.81587362007162523),
    (u'girl', 0.79950702967210407),
    (u'young', 0.78944050406331179),
    (u'spider', 0.78827287082192377),
    (u'wise', 0.7662819233076561),
    (u'men', 0.70576506880860157),
    (u'beautiful', 0.69492684203254429),
    (u'evil', 0.6887102864856347)]

   glove.most_similar('frog', number=10)
   ```

[109]

```
Out[13]:
[(u'shark', 0.75775974484778419),
 (u'giant', 0.71914687122031595),
 (u'dodo', 0.70756087345768237),
 (u'dome', 0.70536309001812902),
 (u'serpent', 0.69089042980042681),
 (u'vicious', 0.68885819147237815),
 (u'blonde', 0.68574786672123234),
 (u'panda', 0.6832336174432142),
 (u'penny', 0.68202780165909405)]

glove.most_similar('girl', number=10)
Out[14]:
[(u'man', 0.79950702967210407),
 (u'woman', 0.79380171669979771),
 (u'baby', 0.77935645649673957),
 (u'beautiful', 0.77447992804057431),
 (u'young', 0.77355323458632896),
 (u'wise', 0.76219894067614957),
 (u'handsome', 0.74155095749823707),
 (u'girls', 0.72011371864695584),
 (u'atelocynus', 0.71560826080222384)]

glove.most_similar('car', number=10)
Out[15]:
[(u'driver', 0.88683873415652947),
 (u'race', 0.84554581794165884),
 (u'crash', 0.76818020141393994),
 (u'cars', 0.76308628267402701),
 (u'taxi', 0.76197230282808859),
 (u'racing', 0.7384645880932772),
 (u'touring', 0.73836030272284159),
 (u'accident', 0.69000847113708996),
 (u'manufacturer', 0.67263805153963518)]

glove.most_similar('queen', number=10)
Out[16]:
[(u'elizabeth', 0.91700558183820069),
 (u'victoria', 0.87533970402870487),
 (u'mary', 0.85515424257738148),
 (u'anne', 0.78273531080737502),
 (u'prince', 0.76833451608330772),
 (u'lady', 0.75227426771795192),
 (u'princess', 0.73927079922218319),
 (u'catherine', 0.73538567181156611),
 (u'tudor', 0.73028985404704971)]
```

Chapter 4

Text classification with GloVe

Now we can see how it's possible to use these vectorized representations to tackle some text classification tasks. This tutorial is a modification of a python tutorial from Robert Guthrie.

After downloading the embedding from GloVe's website (https://nlp.stanford.edu/projects/glove/) we will need to decide which representation we will be using. There are four choices based on the length of the vector (50, 100, 200, 300). We will try the representation with 50 values for each vector:

```
possible_word_vectors = (50, 100, 200, 300)
word_vectors = possible_word_vectors[0]
file_name = f'glove.6B.{word_vectors}d.txt'
filepath = '../data/'
pretrained_embedding = os.path.join(filepath, file_name)
```

Now we will need to create a better structure for the association word/index, we want to have a dictionary where each word is the key and the vectorized representation is the vector. This will be handy after to quickly transform each word into a vector.

We will then use a class that follows the APIs of scikit-learn to transform our document into an average of all its embedding vectors:

```
class EmbeddingVectorizer(object):
    """
    Follows the scikit-learn API
    Transform each document in the average
    of the embedding of the words in it
    """
    def __init__(self, word2vec):
        self.word2vec = word2vec
        self.dim = 50
    def fit(self, X, y):
        return self
    def transform(self, X):
        """
        Find the embedding vector for each word in the dictionary
        and take the mean for each document
        """
        # Renaming it just to make it more understandable
        documents = X
        embedded_docs = []
        for document in documents:
            # For each document
            # Consider the mean of all the embeddings
            embedded_document = []
            for words in document:
```

```
            for w in words:
                if w in self.word2vec:
                    embedded_word = self.word2vec[w]
                else:
                    embedded_word = np.zeros(self.dim)
                embedded_document.append(embedded_word)
            embedded_docs.append(np.mean(embedded_document, axis=0))
        return embedded_docs
```

Now we can finally create the embeddings as follows:

```
# Creating the embedding
e = EmbeddingVectorizer(embeddings_index)
X_train_embedded = e.transform(X_train)
```

With those it's now possible to train our classifier and test it on unseen data:

```
# Train the classifier
rf = RandomForestClassifier(n_estimators=50, n_jobs=-1)
rf.fit(X_train_embedded, y_train)
X_test_embedded = e.transform(X_test)
predictions = rf.predict(X_test_embedded)
```

We then check the predictions' AUC and the confusion matrix to evaluate the performances:

```
print('AUC score: ', roc_auc_score(predictions, y_test))
confusion_matrix(predictions, y_test)
The performances are acceptable, but they could be improved.
AUC score:  0.7390774760383386
array([[224,  89],
       [ 95, 305]])
```

Summary

In this chapter, we learned about machine learning for NLP and word embedding in detail, along with its applications. We also covered GloVe in detail, which involved global matrix factorization and using the GloVe model.

In the next chapter, we will introduce a more sophisticated type of network, **recurrent neural networks (RNNs)**, as well as the math and the concepts behind them.

5
Working with RNNs

So far, we've explored solutions for tasks that are not sequence-based, which means they don't require any history and it will not make any difference knowing what image came before the one that is being classified at the moment. In many other tasks it's very important to know the information that accompanies a piece of information. For example, when we speak, a letter might be pronounced in a different way based on what letter comes before after the concerned letter.

Our brain is able to process this information seemingness, and you could argue that providing more information to the **Neural Networks (NNs)** we saw so far we would be able to process new text.

There is a particular architecture of NNs that aims to solve this problem: **Recurrent Neural Networks (RNNs)**

The important addition that we will discuss in this chapter is a way to extend the type of computational graphs we create to process. A computational graph is a way to structure multiple computations, for example, computing gradients.

The computational graphs we explored only had connections between one layer and the next. An RNN is a network that has one additional type of connection, a recurrent one, which forms a cycle.

In this chapter, we will explore what is achievable with an RNN and how we can build one in Keras to solve a particular problem and following are some main topics that we will cover:

- Recurrent Neural Networks
- Long Short-Term Memory
- LSTMs in Keras

Working with RNNs

Understanding RNNs

RNNs are a family of networks used to solve problems, where it's important to know the sequence of events. They are very similar to **Convolutional Neural Networks (CNNs)**, which are good at predicting grid data, like the below image.

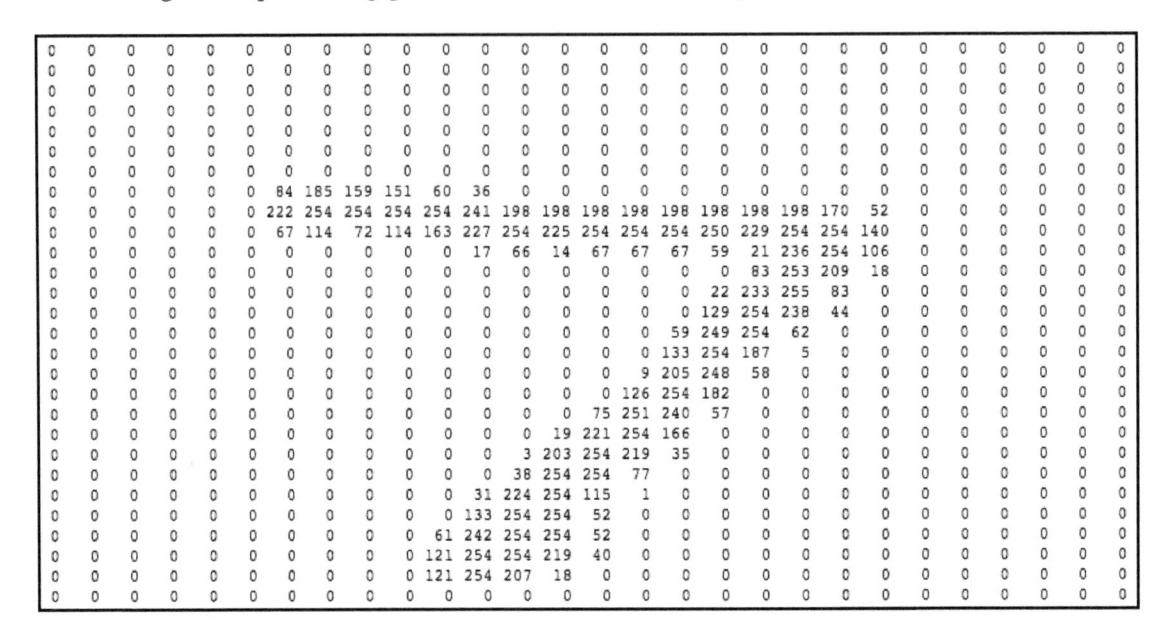

```
0 0 0 0 0 0 0 0 0 0 0 0 0 0 0 0 0 0 0 0 0 0 0 0 0 0 0 0
0 0 0 0 0 0 0 0 0 0 0 0 0 0 0 0 0 0 0 0 0 0 0 0 0 0 0 0
0 0 0 0 0 0 0 0 0 0 0 0 0 0 0 0 0 0 0 0 0 0 0 0 0 0 0 0
0 0 0 0 0 0 0 0 0 0 0 0 0 0 0 0 0 0 0 0 0 0 0 0 0 0 0 0
0 0 0 0 0 0 0 0 0 0 0 0 0 0 0 0 0 0 0 0 0 0 0 0 0 0 0 0
0 0 0 0 0 0 0 0 0 0 0 0 0 0 0 0 0 0 0 0 0 0 0 0 0 0 0 0
0 0 0 0 0 0 0 0 0 0 0 0 0 0 0 0 0 0 0 0 0 0 0 0 0 0 0 0
0 0 0 0 0 0 84 185 159 151 60 36 0 0 0 0 0 0 0 0 0 0 0 0 0 0 0 0
0 0 0 0 0 0 222 254 254 254 254 241 198 198 198 198 198 198 198 198 170 52 0 0 0 0 0 0
0 0 0 0 0 0 67 114 72 114 163 227 254 225 254 254 254 250 229 254 254 140 0 0 0 0 0 0
0 0 0 0 0 0 0 0 0 0 0 17 66 14 67 67 67 59 21 236 254 106 0 0 0 0 0 0
0 0 0 0 0 0 0 0 0 0 0 0 0 0 0 0 0 0 83 253 209 18 0 0 0 0 0 0
0 0 0 0 0 0 0 0 0 0 0 0 0 0 0 0 0 22 233 255 83 0 0 0 0 0 0 0
0 0 0 0 0 0 0 0 0 0 0 0 0 0 0 0 0 129 254 238 44 0 0 0 0 0 0 0
0 0 0 0 0 0 0 0 0 0 0 0 0 0 0 0 59 249 254 62 0 0 0 0 0 0 0 0
0 0 0 0 0 0 0 0 0 0 0 0 0 0 0 0 133 254 187 5 0 0 0 0 0 0 0 0
0 0 0 0 0 0 0 0 0 0 0 0 0 0 0 9 205 248 58 0 0 0 0 0 0 0 0 0
0 0 0 0 0 0 0 0 0 0 0 0 0 0 0 126 254 182 0 0 0 0 0 0 0 0 0 0
0 0 0 0 0 0 0 0 0 0 0 0 0 0 75 251 240 57 0 0 0 0 0 0 0 0 0 0
0 0 0 0 0 0 0 0 0 0 0 0 0 19 221 254 166 0 0 0 0 0 0 0 0 0 0 0
0 0 0 0 0 0 0 0 0 0 0 0 3 203 254 219 35 0 0 0 0 0 0 0 0 0 0 0
0 0 0 0 0 0 0 0 0 0 0 0 38 254 254 77 0 0 0 0 0 0 0 0 0 0 0 0
0 0 0 0 0 0 0 0 0 0 0 31 224 254 115 1 0 0 0 0 0 0 0 0 0 0 0 0
0 0 0 0 0 0 0 0 0 0 0 133 254 254 52 0 0 0 0 0 0 0 0 0 0 0 0 0
0 0 0 0 0 0 0 0 0 0 61 242 254 254 52 0 0 0 0 0 0 0 0 0 0 0 0 0
0 0 0 0 0 0 0 0 0 0 121 254 254 219 40 0 0 0 0 0 0 0 0 0 0 0 0 0
0 0 0 0 0 0 0 0 0 0 121 254 207 18 0 0 0 0 0 0 0 0 0 0 0 0 0 0
0 0 0 0 0 0 0 0 0 0 0 0 0 0 0 0 0 0 0 0 0 0 0 0 0 0 0 0
```

RNNs are better at predicting a sequence of inputs that span over multiple time steps. The input in this case looks as follows:

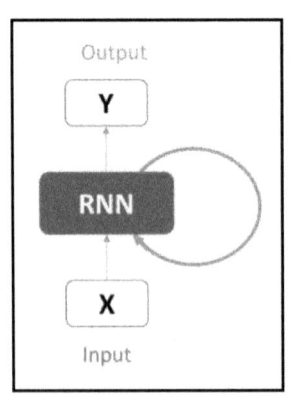

Here, $X(\tau)$ is the value at the time period, τ.

Chapter 5

An example of a sequential task could be to categorize and segment continuous handwritten characters. In this case, to find out when a letter ends and when another starts, it's important to know not only the current information (that is, the pixels), but also the related information:

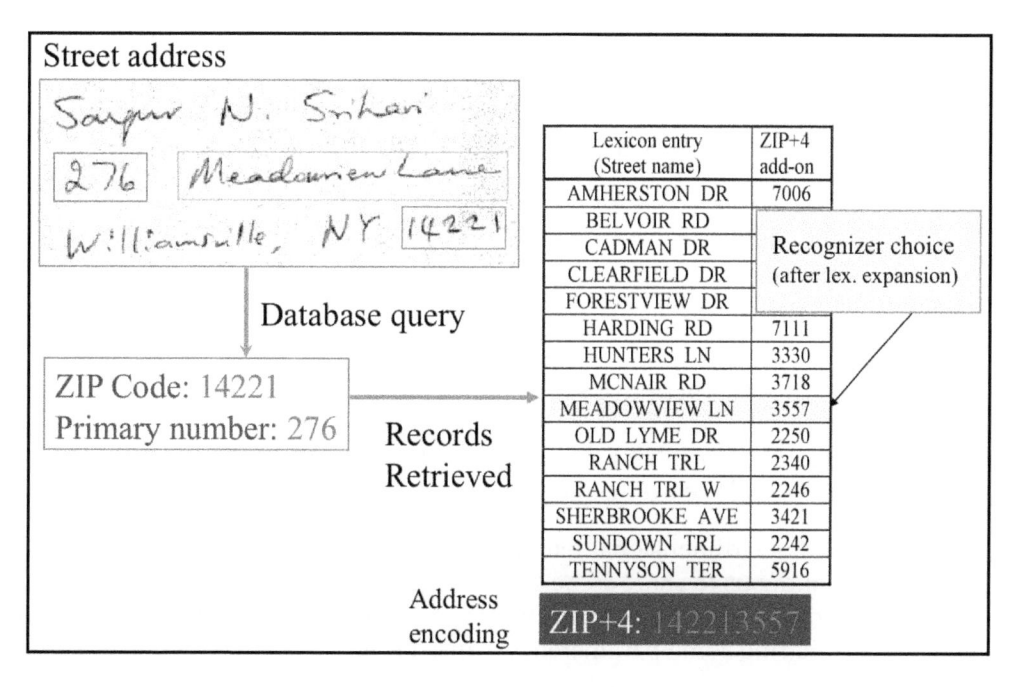

RNNs have been successfully applied to many fields; some of these fields are as follows:

- Speech recognition
- Video sequence prediction
- Machine translation
- Time series predictions
- Music composition
- Handwriting recognition
- Grammar learning

> Some RNNs are Turing complete, meaning that they can simulate any Turing machine. In other words, RNNs can be used to approximate any algorithm.

[115]

Theory behind CNNs

An important concept of RNNs is stemmed from an idea from the 1980s, like many other things in Machine Learning and its related fields. The idea was that it might be possible to share parameters across the model, in this way it is possible to apply the model to instances of different forms and come up with a generalization.

Otherwise, if we take as an example a time series, by having separate values for each parameter, we would not be able to generalize to a sequence that has a length different from a training one.

We saw how convolutional networks can deal with image with large width and height, similarly, RNNs can scale to very long sequences that wouldn't be practical for networks without the recurrent layer. Additionally, as some CNNs can process images of various dimensions, RNNs can also process sequences of variable length.

As an example, let's consider these two sentences: *In 2011, I met my wife* and *I met my wife in 2011*. Here, we want to recognize 2011 as an important year. In a fully connected **feedforward neural network** (**FFNN**) we would need to separate the parameters for each input feature so that it would learn the language rules separated by position.

Using a CNN across a one-dimensional temporal sequence and the same sequence with a time delay, it could allow us to share some of the weights across time, but in a shallow manner, as the convolution would be made only on a closed neighborhood of the network. In this way, we are sharing some parameters because of the convolution with the kernels.

In RNNs, each member of the output is a function of the previous members of the output; this is by applying the same update rule to previous outputs. In this manner, it is possible to share weights through a very deep convolutional graph, such as the following diagram:

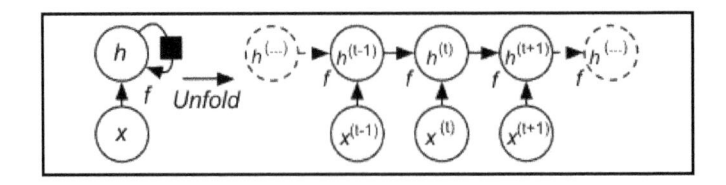

We denote the input of an RNN with a vector, $x^{(t)}$, with the time step that goes from 1 to τ. Most of the time, an RNN operates on mini-batches composed by sequences with different lengths for each member.

An RNN can also be applied on sequences with multiple dimensions that are linked through time, for example, a video.

The advantages of RNNs are as follows:

- There is no limitation on the input length, without impacting the model size
- They are able to take sequential history into account
- Weights are shared across time

On the other hand, the disadvantages of RNNs are as follows:

- They are time-intensive
- They have difficulty accessing information from a long time ago
- They cannot consider any future input for the current state

Types of RNNs

There are several types of RNNs that connect the same unit through time (each in a different way). Let's consider the classical form of a dynamic system driven by the external signal, *x(t)*, and composed by state, *s*, as follows:

$$s(t) = f(s(t-1), x(t); \theta)$$

This equation is recurrent as it's referring to the state at the time, *t-1*. However, *t-1* would also depend on *t-2*, therefore, we could define this equation as follows:

$$s(t) = f(s(t-1); \theta) = f(f(s(t-2); \theta); \theta)$$

At the time, *t=3*, the equation will be updated to the following formula:

$$s(3) = f(s(2); \theta) = f(f(s(1); \theta); \theta)$$

To make it more explicit that we are talking about the hidden state of the unit, we can use *h* instead of *s*, and rewrite the formula as follows:

$$h(t) = f(h(t-1), x(t); \theta),$$

Any recurrent function can be described with RNNs. All the previous states are summarized by the current state, *h(t)*; because of this, we can say that *h(t)* is a lossy compression of the previous information.

Working with RNNs

Use h(t) as a type of lossy summary of the task-relevant aspects of the past sequence of inputs up to the current one. This summary is necessarily lossy, since it maps an arbitrary length, that is, *sequence(x(t), x(t–1), x(t–2), . . . , x(2), x(1))*, to a fixed length vector, *h(t)*. How far back we want to go will depend on the type of problem; for example, if we want to predict the next word, we will only consider a few prior positions, such as two or three previous words or outputs.

The main types of RNN are as follows:

- An RNN with a recurrent connection between hidden units, which fires an output at each time step
- An RNN that has a recurrent connection between the output and the hidden unit at the next time step
- Recurrent connections between the hidden units and the output are obtained only after processing the whole sequence

For each time step, *t*, the activation, *a(t)*, and the output, *y(t)*, are expressed as follows:

$$a(t) = g1(Waata(t-1) + Waxx(t) + ba$$

If we denote with **Wax, Waa, Wya, ba, by, Wax, Waa, Wya,** and **ba,** by the coefficients that are shared temporally and with the **g1, g2, g1, g2** activation functions, as shown in the following diagram:

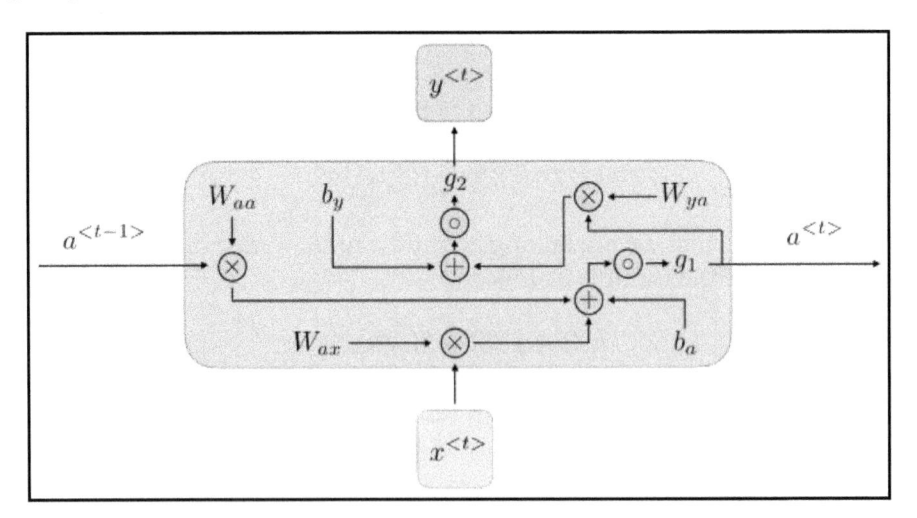

Based on different time differences we will have different types of RNNs.

[118]

One-to-one

When we have both the input and the output used to only compute the same time step, we will have a simple NN, as follows:

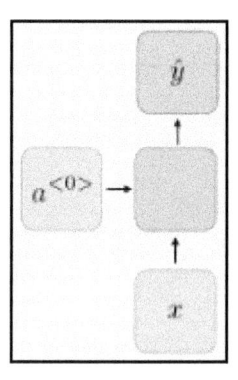

One-to-many

Some networks will only use the current input but they will also consider the output from the previous time step. This type of architecture is used in music generation, where the notes must somehow follow a pleasant pattern:

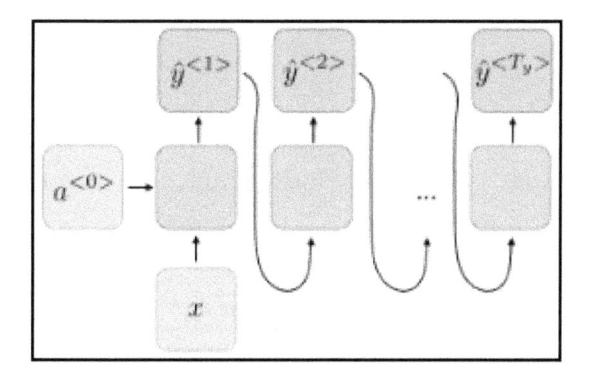

Many-to-many

For some tasks, it's important to have information not only from the previous inputs but also the previous output.

We can further distinguish between two different types of architecture based on the time difference that we are interested in.

Working with RNNs

The same lag
This is when both the input and output are considered with the same time window. This commonly used for sentiment classification. In this case, the network architecture will look like this:

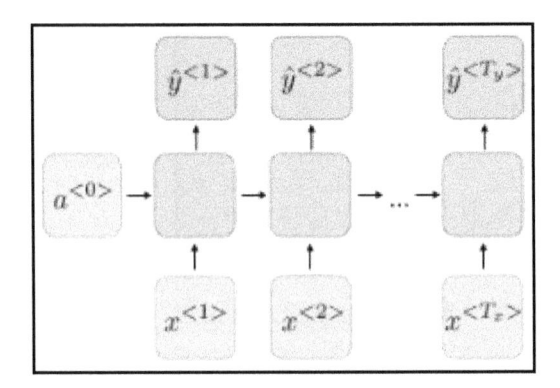

A different lag
Sometimes it's useful to remove the restriction of having the same temporal difference. This type of architecture is used for machine translation:

Loss functions
The loss function, in this case, is the sum of the loss functions over the time window, defined as follows:

$$Loss(y, y') = \sum_{t=1}^{T} Loss(y^t, y'^t)$$

As an activation function, it's common to use sigmoid, tanh, and ReLU. One of the problems that we might have in an RNN (which we might not encounter in FFNN) is that the gradient of the loss function can also explode (not only vanish). This because of the recurrent connections that provide a history of the past instances, which creates a multiplicative gradient that can exponentially increase or decrease. Gradient clipping is used to avoid the explosion of the gradient and this is done by limiting its maximum value, as shown in the following graph:

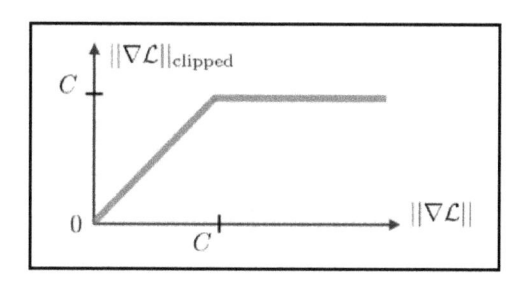

Another way to control the gradient is by using some specific type of gates. Gates are usually indicated with Γ and are defined as follows:

$$\Gamma = \sigma(Wx^t + Ua^{t-1} + b)$$

Here, W, U, and b are coefficients specific to the gate and σ is the sigmoid function. The main ones are summed up in the following table:

Type of gate	Role
Update gate ΓuΓu	Decides how much past information will affect the result
Relevance gate ΓrΓr	Decides whether we should drop the previous information
Forget gate ΓfΓf	Decides whether we should erase the cell

Long Short-Term Memory

One of the main problems in RNNs is that the gradient vanishes pretty quickly with an increase in the time steps. There are some architectures that help alleviate this problem, and the most common one is **Long Short-Term Memory (LSTM)**.

A very common type of RNN is LSTM. This type of network is much better at capturing long-term dependencies than simple RNNs. The only unusual thing about LSTMs is the way that they compute the hidden state.

Working with RNNs

Essentially, an LSTM is composed of a cell, an **Input Gate**, an **Output Gate**, and a **Forget Gate**, which is the unusual thing about it, as shown in the following diagram:

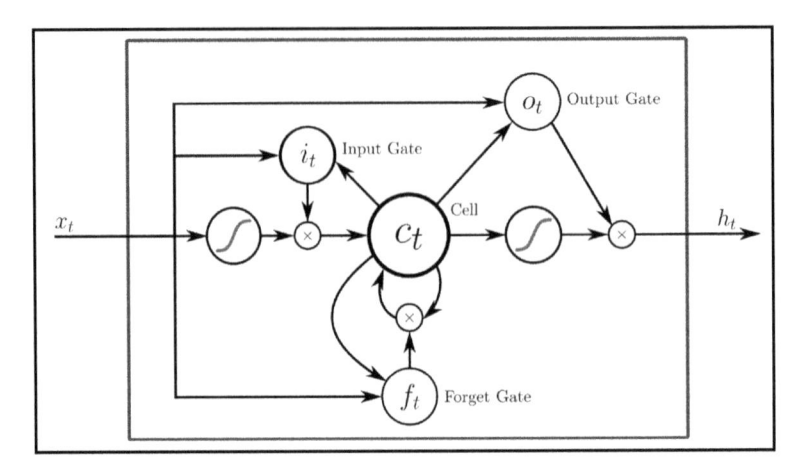

LSTM architecture

This type of network is used to classify and make predictions from time series data. For example, some LSTM applications include handwriting recognition or speech recognition.

One of the properties of LSTM architecture is the ability to deal with lags of different durations (which it does better than RNNs).

The equation of an LSTM with a forget gate is given as follows:

$$f_t = \sigma_g(W_f x_t + U_f h_{t-1} + b_f)$$
$$i_t = \sigma_g(W_i x_t + U_i h_{t-1} + b_i)$$
$$o_t = \sigma_g(W_o x_t + U_o h_{t-1} + b_o)$$
$$c_t = f_t \circ c_{t-1} + i_t \circ \sigma_c(W_c x_t + U_c h_{t-1} + b_c)$$
$$h_t = o_t \circ \sigma_h(c_t)$$

Now take a look at the following notation:

$x_t \in \mathbb{R}^a$: input vector to the LSTM unit
$f_t \in \mathbb{R}^h$: forget gate's activation vector
$i_t \in \mathbb{R}^h$: input gate's activation vector
$o_t \in \mathbb{R}^h$: output gate's activation vector
$h_t \in \mathbb{R}^h$: hidden state vector also known as output vector of the LSTM unit
$c_t \in \mathbb{R}^h$: cell state vector
$W \in \mathbb{R}^{h \times d}, U \in \mathbb{R}^{h \times h}$ and $b \in \mathbb{R}^h$: weight matrices and bias vector parameters which need to be learned during training

Here, the LSTM needs to decide what information we're going to throw away from the cell. This is done by a type of gate called the **forget layer**. It's implemented using a sigmoid function that evaluates the hidden state and the current input in order to decide whether we keep the information or get rid of it.

If we want to predict the next word based on the previous one, the information of the cell might store is the gender of the noun, to predict the next world correctly. If we change the subject we want to forget the previous gender information, and that what this gate is used to:

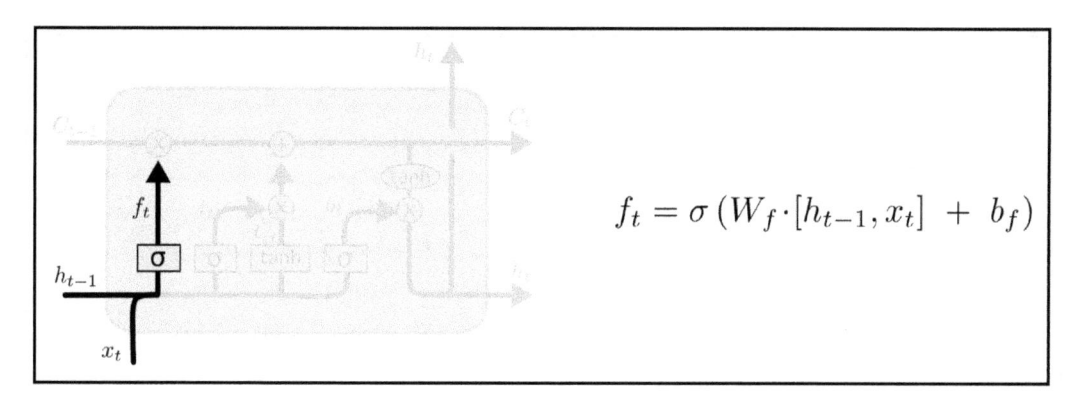

$$f_t = \sigma\left(W_f \cdot [h_{t-1}, x_t] + b_f\right)$$

Working with RNNs

The second step would be to decide what information the cell should store. In our example, it would be to determine the gender we should store once we forget the previous one. This is done in two parts; the first part is composed of a sigmoid that decides which value we should update. Then, another layer, which uses *tanh*, is used to create a vector of candidates:

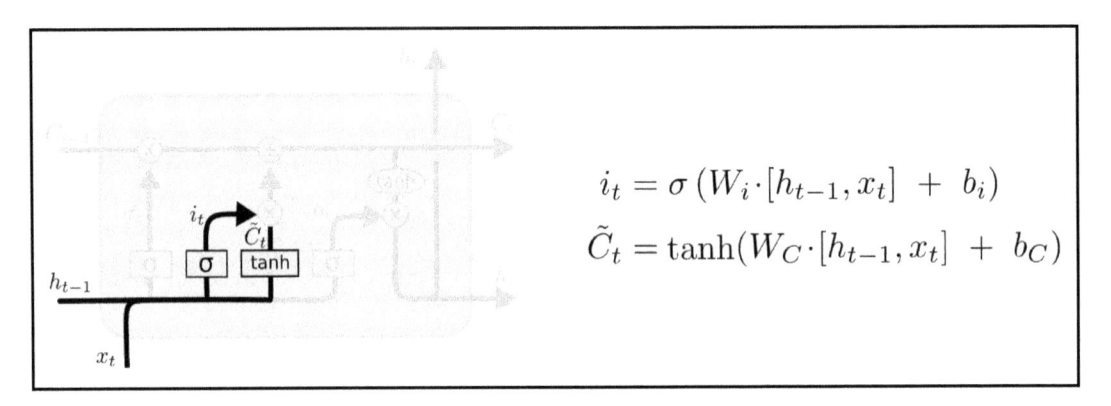

$$i_t = \sigma\left(W_i \cdot [h_{t-1}, x_t] + b_i\right)$$

$$\tilde{C}_t = \tanh(W_C \cdot [h_{t-1}, x_t] + b_C)$$

Now we have the decision as to whether we should drop the information *and* the new potential value:

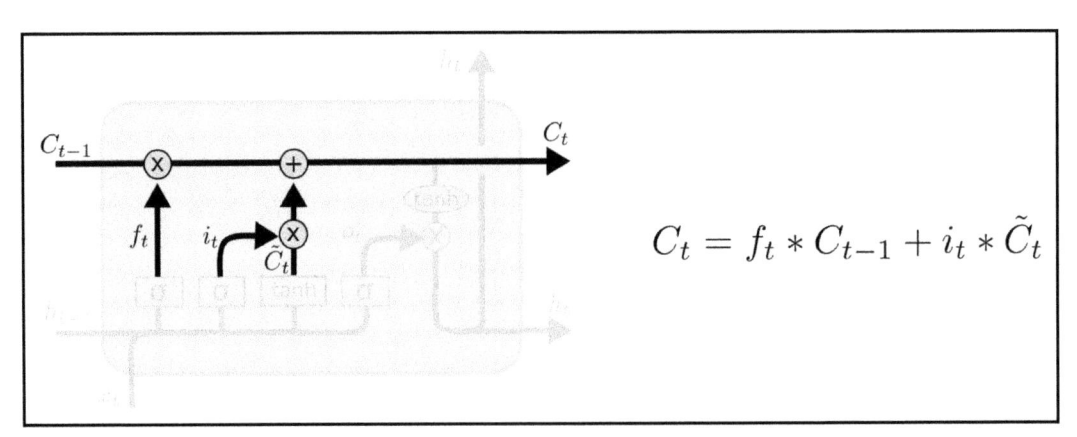

$$C_t = f_t * C_{t-1} + i_t * \tilde{C}_t$$

At the end of the notation, the cell decides what to output. The first part is to decide what part of the cell we are going to output. This is determined by a sigmoid. The second part is to squash the values between **-1** and **1**, and then multiply it by the sigmoid gate:

$$o_t = \sigma\left(W_o\left[h_{t-1}, x_t\right] + b_o\right)$$

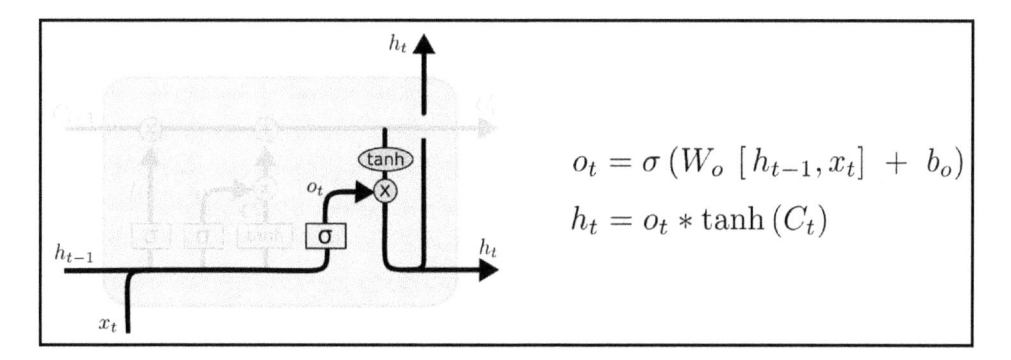

$$h_t = o_t * \tanh\left(C_t\right)$$

In our language model task, we can decide to output information about whether the subject is plural or singular, to inform, for example, the next verb conjugation.

Gated Recurrent Units (GRUs) operate in a similar way to LSTMs but with fewer parameters, as they do not have an output gate. It has a similar performance in some tasks, but in general, LSTM architecture provides better performance:

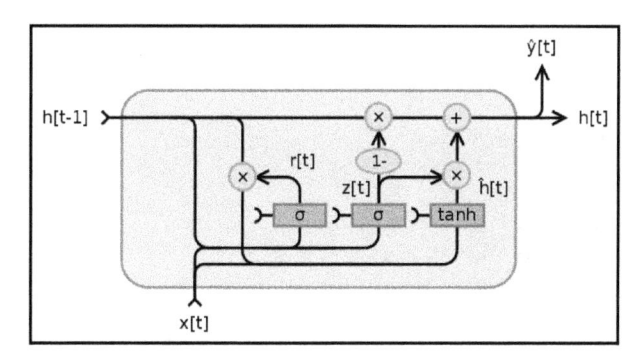

LSTMs in Keras

We will now demonstrate an example of an LSTM implemented in keras to solve a simple time series prediction problem:

1. Import all the required libraries as follows:

```
%matplotlib inline
import numpy
import matplotlib.pyplot as plt
from pandas import read_csv
import math
from keras.models import Sequential
```

```
from keras.layers import Dense
from keras.layers import LSTM
from sklearn.preprocessing import MinMaxScaler
from sklearn.metrics import mean_squared_error
import os
import numpy as np
import math

# Necessary for some OSX version
os.environ['KMP_DUPLICATE_LIB_OK'] = 'True'

# fix a random seed for reproducibility
numpy.random.seed(11)
```

2. Define a few parameters that will be important for later on, as follows:

```
LEN_DATASET = 100
EPOCHS = 50
BATCH_SIZE = 1

# It's going to be used to
# reshape into X=t and Y=t+1
look_back = 1
```

3. Create the dataset as follows:

```
sin_wave = np.array(
    [math.sin(x) + i * 0.1 for i, x in
enumerate(np.arange(LEN_DATASET))])
dataset = sin_wave.reshape(len(sin_wave), 1)
```

The preceding commands generate the time series that we have to model:

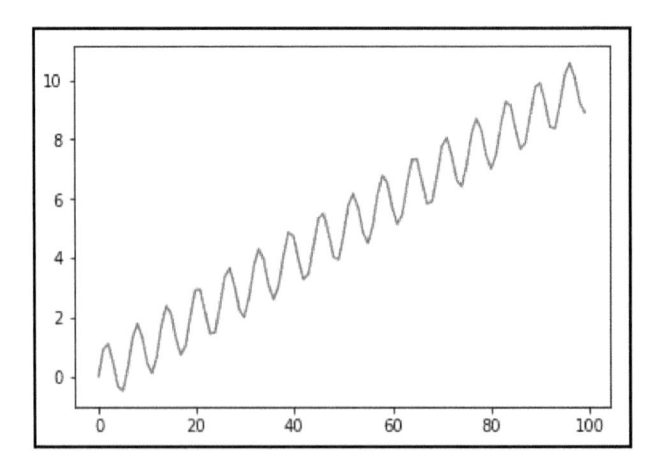

Chapter 5

4. Define a function to reshape the input data, as follows:

```
def create_dataset(dataset, look_back=1):
    X, Y = [], []
    for i in range(len(dataset) - look_back - 1):
        a = dataset[i:(i + look_back), 0]
        X.append(a)
        Y.append(dataset[i + look_back, 0])
    return numpy.array(X), numpy.array(Y)
```

5. Create a training set to fit our model and a test set to verify the performances by executing the following commands:

```
# normalize the dataset
scaler = MinMaxScaler(feature_range=(0, 1))
dataset = scaler.fit_transform(dataset)
# split into train and test sets
train_size = int(len(dataset) * 2/3)
test_size = len(dataset) - train_size
train, test = dataset[0:train_size, :],
dataset[train_size:len(dataset), :]

X_train, y_train = create_dataset(train, look_back)
X_test, y_test = create_dataset(test, look_back)
# reshape input to be [samples, time steps, features]
X_train = numpy.reshape(X_train, (X_train.shape[0], 1,
X_train.shape[1]))
X_test = numpy.reshape(X_test, (X_test.shape[0], 1,
X_test.shape[1]))
```

6. Define a simple network; to accomplish this, we will use the LSTM function from `keras`, as follows:

```
# create and fit the LSTM network
model = Sequential()
model.add(LSTM(4, input_shape=(1, look_back)))
model.add(Dense(1))
model.compile(loss='mean_squared_error', optimizer='adam')
model.fit(X_train, y_train, epochs=EPOCHS, batch_size=BATCH_SIZE,
verbose=2)
```

7. Make the predictions as follows:

```
# Making the predictions
predictions_train = model.predict(X_train)
predictions_test = model.predict(X_test)
```

Working with RNNs

8. Invert the scaler we applied to the input data:

   ```
   # Re-applying the scaling to the predictions
   predictions_train = scaler.inverse_transform(predictions_train)
   predictions_test = scaler.inverse_transform(predictions_test)
   y_train = scaler.inverse_transform([y_train])
   y_test = scaler.inverse_transform([y_test])
   ```

9. Calculate the root mean square error, as follows:

   ```
   # calculate root mean squared error
   trainScore = math.sqrt(mean_squared_error(y_train[0],
   predictions_train[:, 0]))
   testScore = math.sqrt(mean_squared_error(y_test[0],
   predictions_test[:, 0]))

   print('Train RMSE: %.2f ' % (trainScore))
   print('Test RMSE: %.2f ' % (testScore))
   ```

   This will produce the following output:

   ```
   Epoch 1/50
    - 5s - loss: 0.0991
   Epoch 2/50
    - 0s - loss: 0.0559
   Epoch 3/50
    - 0s - loss: 0.0331
   Epoch 4/50
    - 0s - loss: 0.0236
   Epoch 5/50
    - 0s - loss: 0.0203
   Epoch 6/50
    - 0s - loss: 0.0186
   Epoch 7/50
    - 0s - loss: 0.0176
   ```

10. Verify the accuracy of the predictions graphically, as follows:

    ```
    # shift train predictions for plotting
    predictions_train_plot = numpy.empty_like(dataset)
    predictions_train_plot[:, :] = numpy.nan
    predictions_train_plot[look_back:len(predictions_train) +
    look_back, :] = predictions_train

    # shift test predictions for plotting
    predictions_test_plot = numpy.empty_like(dataset)
    predictions_test_plot[:, :] = numpy.nan
    predictions_test_plot[len(predictions_train) + (look_back * 2) +
    ```

[128]

```
1:len(dataset) -1, :] = predictions_test

# plot baseline and predictions
plt.plot(scaler.inverse_transform(dataset))
plt.plot(predictions_train_plot, label='Training set')
plt.plot(predictions_test_plot, label='Test set')
plt.legend(loc='upper left')
plt.show()
```

The preceding commands, if executed, will produce the following graph:

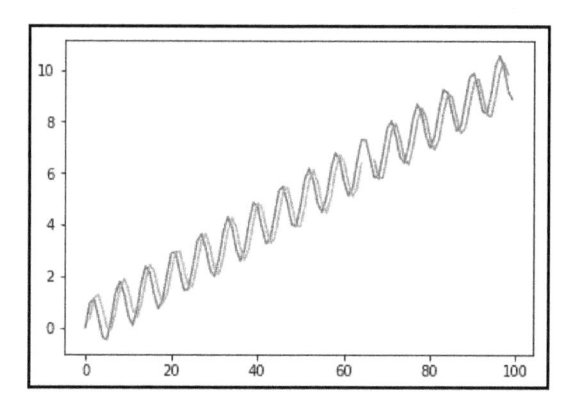

The blue line represents the whole time series; in red, we see the training set, and our predictions are in green.

PyTorch basics

PyTorch is another deep learning framework that aims to provide an efficient way to compute graphs using Pythonic APIs. According to the authors, it has the following two goals:

- To provide an equivalent to NumPy that is capable of using the computational power of **Graphics Processing Units (GPUs)**
- To create a deep learning research platform

What really distinguishes PyTorch from other popular frameworks is the adoption of a **Dynamic Computational Graph (DCG)**. Usually, a static graph is used as it's possible to optimize it and run it in parallel in the target GPU. This can be a problem if we require more flexibility; for example, by changing the execution graph as we train the algorithm. This is especially useful in **natural language processing (NLP)** when spoken expression can be of different lengths.

Working with RNNs

To accomplish these goals, it relies on tensors, which are the equivalent of `ndarray` in NumPy but with the addition that they can also be computed on a GPU:

```
import torch
x, y = 3, 2
# Create a matrix
# of dimension x and y
x = torch.Tensor(x, y)
print(x)
```

A fundamental part of PyTorch is the `autograd` package. It provides auto-differentiation for all operations on tensors. To define the operation in a tensor, we need to initiate `tensor` in `torch.Tensor`. If we set `requires_grad` as `True`, PyTorch starts recording the operations on it. Then, we call `backwards()` on our `tensor`.

To be able to do this, we will need to set the `requires_grad` parameter to `true`. This will make sure that `torch.autograd` records operations on `tensor` for automatic differentiation:

```
x = torch.tensor([[1., -1.], [1., 1.]], requires_grad=True)
```

Then, to differentiate, it's enough to specify the following command:

```
my_tensor.backward()
```

We will have the gradient computed automatically. So, we don't need to explicitly define the gradient as we did before. We will now take a look at an example of an NLP prediction task using PyTorch to solve it.

Time series prediction

We will now demonstrate how to use an RNN to perform **Part-of-Speech** (**PoS**) tagging on a very simple dataset by performing the following steps:

1. Import the main libraries as follows:

    ```
    # Author: Robert Guthrie

    import torch
    import torch.nn as nn
    import torch.nn.functional as F
    import torch.optim as optim

    torch.manual_seed(1)
    ```

2. Create the dataset; we are going to use a toy example, as follows:

```
#
https://pytorch.org/tutorials/beginner/nlp/sequence_models_tutorial
.html#example-an-lstm-for-part-of-speech-tagging
import numpy as np

def prepare_sequence(seq, to_ix):
    idxs = [to_ix[w] for w in seq]
    return torch.tensor(idxs, dtype=torch.long)


training_data = [
    ("My grandmother ate the polemta".split(), ["DET", "NN", "V",
    "DET", "NN"]),
    ("Marina read my book".split(), ["NN", "V", "DET", "NN"])
]
word_index = {}
for sent, tags in training_data:
    for word in sent:
        if word not in word_index:
            word_index[word] = len(word_index)

print(word_index)
tag_to_ix = {"DET": 0, "NN": 1, "V": 2}

# These will usually be more like 32 or 64 dimensional.
# We will keep them small, so we can see how the weights change as we train.
EMBEDDING_DIM = 6
HIDDEN_DIM = 6
```

The preceding commands generates the following output:

```
{'My': 0, 'grandmother': 1, 'ate': 2, 'the': 3, 'polemta': 4,
'Linda': 5, 'read': 6, 'my': 7, 'book': 8}
```

3. Define the LSTM model as follows:

```
class LSTMTagger(nn.Module):

    def __init__(self, embedding_dim, hidden_dim, vocab_size,
    tagset_size):
        super(LSTMTagger, self).__init__()
        self.hidden_dim = hidden_dim

        self.word_embeddings = nn.Embedding(vocab_size,
        embedding_dim)
```

Working with RNNs

```
        # The LSTM takes word embeddings as inputs, and outputs
        hidden states
        # with dimensionality hidden_dim.
        self.lstm = nn.LSTM(embedding_dim, hidden_dim)

        # The linear layer that maps from hidden state space to tag
        space
        self.hidden2tag = nn.Linear(hidden_dim, tagset_size)

    def forward(self, sentence):
        embeds = self.word_embeddings(sentence)
        lstm_out, _ = self.lstm(embeds.view(len(sentence), 1, -1))
        tag_space = self.hidden2tag(lstm_out.view(len(sentence),
        -1))
        tag_scores = F.log_softmax(tag_space, dim=1)
        return tag_scores
```

4. Train the network as follows:

```
# Training the model

model = LSTMTagger(EMBEDDING_DIM, HIDDEN_DIM, len(word_index),
len(tag_to_ix))
loss_function = nn.NLLLoss()
optimizer = optim.SGD(model.parameters(), lr=0.1)


for epoch in range(300): # again, normally you would NOT do 300
epochs, it is toy data
    for sentence, tags in training_data:
        # Step 1. Remember that Pytorch accumulates gradients.
        # We need to clear them out before each instance
        model.zero_grad()

        # Step 2. Get our inputs ready for the network, that is,
        turn them into
        # Tensors of word indices.
        sentence_in = prepare_sequence(sentence, word_index)
        targets = prepare_sequence(tags, tag_to_ix)

        # Step 3. Run our forward pass.
        tag_scores = model(sentence_in)

        # Step 4. Compute the loss, gradients, and update the
        parameters by
        # calling optimizer.step()
        loss = loss_function(tag_scores, targets)
        loss.backward()
```

```
        optimizer.step()

# See what the scores are after training
with torch.no_grad():
    inputs = prepare_sequence(training_data[0][0], word_index)
    tag_scores = model(inputs)

    # The sentence is "my grandmother ate the polenta". i,j
    corresponds to score for tag j
    # for word i. The predicted tag is the maximum scoring tag.
    # Here, we can see the predicted sequence below is 0 1 2 0 1
    # since 0 is index of the maximum value of row 1,
    # 1 is the index of maximum value of row 2, etc.
    # Which is DET NOUN VERB DET NOUN, the correct sequence!
    print(tag_scores)
```

The preceding commands generate the following result:

```
tensor([[-0.3892, -1.2426, -3.3890],
        [-2.1082, -0.1328, -5.8464],
        [-3.0852, -5.9469, -0.0495],
        [-0.0499, -3.4414, -4.0961],
        [-2.4540, -0.0929, -5.8799]])
```

Note that we cannot check whether the algorithm has learned:

```
import numpy as np

ix_to_tag = {0: "DET", 1: "NN", 2: "V"}

def get_max_prob_result(inp, ix_to_tag):
    idx_max = np.argmax(inp, axis=0)
    return ix_to_tag[idx_max]

test_sentence = training_data[0][0]
inputs = prepare_sequence(test_sentence, word_index)
tag_scores = model(inputs)
for i in range(len(test_sentence)):
    print('{}: {}'.format(test_sentence[i],
        get_max_prob_result(tag_scores[i].data.numpy(),
        ix_to_tag)))
```

Now we can verify that the following output is the one that was expected:

```
The: DET
dog: NN
ate: V
the: DET
apple: NN
```

Summary

In this chapter, we demonstrated how to replicate any function, as RNNs are Turing complete. In particular, we explored how to solve time-dependent series data or time series data.

In particular, we learned how to implement an LSTM and its architecture. We learned about its ability to capture both long- and short-term dependencies. LSTM has a chain-like structure, which is similar to a simple RNN; however, instead of one, it has four neural network layers. These layers form a gate that allows the network to add or remove information if certain conditions are met.

Additionally, we learned how to implement an RNN using `keras`. We also introduced another tool, which is particularly useful for complex tasks, such as NLP with PyTorch. PyTorch allows you to compute the execution graph dynamically, which is particularly useful for tasks that have variable data.

In the next chapter, we will explore how to make use of networks to train and solve one task for different tasks that they have been trained on.

6
Reusing Neural Networks with Transfer Learning

There is a fundamental difference between the way humans learn and the way machines learn. A clear advantage for humans is our ability to transfer knowledge between different domains. So far, we have only explored techniques that make our models learn tasks, such as image recognition. In this chapter, we will see how it's possible to generalize learning and use a model trained for another task to solve different problems. We will also explore a code example of transfer learning, in PyTorch.

Following are the topics that will be covered in this book:

- Transfer learning theory
- Implementing multi-task learning
- Feature extraction
- Implementation in PyTorch

Transfer learning theory

As we have said in previous chapters, hidden layers of neural networks can be used to automatically build features on top of each other. This way of building features automatically from raw data is quite efficient. For example, if we want to build an image classification algorithm that classifies different types of artwork, we don't need to hand-craft features; we can outsource this process to the network.

This also has the advantage of creating a different and compact representation of the main features that are important in our task. These can potentially be used to algorithmically generate new instances of the object of our classification. In our example, we would be able to generate realistic artwork. We will see how we can generate new instances in more detail in `Chapter 7`, *Working with Generative Algorithms*.

There is another important aspect of **Neural Networks** (**NNs**). You might wonder how specific these features are to the task they have been trained on. Turns out that it's possible to re-use networks that have been trained for one task to solve similar tasks with minor adjustments.

This process is called **transfer learning** (**TL**), and it can be especially useful when you don't have much available data but do have a very high-performing network that was trained for a similar task. For example, a network trained to recognize cars could be re-used to recognize trucks. Of course, it would be necessary to make some modifications, but re-using part of the network has several advantages as follows:

- Less time needed to train the network
- Less data needed
- Cheaper to train

On the other hand, we also have some problems and limitations. One of the problems you might experience with TensorFlow is that your assumptions on the similarity of the tasks is not accurate. Also, if you don't have a good understanding of the theory behind TensorFlow, you might lose visibility and make the problem much more difficult to solve. This is because, by hiding one of the complexities, it will also be more difficult to find out why the network is not performing as expected.

Introducing multi-task learning

Multi-task learning (**MTL**) is a type of algorithm in which a model is trained on different tasks at the same time. In this way, the network creates weights that are more generic and not tied to a specific task. In general, these models are more adaptable and flexible.

Refer to `https://www.datacamp.com/community/tutorials/transfer-learning` for more information.

With this task, we will have a few initial shared layers.

The assumption is that training a network on different tasks will make the network able to generalize to more tasks, maintaining a good level of performance. The way it will achieve that is to create some layers that are more generic.

Reusing other networks as feature extractors

Another popular application of TL is using pre-trained networks to extract useful features. To be able to apply this technique, we will need to find a pre-trained network on a similar task, after which we need to customize it for our task.

Implementing MTL

Now, we will see in more detail what we need to do in an MTL task.

There are different ways to implement MTL. Two methods that are commonly used are as follows:

- **Hard parameter sharing**: This is the most common way to implement MTL, and it consists of sharing some of the hidden layers across all tasks, while other layers are kept specific for each single task:

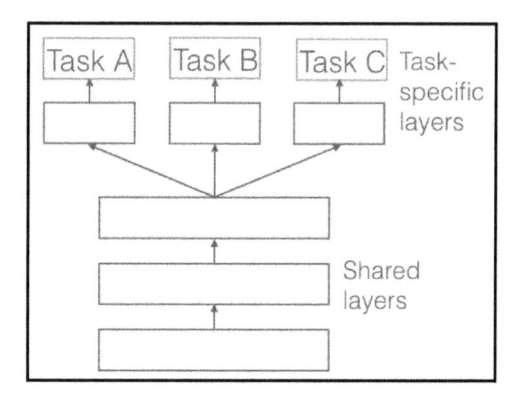

    The main advantage of this method is that it's difficult to overfit. Overfitting is particularly a problem for NNs, but in this case, the more tasks, the lower the danger of overfitting. This is quite clear, because overfitting is creating a solution that is too specific for the dataset we provide, while in this case, by design, we have a more generic task and a variegated dataset.

- **Soft parameter sharing**: With soft parameter sharing, we have one model, but each task will have its own parameters. In this case, we train the full network on different tasks, but then we add a constraint to make sure the parameters will be similar overall. Regularization techniques are often used to accomplish that, in particular the L2 norm. This type of normalization imposes a penalty on large differences among the parameters at the same level of the network:

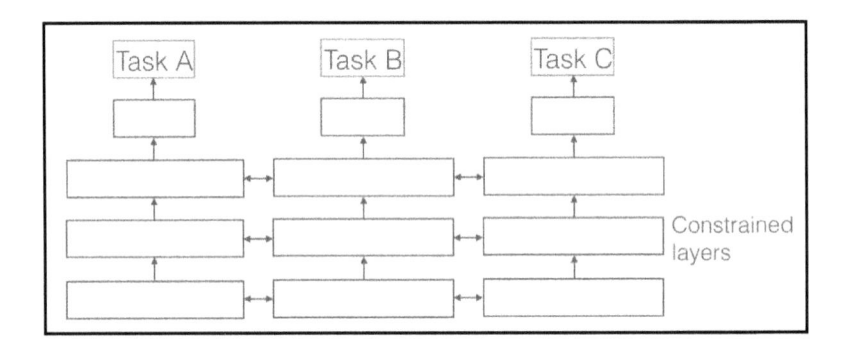

Implementing any MLT strategy has some advantages over classical learning. In particular, some of the main things we can accomplish are as follows:

- **Increases the dataset**: By using different tasks, we will have more data available to train out network.
- **Regularization**: By having constraints on the weights, we attain regularization.
- **Increases the importance of generic features**: MLT will make sure that more generic features will be remembered by the weights, since task-specific features would increase the error of the other tasks. If that does not happen, we will have something called **negative transfer**, where task-specific features will contribute negatively to another task.
- **Eavesdrop**: Some features are easy to learn in one task and difficult to learn from another. MLT increases the chance of learning more interesting features by working on a multitude of tasks.

Feature extraction

Another simpler but usually less effective way of doing TL is to use a network trained on a specific task as a feature extractor. In this way, the feature we will extract will be very dependent on the task.

But we also know that the features created in different layers follow a hierarchical structure that will learn a high-level representation of the image in the following different layers:

- **Lower layer**: Features in lower layers will be very low-level. This means that they are quite generic and simple. Examples of features extracted in the first layer can be lines, edges, or linear relationships; we saw previously that, with one layer, we can describe linear relationships. The second layer will be able to capture more complex shapes, such as curves.
- **Higher layer**: Features in higher layers will be more high-level descriptions of our inputs. Parts of it might be too specific to one task, and other parts can be adapted. For example, if the task is to classify a bird, you would be able to see the beak and part of the head.
- **Last layer**: Depending on the task, this is where feature creation ends and where classification starts.

Depending on how similar the two tasks are, we will determine how much of the network we should retrain with data from the new task.

Implementing TL in PyTorch

Now we will see how it's possible to implement TL in PyTorch by performing the following steps. We will use a standard training set, cats and dogs, and a pre-trained network:

1. Import the necessary libraries as follows:

    ```
    import torch
    import torchvision
    import torch.nn as nn
    import numpy as np
    import torch.optim as optim
    from torchvision import models
    from torchvision import transforms
    import copy
    import os
    from os import listdir
    import shutil
    ```

Reusing Neural Networks with Transfer Learning

```
from torchvision import datasets
import random
from torch.optim import lr_scheduler
import matplotlib.pyplot as plt
```

2. Now, we will use a handy PyTorch function:

```
# # Create train and test dataset

data_dir = os.path.join('kagglecatsanddogs_3367a','PetImages')

# # Create the train and test set folder
train_dir = os.path.join(data_dir, 'train')
validation_dir = os.path.join(data_dir, 'validation')
train_dir_cat = os.path.join(train_dir,'Cat')
train_dir_dog = os.path.join(train_dir,'Dog')
validation_dir_cat = os.path.join(validation_dir,'Cat')
validation_dir_dog = os.path.join(validation_dir,'Dog')

try:
    os.mkdir(train_dir)
    os.mkdir(train_dir_dog)
    os.mkdir(train_dir_cat)
    os.mkdir(validation_dir)
    os.mkdir(validation_dir_dog)
    os.mkdir(validation_dir_cat)
except FileExistsError:
    print('File exists')

dir_cat = os.path.join(data_dir,'Cat')
dir_dog = os.path.join(data_dir,'Dog')

files_cat = [os.path.join(dir_cat, f) for f in os.listdir(dir_cat)
if os.path.isfile(os.path.join(dir_cat, f))]
files_dog = [os.path.join(dir_dog, f) for f in os.listdir(dir_dog)
if os.path.isfile(os.path.join(dir_dog, f))]

msk_cat = np.random.rand(len(files_cat)) < 0.8
msk_dog = np.random.rand(len(files_dog)) < 0.8

rand_items_cats = random.sample(files_cat, int(len(files_cat)*0.8))
rand_items_dogs = random.sample(files_dog, int(len(files_dog)*0.8))


# # validation_data
# # train_data
```

```python
def move_file_list(directory, file_list):
    for f in file_list:
        f_name = f.split('/')[-1]
        shutil.move(f, os.path.join(directory, f_name))

move_file_list(train_dir_dog, rand_items_dogs)
move_file_list(train_dir_dog, rand_items_dogs)

files_cat_v = [os.path.join(dir_cat, f) for f in
os.listdir(dir_cat) if os.path.isfile(os.path.join(dir_cat, f))]
files_dog_v = [os.path.join(dir_dog, f) for f in
os.listdir(dir_dog) if os.path.isfile(os.path.join(dir_dog, f))]

move_file_list(validation_dir_cat, files_cat_v)
move_file_list(validation_dir_dog, files_dog_v)
```

3. Now that we have created the dataset, we can load the data as follows:

```
# !!!!!!Original!!!!
# Data augmentation and normalization for training
# Just normalization for validation
mean = np.array([0.5, 0.5, 0.5])
std = np.array([0.25, 0.25, 0.25])

data_transforms = {
    'train': transforms.Compose([
        transforms.RandomResizedCrop(224),
        transforms.RandomHorizontalFlip(),
        transforms.ToTensor(),
        transforms.Normalize(mean, std)
    ]),
    'validation': transforms.Compose([
        transforms.Resize(256),
        transforms.CenterCrop(224),
        transforms.ToTensor(),
        transforms.Normalize(mean, std)
    ]),
}

image_datasets = {x: datasets.ImageFolder(os.path.join(data_dir, x),
                                          data_transforms[x])
                  for x in ['train', 'validation']}
dataloaders = {x: torch.utils.data.DataLoader(image_datasets[x],
batch_size=4, shuffle=True, num_workers=4)
              for x in ['train', 'validation']}
dataset_sizes = {x: len(image_datasets[x]) for x in ['train',
'validation']}
```

```
class_names = image_datasets['train'].classes

device = torch.device("cpu")
```

4. Let's also create a function to visualize the images from `tensor` as follows:

```
def imshow(input_image, title=None):
    """Plot the input tensor as animage"""
    input_image = input_image.numpy()
    input_image = input_image.transpose((1, 2, 0))
    input_image = std * input_image + mean
    plt.imshow(input_image)
    plt.title(title)
```

5. Let's see the output; using the following code:

```
# Get a batch of training data
inputs, classes = next(iter(dataloaders['train']))

# Make a grid from batch
out = torchvision.utils.make_grid(inputs)

imshow(out, title=[class_names[x] for x in classes])
```

The preceding commands generate the following output:

6. Retrain the model by executing the following code block:

```
def train_model(model, criterion, optimizer, scheduler, epochs=10):

    best_model_wts = copy.deepcopy(model.state_dict())
    best_acc = 0.0

    for epoch in range(epochs):
        print('Epoch {} of a total of {}'.format(epoch, epochs - 1))

        # Each epoch has a training and validation phase
        for phase in ['train', 'validation']:
```

[142]

```python
            if phase == 'train':
                scheduler.step()
                model.train()  # Set model to training mode
            else:
                model.eval()   # Set model to evaluate mode

            running_loss = 0.0
            running_corrects = 0

            # Iterate over data.
            for inputs, labels in dataloaders[phase]:
                inputs = inputs.to(device)
                labels = labels.to(device)

                # zero the parameter gradients
                optimizer.zero_grad()

                # forward
                # track history if only in train
                with torch.set_grad_enabled(phase == 'train'):
                    outputs = model(inputs)
                    _, preds = torch.max(outputs, 1)
                    loss = criterion(outputs, labels)

                    # backward + optimize only if in training phase
                    if phase == 'train':
                        loss.backward()
                        optimizer.step()

                # statistics
                running_loss += loss.item() * inputs.size(0)
                running_corrects += torch.sum(preds == labels.data)
            epoch_loss = running_loss / dataset_sizes[phase]
            epoch_acc = running_corrects.double() / dataset_sizes[phase]

            print('{} Loss: {:.4f} Acc: {:.4f}'.format(
                phase, epoch_loss, epoch_acc))

            # deep copy the model
            if phase == 'val' and epoch_acc > best_acc:
                best_acc = epoch_acc
                best_model_wts = copy.deepcopy(model.state_dict())

        print()

print('Training finish')
```

Reusing Neural Networks with Transfer Learning

```
print('Best val Acc: {:4f}'.format(best_acc))

# load best model weights
model.load_state_dict(best_model_wts)
return model
```

And now we can finally define the model. To do that, we will use a famous pre-trained model that is available in `torchvision`.

We will use a model called `resnet18`. ResNet is a family of networks that use **deep residual learning,** where the layers explicitly refer to learning residual functions with reference to the input layers. In this way, it's possible to train deeper networks:

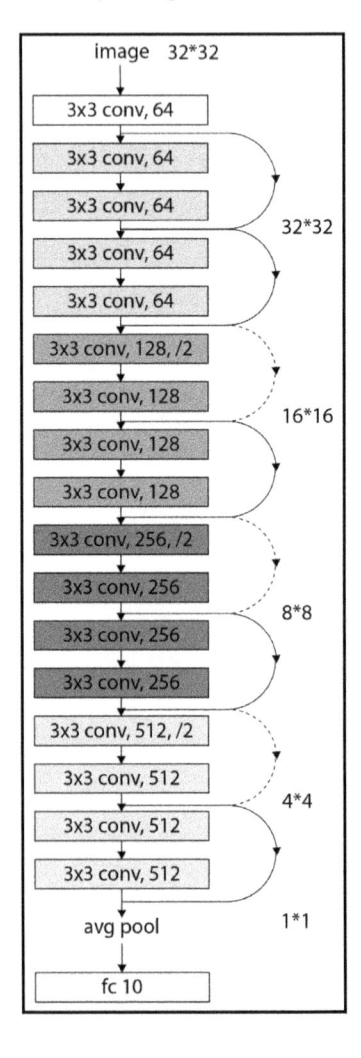

image 32*32

3x3 conv, 64

3x3 conv, 64
3x3 conv, 64   32*32
3x3 conv, 64
3x3 conv, 64

3x3 conv, 128, /2
3x3 conv, 128   16*16
3x3 conv, 128
3x3 conv, 128

3x3 conv, 256, /2
3x3 conv, 256   8*8
3x3 conv, 256
3x3 conv, 256

3x3 conv, 512, /2
3x3 conv, 512   4*4
3x3 conv, 512
3x3 conv, 512

avg pool   1*1

fc 10

There is empirical evidence that these networks are easier to optimize and can increase accuracy with increased depth. Now that we have a good model, we can apply the principles that we learned about TL.

ResNet-18 was trained on the ImageNet dataset, an open source dataset for general object recognition consisting of one million images. The following are the results:

Network	Top-1 error	Top-5 error
ResNet-18	30.24	10.92

Now, let's load the trained model:

```
model_ft = models.resnet18(pretrained=True)
```

Now we want to use the features the network already has, but adapt them to a new task. As we said, the layer we need to change is the last one, where classification happens. We need this because we previously had multiple outputs, while for this task we want binary output only.

In PyTorch, this is pretty simple: it's enough to overwrite the last layer with a binary classifier. We decided to use a linear function. To create a suitable linear classifier, we need to keep in mind not only the number of outputs we want (2) but also the number of features we will receive as input from the network:

```
model_ft.fc = nn.Linear(num_features, 2)
criterion = nn.CrossEntropyLoss()
# criterion = nn.BCEWithLogitsLoss()
# criterion = nn.BCELoss()
# Observe that all parameters are being optimized
optimizer_ft = optim.SGD(model_ft.parameters(), lr=0.001, momentum=0.9)
# Decay LR by a factor of 0.1 every 7 epochs
exp_lr_scheduler = lr_scheduler.StepLR(optimizer_ft, step_size=4, gamma=0.1)
```

Now we can train it as follows:

```
model_ft = train_model(model_ft, criterion, optimizer_ft, exp_lr_scheduler,
dataloader_training=dataloaders_train,
Sdataloader_validation=dataloaders_validation, epochs=1)
```

Summary

In this chapter, we explained the main concepts of TL. We also learned about multi-task learning and implementation of MTL. Then, we learned feature extraction. Finally, we learned how to implement TL in PyTorch.

In the next chapter, we will see how the differences between the generator and the discriminator help form the foundations of a GAN.

Section 3: Advanced Applications

In this section, we will learn more advanced concepts and how they are used in a multitude of tasks, from generation to sequential decision-making.

The following chapters are included in this section:

- Chapter 7, *Working with Generative Algorithms*
- Chapter 8, *Implementing Autoencoders*
- Chapter 9, *Deep Belief Networks*
- Chapter 10, *Reinforcement Learning*
- Chapter 11, *What's Next?*

7
Working with Generative Algorithms

Generative algorithms are part of unsupervised learning techniques. They underpin one of the most innovative concepts in machine learning in the past decade: **Generative Adversarial Networks** (**GANs**). In this chapter, we will be looking at the variations and developments in generative models in recent times.

A generative model can learn to mimic any distribution of it. Their potential is huge as they can be taught to recreate similar models in any domain. Some of these domains include, but are not limited, to the following:

- Images
- Music
- Speech
- Text
- Videos

There are a host of published papers outlining the advancements in GANs, and links to some of those most noteworthy have been listed at the end of this chapter.

Specifically, we will be covering the following topics in this chapter:

- Discriminative versus generative algorithms
- Different types of GANs, including those that have achieved some state-of-the-art results
- GAN applications

Discriminative versus generative algorithms

In order to comprehend generative algorithms, it can be helpful to contrast them with **discriminative algorithms**. When input data is fed into a discriminative algorithm, it aims to predict the label to which the data belongs. As such, the algorithm aims to map features to labels. Generative algorithms, on the other hand, do the opposite; they aim to predict features given a certain label.

Let's compare these two types of models in the context of whether an email is spam. We can consider x to be the model feature; for example, all of the words in the email. We can also consider the target variable, y, to state whether the email is actually spam. In such a scenario, the discriminative and generative models will aim to answer the following questions:

- **Discriminative model p(y|x)**: Given the input features, x, what is the probability of the email being spam?
- **Generative model p(x|y)**: Given that the email is spam, how likely are the input features to be x?

In other words, discriminative models learn the boundary between classes, whereas generative models learn to model the distribution of individual classes, as shown in the following diagram:

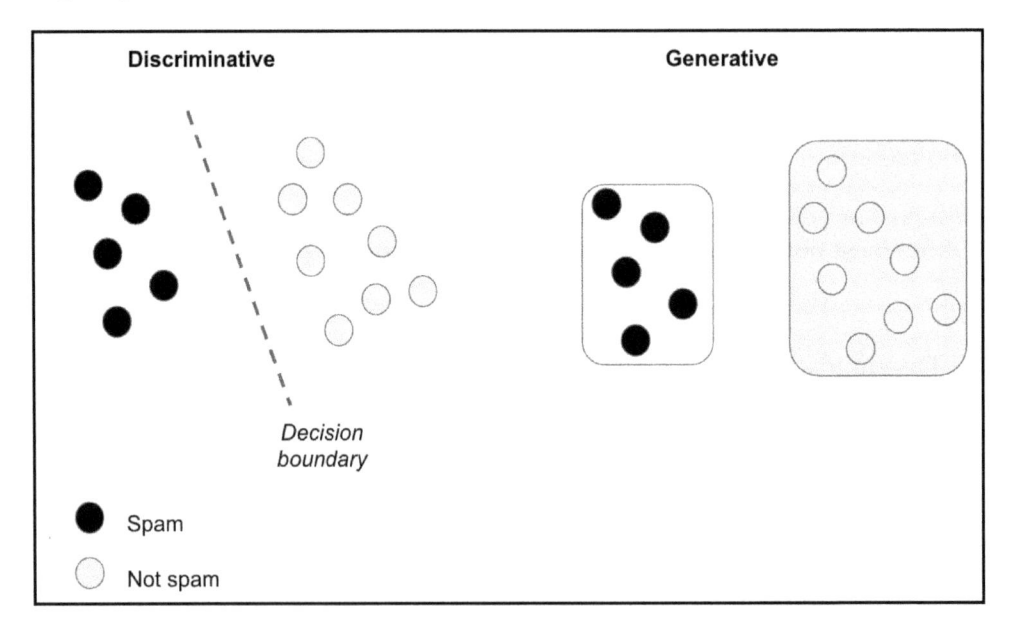

Chapter 7

The generative model learns to predict the joint probability with the help of the following **Bayes Theorem**:

$$p(x|y) = \frac{p(y|x)p(x)}{p(y)}$$

Here, let's explore the preceding terms:

- $p(x|y)$ is a conditional probability, the likelihood of y, given x
- $p(x|y)$ is also a conditional probability, the likelihood of x, given y
- $p(x)$ and $p(y)$ are the probabilities of observing x and y independently of each other

The following are some examples of discriminative classifiers:

- Logistic regression
- Nearest neighbors
- **Support vector machines (SVMs)**

The following are some examples of generative classifiers:

- Naive Bayes
- **Hidden Markov Models (HMMs)**
- Bayesian networks

Understanding GANs

GANs are comprised of two neural networks: a generator and a discriminator. They are able to generate new, synthetic data. The generator outputs new instances of the data, while the discriminator determines whether each instance of the data that is fed to it belongs to the training dataset.

Working with Generative Algorithms

The following screenshot gives an illustration of the output from a GAN on the **MNIST** and **Toronto Face** datasets. In both cases, the images on the far-right side of the grid are the true values and the others are generated by the model:

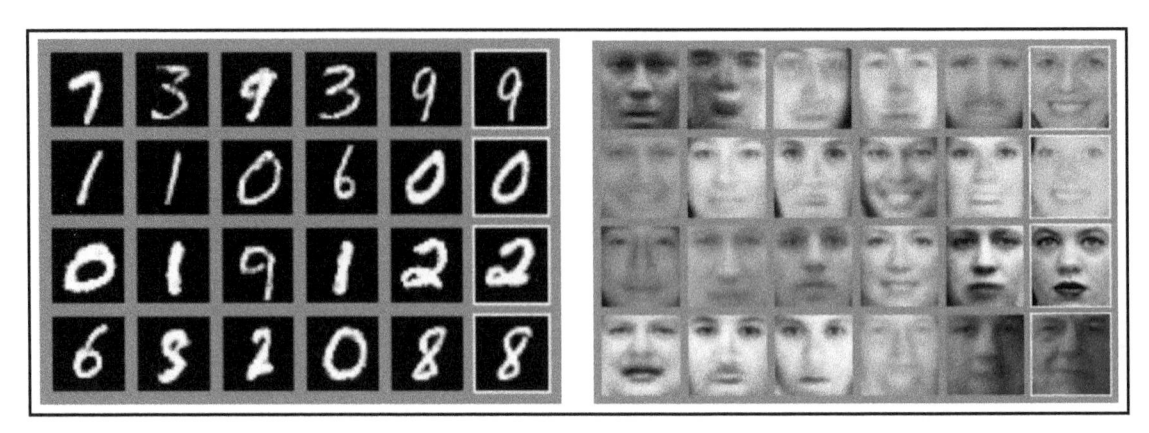

The source for this image can be found at: `https://arxiv.org/pdf/1406.2661.pdf`

Let's consider this further in the context of using the MNIST dataset, where the goal of the GAN is to generate similar images of handwritten digits. The role of the generator in the network is to create new synthetic images. These images are then passed to the discriminator. The goal of the discriminator is to identify whether the images from the generator are authentic or fake. The goal of the generator, on the other hand, is to generate images that won't be classed as fake by the discriminator. As such, the discriminator and generator have opposing objective (`loss`) functions, which means that if one of the models changes their behavior, then so does the other.

The following are the steps that a GAN takes:

1. Random numbers are fed into the generator and an image is generated
2. The generated image is fed into the discriminator along with other images taken from the real dataset
3. The discriminator considers all of the images fed into it and returns a probability as to whether it thinks the image is real or fake

Take a look at the following diagram:

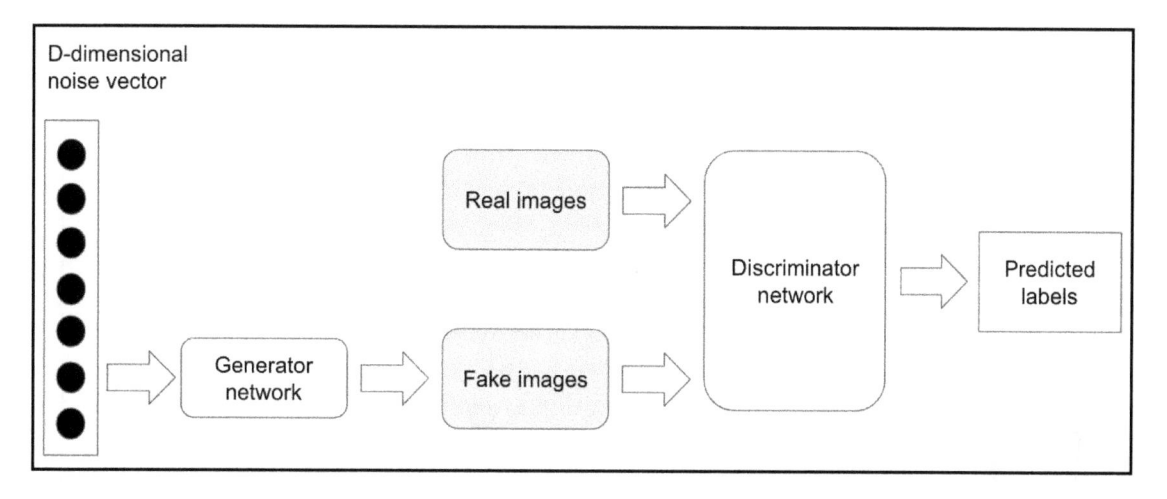

The discriminator network is simply a standard convolutional network that categorises images being fed to it. It performs downsampling and classifies the images in a binary fashion, labeling each image as real or fake:

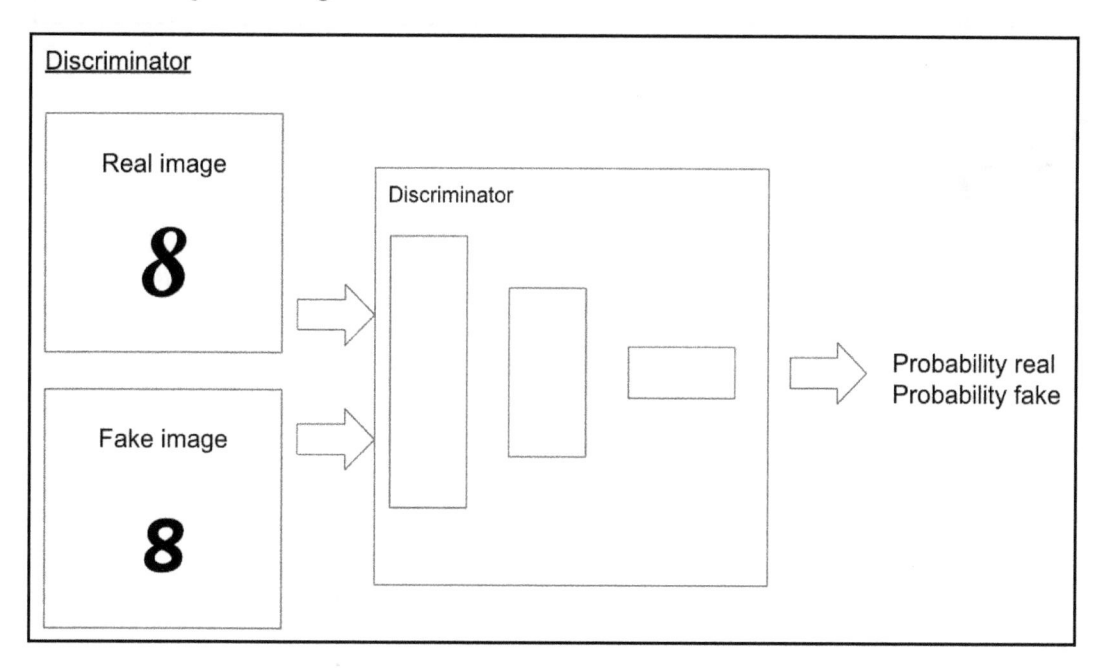

Conversely, the generator is essentially the reverse of a convolutional network. The generator takes the random noise and performs upsampling in order to output the image:

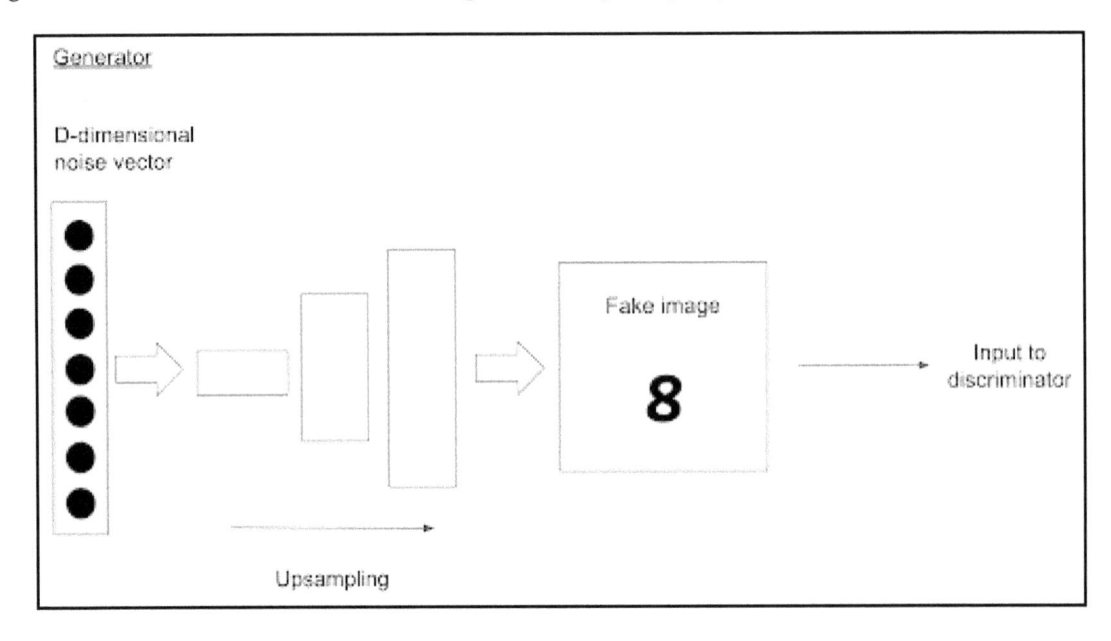

Training GANs

The training process of a GAN is as follows:

- **Training the discriminator**: Generator values should be held constant
- **Training the generator**: The discriminator should be pretrained against the original dataset

Either side of the GAN can overpower the other if one is significantly higher-performing than the other. For example, if the discriminator is too high-performing, it will return a value that is very close to either 0 or 1, and the generator will have difficulties reading the gradient. On the other hand, if the performance of the generator is too high, then it will continually exploit weaknesses in the discriminator that lead to false negatives.

Such a dilemma during training is illustrated in the following graph for the case of a binary classification problem. We want to stop one side of the GAN from winning so that both sides can continue to learn together for an extended period of time:

Logistic Sigmoid Function

f(x)

slopes near zero

x

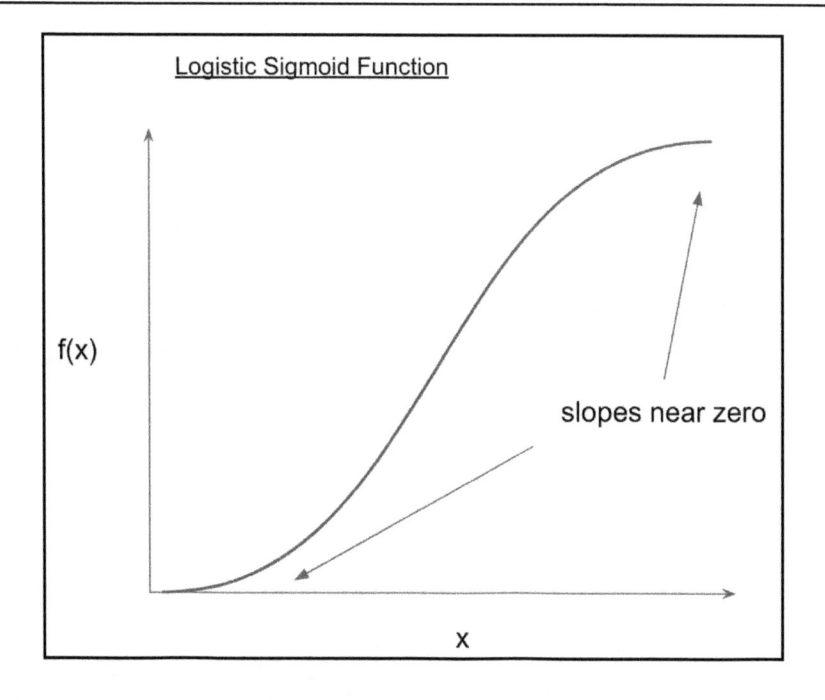

GAN challenges

GANs often face the following major challenges:

- **Mode collapse**: When the generator collapses and produces limited varieties of samples
- **Diminished gradient**: When the discriminator performs too well that the generator gradient vanishes and learns nothing
- **High sensitivity**: They are highly sensitive to the hyperparameter selections
- **Overfitting**: An imbalance between the generator and discriminator can cause overfitting
- **Long training time**: If the model is trained on a GPU, it can take hours
- **Non-convergence**: The models may never converge, as the parameters can oscillate and destabilize

Working with Generative Algorithms

We will consider the MNIST dataset, where there are 10 major modes: digits 0 to 9. The samples in the following screenshot are generated by two different GANs. The top row in the grid outputs all 10 modes (that is, all digits from 0 to 9), whereas the second row only outputs a single mode (the digit 6). This is an example of **mode collapse**:

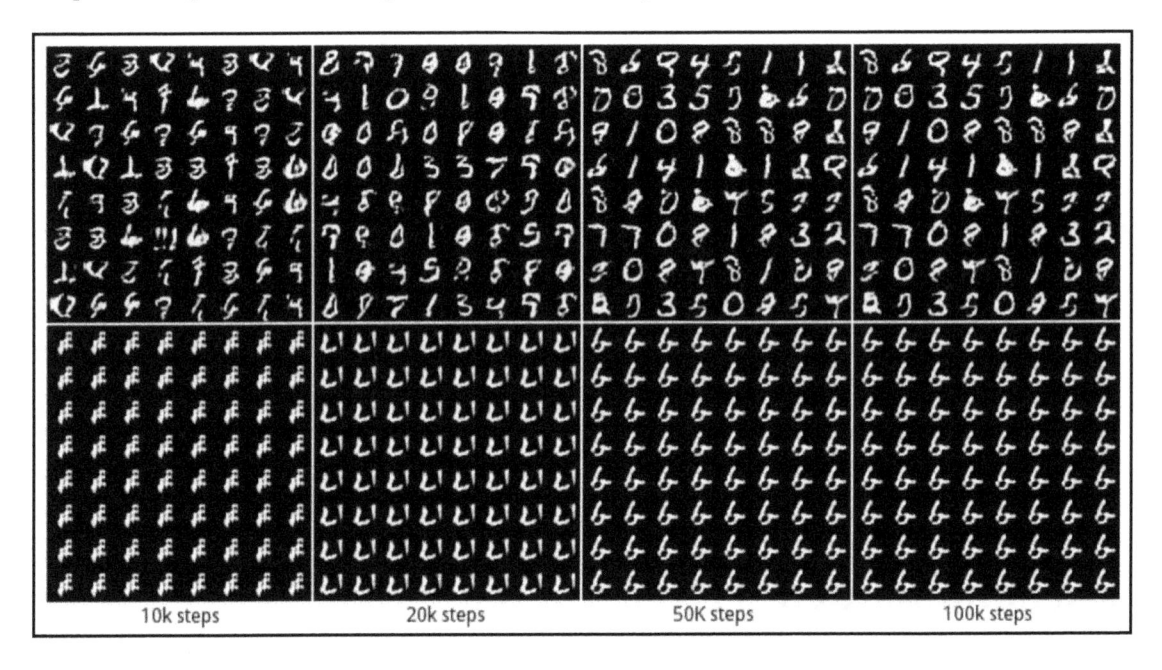

The source for this image can be found at: `https://arxiv.org/pdf/1611.02163.pdf`

Mode collapse is one of the most difficult problems to solve in GANs. While a complete collapse is uncommon, a partial collapse happens often. The following diagram shows that photos with the same underlined color look similar when the mode begins collapsing:

The source can be found at: `https://arxiv.org/pdf/1703.10717.pdf`

[156]

Overcoming mode collapse is currently an active area of research. There are a number of different ways in which mode collapse has been dealt with, but there is not one single silver bullet to solve the problem completely. Some of the known techniques that can be used to reduce the severity of the problem are as follows:

- **Minibatch discrimination**: The idea is to use samples within a batch to assess whether the entire batch is real. The generator can be penalized for generating similar-looking samples by incorporating a term that represents the diversity of the samples. This term can be added to the generator's cost function. As such, the generator is forced to generate diverse samples.
- **Experience replay**: In order to prevent the generator from easily fooling the discriminator, we can show previously generated samples to the discriminator.
- **Wasserstein GANs (WGANs)**: Traditional GANs aim to minimize the **Jensen-Shannon divergence** between the distribution of the generator and the distribution of the real data. However, minimising the Wasserstein distance has been proven more effective in terms of reducing mode collapse.

GAN variations and timelines

There have been many significant developments to GAN research in recent times. The following timeline shows some of the most noteworthy advances:

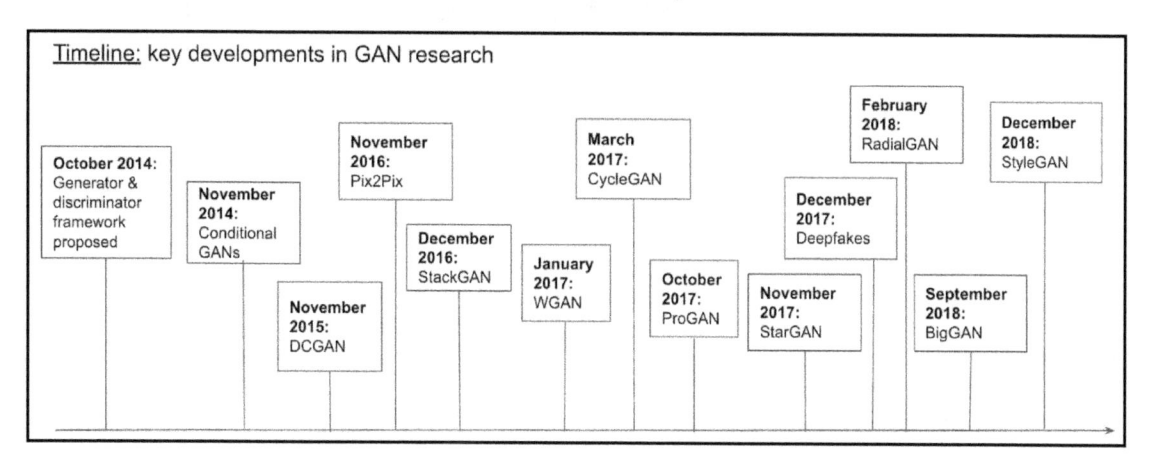

Timeline: key developments in GAN research

- October 2014: Generator & discriminator framework proposed
- November 2014: Conditional GANs
- November 2015: DCGAN
- November 2016: Pix2Pix
- December 2016: StackGAN
- January 2017: WGAN
- March 2017: CycleGAN
- October 2017: ProGAN
- November 2017: StarGAN
- December 2017: Deepfakes
- February 2018: RadialGAN
- September 2018: BigGAN
- December 2018: StyleGAN

This chapter will now give insight into these developments, their applications, and results.

Conditional GANs

Conditional GANs are a central theme that form the building blocks of many state-of-the-art GANs. The paper submitted by Mirza and Osindero in 2014 shows how integrating the class labels of data yields greater stability in GAN training. This idea of conditioning GANs with prior information is a common approach in future GAN research. It is particularly important for papers whose main focus is on image-to-image or text-to-image applications:

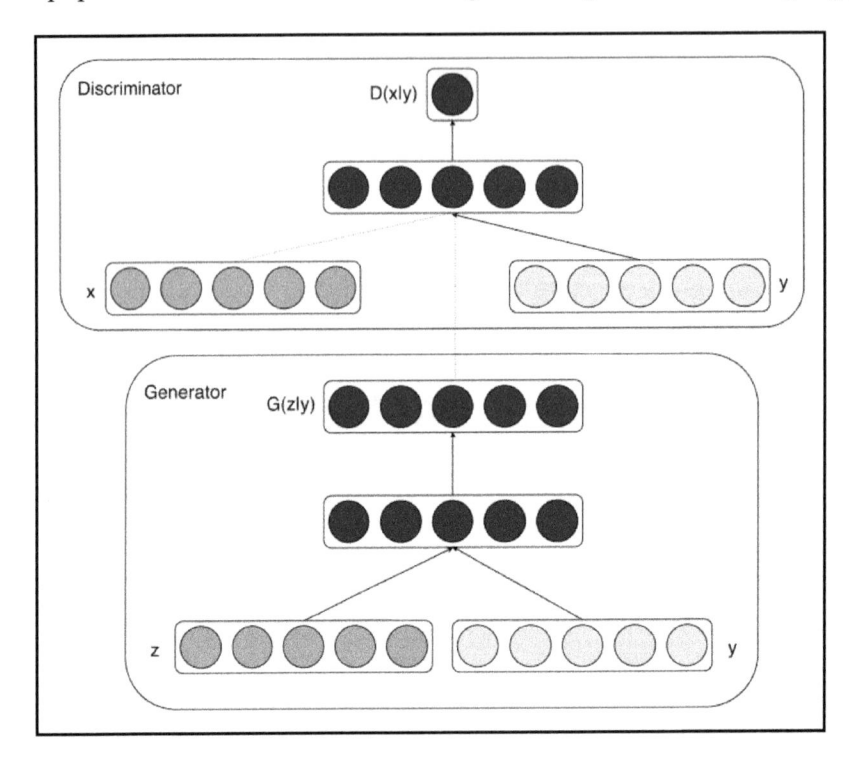

The source for this image can be found at: https://arxiv.org/pdf/1411.1784.pdf

DCGAN

A **Deep Convolutional Generative Adversarial Network (DCGAN)** is a popular network design for GANs. It incorporates key **Convolutional Neural Network (CNN)** concepts in order to overcome some of the challenges outlined previously, and consequently generates better images. The following photos give an example of some of the images generated by a DCGAN when trained on bedroom images:

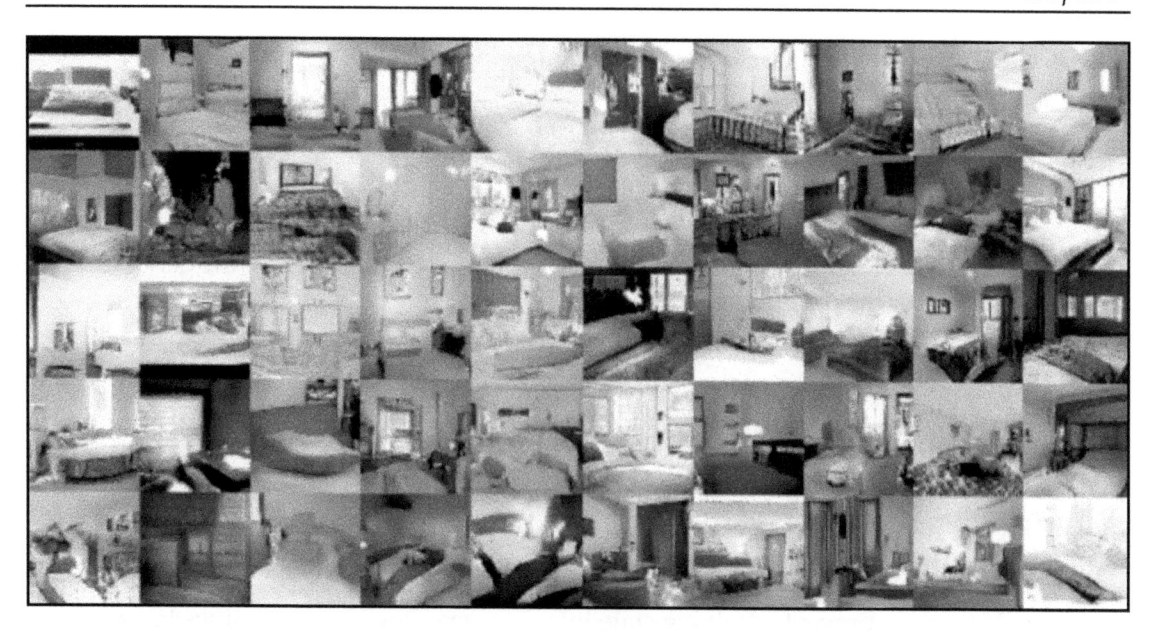

The source for this image can be found at: https://arxiv.org/pdf/1511.06434.pdf

The network design of the generator within the DCGAN is as per the following diagram:

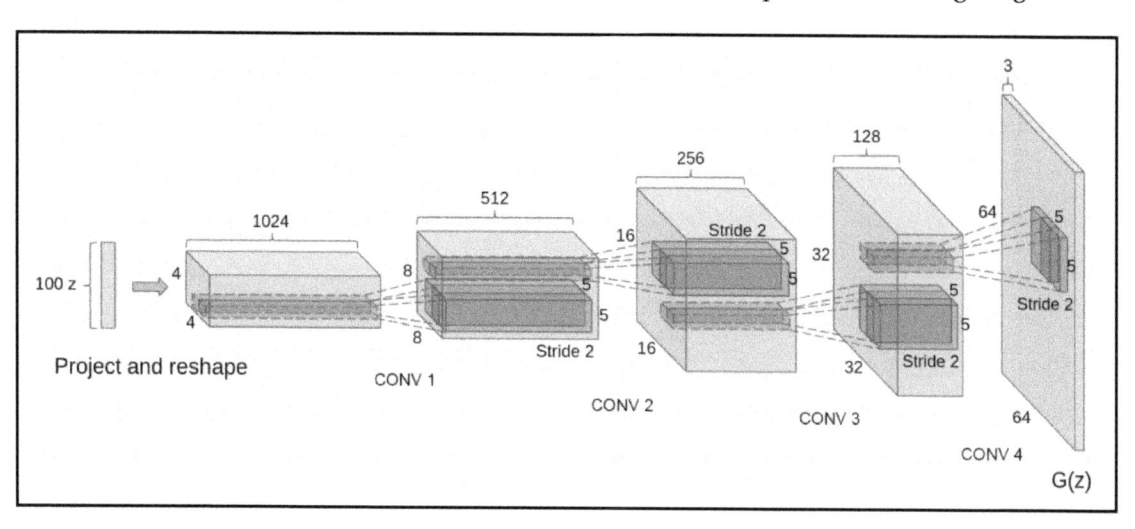

The source for this image can be found at: https://arxiv.org/pdf/1511.06434.pdf

The DCGAN architecture is constituted of the following aspects:

- Batch normalization, is used except for the output layer of the generator and the input layer of the discriminator
- Convolutional stride replaces all max pooling
- Convolutional layers are eliminated
- The **Rectified Linear Unit (ReLU)** activation function is used in the generator, except for the output layer, which uses `tanh`
- The Leaky ReLU activation function is used in the discriminator

ReLU versus Leaky ReLU

The ReLU activation function takes the maximum between the input value and zero. Sometimes, the network gets stuck in a popular state (referred to as the **dying state**) using the ReLU activation function because it produces nothing but zeros for all of the outputs.

Leaky ReLU helps to prevent the dying state by allowing a few negative values to pass through. If the input to a leaky ReLU activation function is positive, then the output will also be positive. Similarly, the output will be a controlled negative value if the input is negative. This negative value is controlled by a parameter called **alpha**, which that introduces tolerance to the network by allowing some negative values to pass through it:

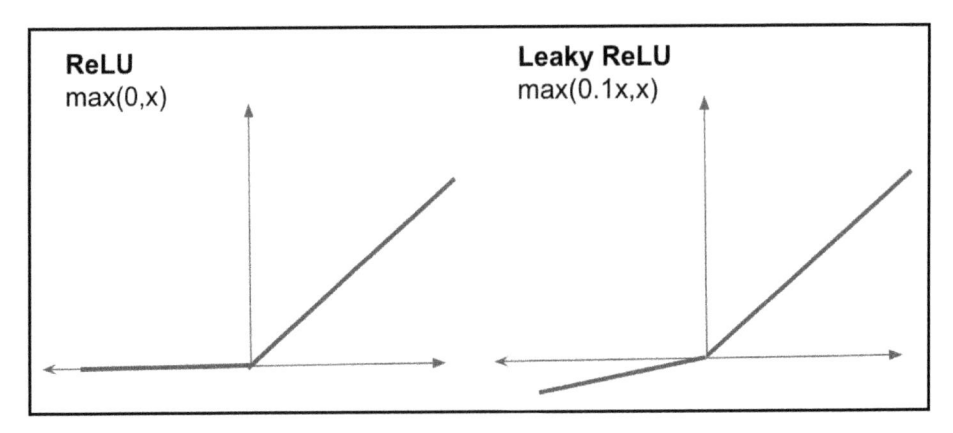

DCGAN – a coded example

Now, let's consider a coded example of training a DCGAN using the Keras library and MNIST dataset, in order to generate synthetic images by performing the following steps:

1. Firstly, import the necessary libraries as follows:

    ```
    from keras.models import Sequential,Model
    from keras.layers import *
    from keras.datasets import mnist
    from keras.optimizers import Adam
    from keras.layers.advanced_activations import LeakyReLU
    from tqdm import tqdm
    ```

2. Now import the MNIST dataset, split it into training and testing datasets, and normalize as follows:

    ```
    (X_train,Y_train),(X_test,Y_test) = mnist.load_data()
    X_train = np.reshape(X_train,(60000,28,28,1)).astype('float32')
    X_test = np.reshape(X_test,(10000,28,28,1)).astype('float32')
    # Normalize the images between -1 to 1
    X_train = (X_train - 127.5)/127.5
    ```

3. From here, define the generator model as follows:

    ```
    def generator_model():
    model = Sequential()
    model.add(Dense(128*7*7,input_dim = 100, activation = LeakyReLU(0.1)))
    model.add(BatchNormalization())
    model.add(Reshape((7,7,128)))
    model.add(UpSampling2D())
    model.add(Conv2D(64, (5,5), padding = 'same', activation = LeakyReLU(0.1)))
    model.add(BatchNormalization())
    model.add(UpSampling2D())
    model.add(Conv2D(1, (5,5), padding = 'same', activation = 'tanh'))
    return model
    generator_model = generator_model()
    ```

The preceding code generates the following output:

```
Layer (type)                 Output Shape              Param #
=================================================================
dense_7 (Dense)              (None, 6272)              633472
_____
batch_normalization_9 (Batch (None, 6272)              25088
_____
reshape_5 (Reshape)          (None, 7, 7, 128)         0
_____
up_sampling2d_9 (UpSampling2 (None, 14, 14, 128)       0
_____
conv2d_13 (Conv2D)           (None, 14, 14, 64)        204864
_____
batch_normalization_10 (Batc (None, 14, 14, 64)        256
_____
up_sampling2d_10 (UpSampling (None, 28, 28, 64)        0
_____
conv2d_14 (Conv2D)           (None, 28, 28, 1)         1601
=================================================================
Total params: 865,281
Trainable params: 852,609
Non-trainable params: 12,672
_____
None
```

4. Define the discriminator model, where the input will be both the real images from the MNIST dataset and the fake images created by the generator:

```
def discriminator_model():
model = Sequential()
model.add(Conv2D(64,(5,5),padding = 'same',input_shape = (28,28,1)
, activation = LeakyReLU(0.1) , subsample = (2,2)))
model.add(Dropout(0.3))
model.add(Conv2D(128,(5,5),padding = 'same', activation =
LeakyReLU(0.1) , subsample = (2,2)))
model.add(Dropout(0.3))
model.add(Flatten())
model.add(Dense(1,activation = 'sigmoid'))
return model
```

The preceding code generates the following output:

```
Layer (type)                    Output Shape              Param #
=================================================================
conv2d_3 (Conv2D)               (None, 14, 14, 64)        1664
_____
dropout_1 (Dropout)             (None, 14, 14, 64)        0
_____
conv2d_4 (Conv2D)               (None, 7, 7, 128)         204928
_____
dropout_2 (Dropout)             (None, 7, 7, 128)         0
_____
flatten_1 (Flatten)             (None, 6272)              0
_____
dense_2 (Dense)                 (None, 1)                 6273
=================================================================
Total params: 212,865
Trainable params: 212,865
Non-trainable params: 0
```

5. Compile both the generator and the discriminator with the Adam optimizer:

```
generator_model.compile(loss = 'binary_crossentropy' , optimizer = Adam())
discriminator_model.compile(loss = 'binary_crossentropy' , optimizer = Adam())
Now we build and compile the adversarial model.
generator_input = Input(shape = (100,))
generator_output = generator_model(generator_input)
discriminator_model.trainable = False
discriminator_output = discriminator_model(generator_output)
adversarial_model = Model(input = generator_input , output = discriminator_output)
adversarial_model.summary()
adversarial_model.compile(loss = 'binary_crossentropy' , optimizer = Adam())
```

[163]

The preceding code generates the following output:

```
Layer (type)                 Output Shape              Param #
=================================================================
input_3 (InputLayer)         (None, 100)               0
_____
sequential_1 (Sequential)    (None, 28, 28, 1)         865281
_____
sequential_2 (Sequential)    (None, 1)                 212865
=================================================================
Total params: 1,078,146
Trainable params: 852,609
Non-trainable params: 225,537
```

6. From here, create a function to train the model:

```
def train(epochs):
batch_size = 128
batch = 400
for i in range(epochs):
for j in tqdm(range(batch)):
# Define the noise to be input into the generator
noise_1 = np.random.rand(batch_size,100)
# Create the random images output from the generator
gen_images = generator_model.predict(noise_1 , batch_size = batch_size )
# Real images from MNIST dataset
image_batch = X_train[np.random.randint(0, X_train.shape[0], size=batch_size)]
# Create the input data for discriminator (real images and fake images from the generator)
disc_inp = np.concatenate([gen_images,image_batch])
# Assign labels where 1 is a real image and 0 is fake for the discriminator training
disc_Y = [0]*batch_size + [1]*batch_size
# Make discriminator model trainable
discriminator_model.trainable = True
# Train the discriminator model
discriminator_model.train_on_batch(disc_inp,disc_Y)
# Generate noise for the adversarial network
noise_2 = np.random.rand(batch_size,100)
# Freeze the weights of the discriminator and train the generator
discriminator_model.trainable = False
# Labels for adversarial model are always 1
y_adv = [1]*batch_size
```

```
# Train the adversarial model
adversarial_model.train_on_batch(noise_2,y_adv)
# Repeat process for 'epoch' no. of times
train(80)
```

7. Now that the model is trained, we can output some synthetic images and see how realistic they appear:

```
import matplotlib.pyplot as plt
def plot_output(text):
# Random noise as the input
try_input = np.random.rand(50, 100)
predictions = generator_model.predict(try_input)
plt.figure(figsize=(20,20))
for i in range(predictions.shape[0]):
plt.subplot(10, 10, i+1)
plt.imshow(predictions[i, :, :, 0], cmap='gray')
plt.axis('off')
plt.tight_layout()
plt.savefig(text)
plot_output('80')
```

The preceding code generates the following output:

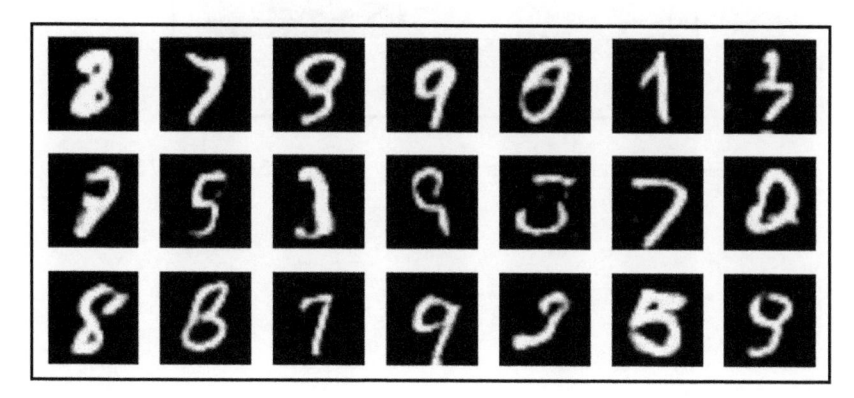

It appears that the model is performing nicely, as the images are similar to those in the original dataset.

Pix2Pix GAN

Another image-to-image translation GAN model is **Pix2Pix**. It has many applications such as **edge maps** to photo-realistic images, and black and white to colour.

The architecture uses paired training samples and incorporates a **PatchGAN**. The PatchGAN looks at individual regions of the image in order to determine whether they are real or fake, versus when considering the whole image.

The following are some examples of images generated by implementing the Pix2Pix GAN:

- Mapping the edges of a handbag to a full realistic image is as follows:

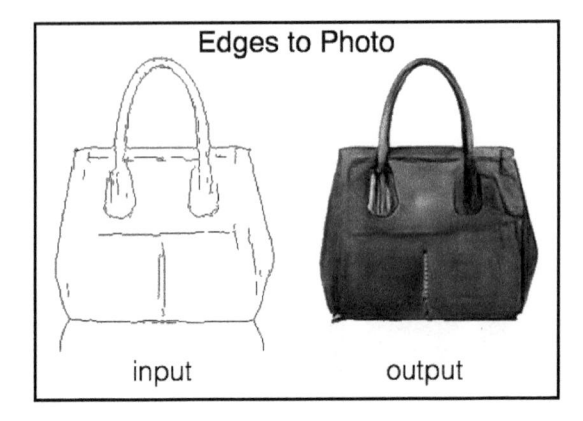

The source for this image can be found at: https://arxiv.org/pdf/1611.07004.pdf

- Mapping black-and-white image to color is as follows:

The source for this image can be found at: https://arxiv.org/pdf/1611.07004.pdf

A TensorFlow implementation of Pix2Pix GAN is available at the GitHub repository: `https://github.com/affinelayer/pix2pix-tensorflow`. This allows you to generate images using your own dataset.

StackGAN

StackGAN is somewhat unique to many other papers of research around GANs because it focuses on translating natural language text to images. This is achieved by altering a text embedding in such a way that it captures visual characteristics.

The following screenshot shows some of the images generated by StackGAN, given the textual description fed into it. This has many real-world applications, such as converting a story to a comic illustration:

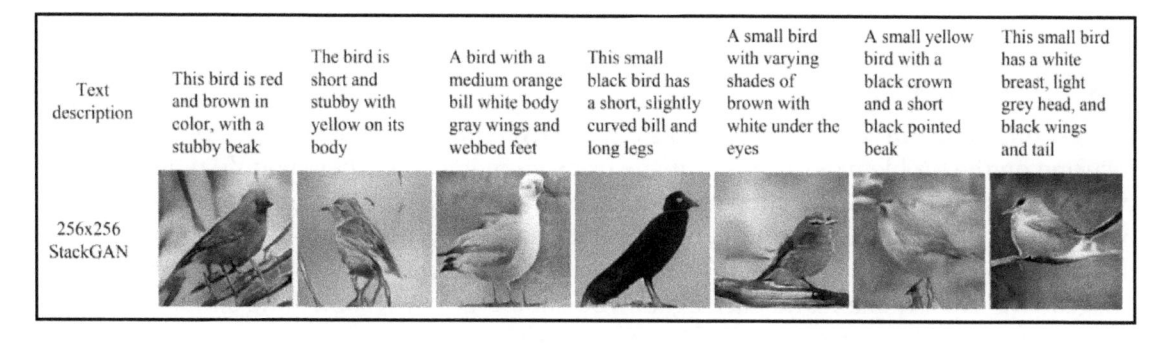

The source for this image can be found at: https://arxiv.org/pdf/1612.03242.pdf

Working with Generative Algorithms

The following diagram shows the overall architecture of StackGAN. It works on multiple scales and first outputs an image of resolution 64 x 64, and then uses this as prior information to generate an image of a 256 x 256 resolution. The stage-one generator draws the low-resolution image by defining the rough shape and basic colors of the object from the given text. It then paints the background from a random noise vector. The stage-two generator corrects defects in the stage-one generator and adds details to the results. This yields a more realistic high-resolution image, as follows:

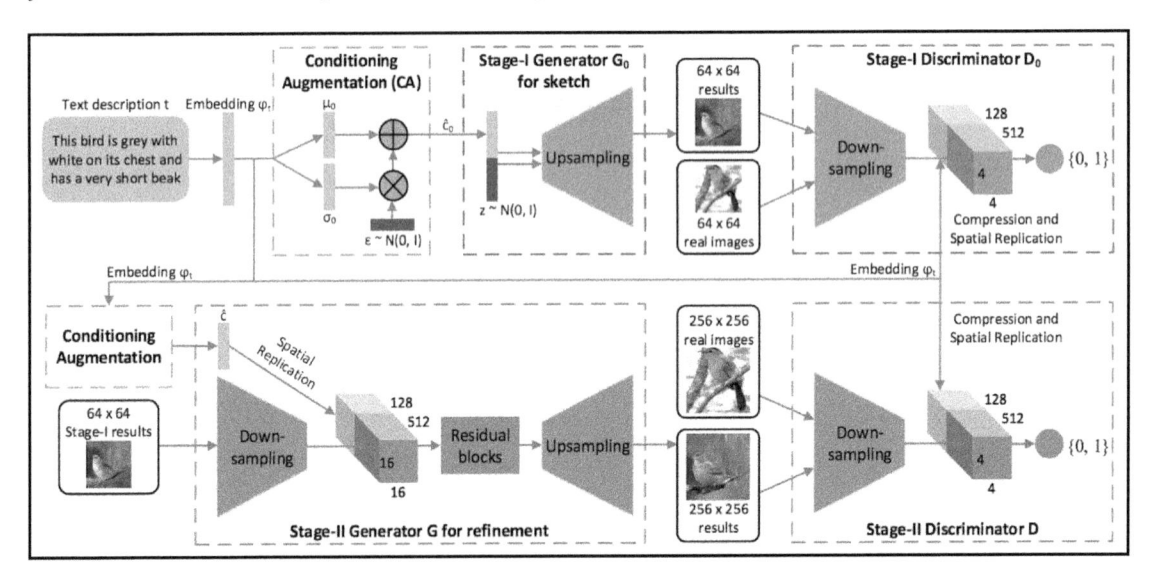

The source for this image can be found at: https://arxiv.org/pdf/1612.03242.pdf

A PyTorch implementation of this model can be downloaded from the GitHub repository at: https://github.com/hanzhanggit/StackGAN-Pytorch.git.

CycleGAN

Cycle-Consistent Adversarial Networks (CycleGANs) were introduced in a paper focusing on the problem of image-to-image translation in cases where you do not have paired training samples. The paper aims to stabilize GAN training through the introduction of the cycle-consistency loss formulation. The central idea behind the `loss` function is illustrated in the following diagram. It relies on the assumption that if you convert an image to the other domain and back again, you should get back something similar to what was put into it. This enforces that $F(G(x)) \approx x$ and $G(F(y)) \approx y$:

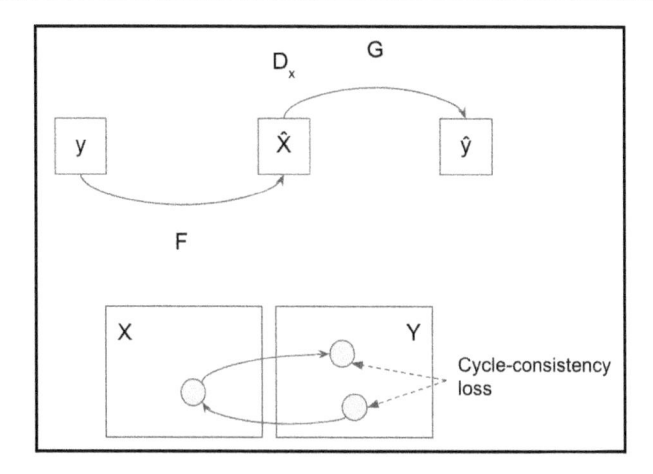

There are many applications of CycleGAN, such as enhanced image resolution and style transfer. More specifically, it can be used for converting pictures to paintings (and vice versa), along with mapping one animal to another, as shown in the following example screenshots.

The following are the examples cited in the CycleGAN paper on implementing CycleGAN:

- Mapping Monet's paintings to a photographic style looks as follows:

The source for this image can be found at: https://arxiv.org/pdf/1703.10593.pdf

- Mapping a horse to a zebra looks as follows:

The source for this image can be found at: https://arxiv.org/pdf/1703.10593.pdf

A Pytorch implementation of CycleGAN is available at the GitHub repository at: `https://github.com/aitorzip/PyTorch-CycleGAN`. This allows you to generate images using your own dataset.

ProGAN

Progressive Growing of GAN (**ProGAN**) is aimed to address some of the problems faced in the original DCGAN architecture. It begins by training both the generator and the discriminator with a low resolution image (for example, 4 x 4 pixels). After that, it adds a higher resolution layer every time it performs its training progressively in order to generate a large high-quality image (for example, 1,024 x 1,042 pixels). This approach to training firstly learns the base features, and then learns more and more details about the image in each subsequent layer. By increasing the resolution gradually in this way, it breaks down the problem into much simpler pieces. This incremental learning process greatly stabilizes training and reduces the possibility of mode collapse occurring.

Chapter 7

The following diagram depicts the individual generator and discriminator networks:

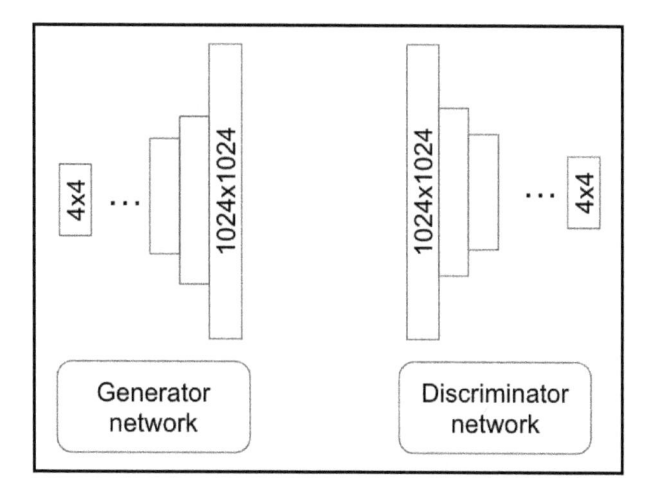

Take a look at the following overall architecture:

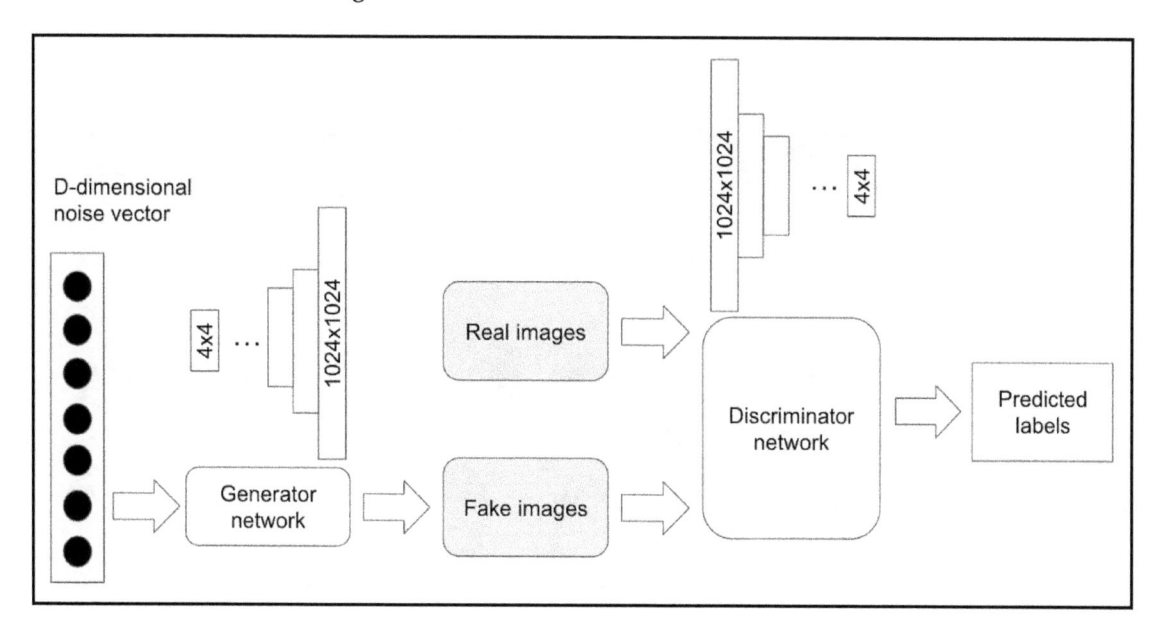

Working with Generative Algorithms

While ProGAN does generate high-quality images, it has very limited ability to control specific features of the image. This is because tweaking the input usually affects multiple features at the same time, rather than just one.

A Pytorch implementation of ProGAN can be found at the GitHub repository at: `https://github.com/akanimax/pro_gan_pytorch`.

StarGAN

A **StarGAN** model can also translate images from one domain to the other. For example, if considering images of people's faces, the model could change the hair color of a person from blonde to brown. In this example, the hair color is known to be the attribute, and the colors blonde and brown are known to be the attribute values. The domain in this scenario would be denoted as a set of images that share the same attribute value. People with blonde hair is one domain and people with brown hair is another.

The following photos show some results of StarGAN when trained on the `CelebA` dataset. This illustrates the performance of facial attribute transfer on photos:

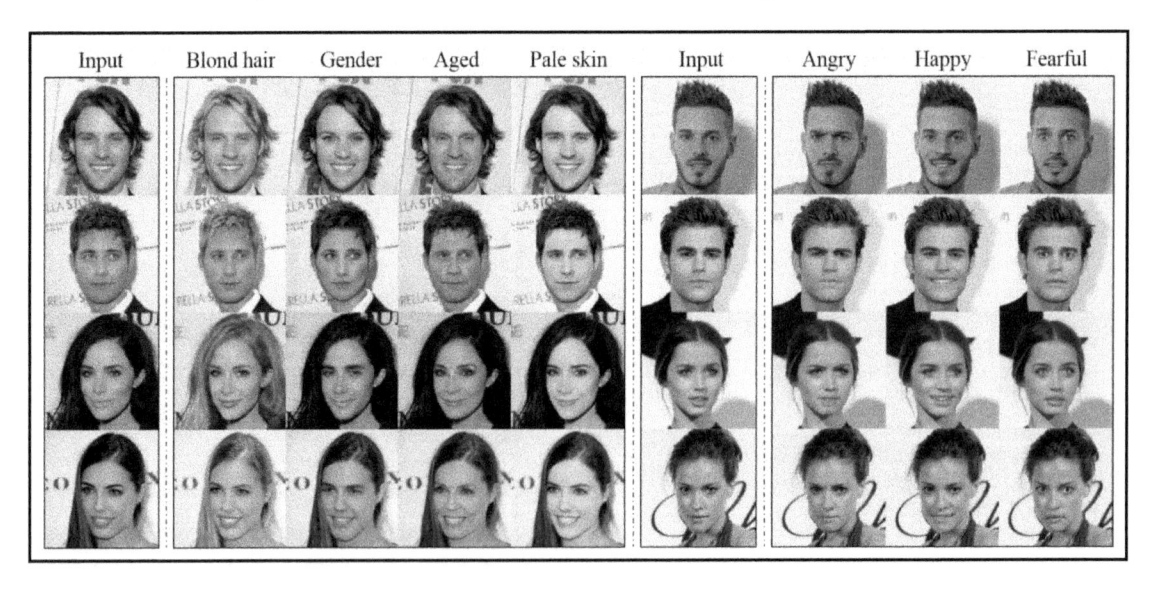

The source for this image can be found at: `https://arxiv.org/pdf/1711.09020.pdf`

Chapter 7

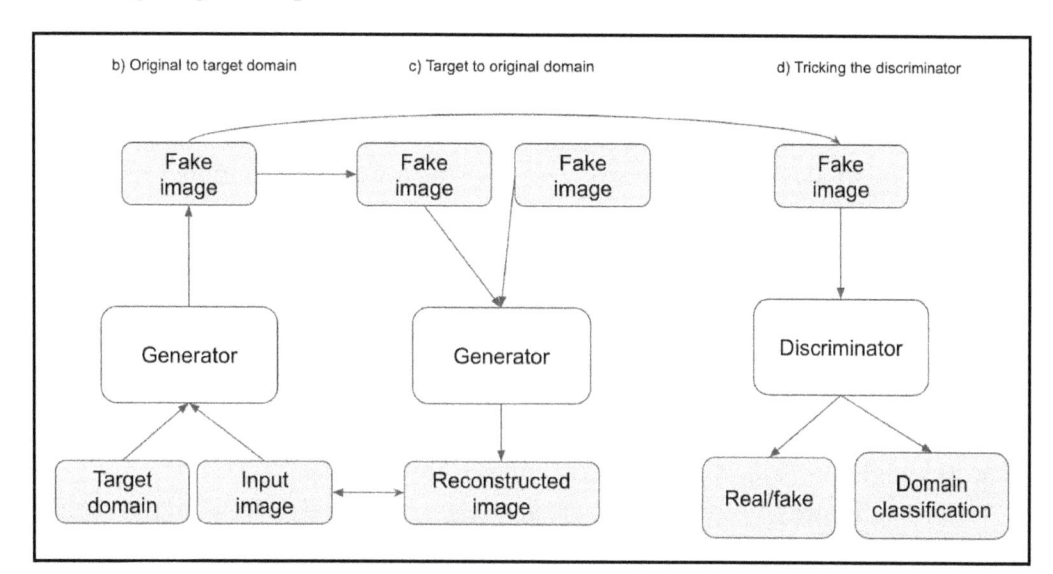

The following diagram depicts the structure of a StarGAN model:

[Diagram showing: b) Original to target domain, c) Target to original domain, d) Tricking the discriminator. Components include Fake image, Generator, Target domain, Input image, Reconstructed image, Discriminator, Real/fake, Domain classification.]

The steps a StarGAN takes are as follows:

1. The **Generator** G takes in as input the image itself, and the domain label (for example, the hair color). It then generates a fake image (step **a** in the preceding diagram).
2. Given the original domain label, the **Generator** G tries to reconstruct the original image from the fake image.
3. The discriminator determines how likely the image is to be fake and also classifies the image to its corresponding domain. The generator attempts to generate images that are indistinguishable from the real images and are classifiable as a target domain by the discriminator. As such, the generator will ultimately learn to generate realistic images corresponding to the given target domain (step **c**).

StarGAN discriminator objectives

The discriminator in StarGAN has the following two objectives:

- To identify whether the image is fake
- To predict the domain of the image input fed into it with the help of an auxiliary classifier

The discriminator learns the mapping of the original image and its domain from the dataset with the auxiliary classifier. When the generator creates a new image conditioned on a target domain (for example, hair color, h), the discriminator can predict the generated images domain, so the generator will create new images until the discriminator predicts it as the target domain, h (for example, blonde hair).

The `loss` function of the discriminator works as per the following equation:

$$L_D = -L_{adv} + \lambda_{hls} L_{hls}^r$$

StarGAN generator functions

The generator in StarGAN has the following three key functions:

- Its weights are adjusted so that the images are realistic.
- Its weights are adjusted so that the generated images are classifiable as a target by the discriminator.
- Given the original domain label, the generator aims to reconstruct the original image from the fake image. A single generator is used twice; firstly, to translate the original image in the target domain, and then, to take the translated image and reconstruct the original image.

The loss function of the generator is as per the following equation:

$$L_G = L_{adv} + \lambda_{hls} L_{hls}^f + \lambda_{reh} L_{reh}$$

The following GitHub repository provides a PyTorch implementation of StarGAN at https://github.com/yunjey/stargan. Users of the repository can either use a pretrained model or train their own model in order to generate synthetic images.

BigGAN

The **BigGAN** model is arguably the current state-of-the-art model in ImageNet generation (at the time of writing). Modifications incorporated into the model focus on the following:

- **Scalability**: The two architectural changes to improve scalability were introduced in order to improve the performance of the GAN, while at the same time improving conditioning by applying orthogonal regularization to the generator.

- **Robustness**: The orthogonal regularization that is applied to the generator makes the model responsive to the truncation trick, so that fine control of the fidelity and variety tradeoffs is possible by truncating the latent space.
- **Stability**: Devised solutions in order to minimize the instabilities.

Samples of photos generated by the BigGAN model at a 512 x 512 resolution are as follows:

The source for this image can be found at: https://arxiv.org/pdf/1809.11096.pdf

StyleGAN

StyleGAN is a GAN design released by researchers at NVIDIA in December 2018. It is essentially an upgraded version of ProGAN. It combined ProGAN with neural style transfer. At the core of the StyleGAN architecture is a style-transfer technique. The model set a new record for face generation tasks and can also be used to generate realistic images of cars, bedrooms, houses, and so on.

Working with Generative Algorithms

As with ProGAN, StyleGAN generates images gradually by starting with a very low resolution and continuing to a high-resolution image. The GAN controls the visual features that are expressed in each level, from coarse features such as the pose and face shape, through to the finer features such as eye and hair color:

The source for this image can be found at: https://arxiv.org/abs/1812.04948

The generator in StyleGAN incorporates a mapping network. The goal of the mapping network is to encode the input vector into an intermediate vector where different elements control different visual features. With the introduction of another neural network, the model can generate a vector that isn't required to follow the training data distribution and can minimize the correlation between features. This mapping network consists of eight fully connected layers where the output is the same size as the input layer, as shown in the following diagram:

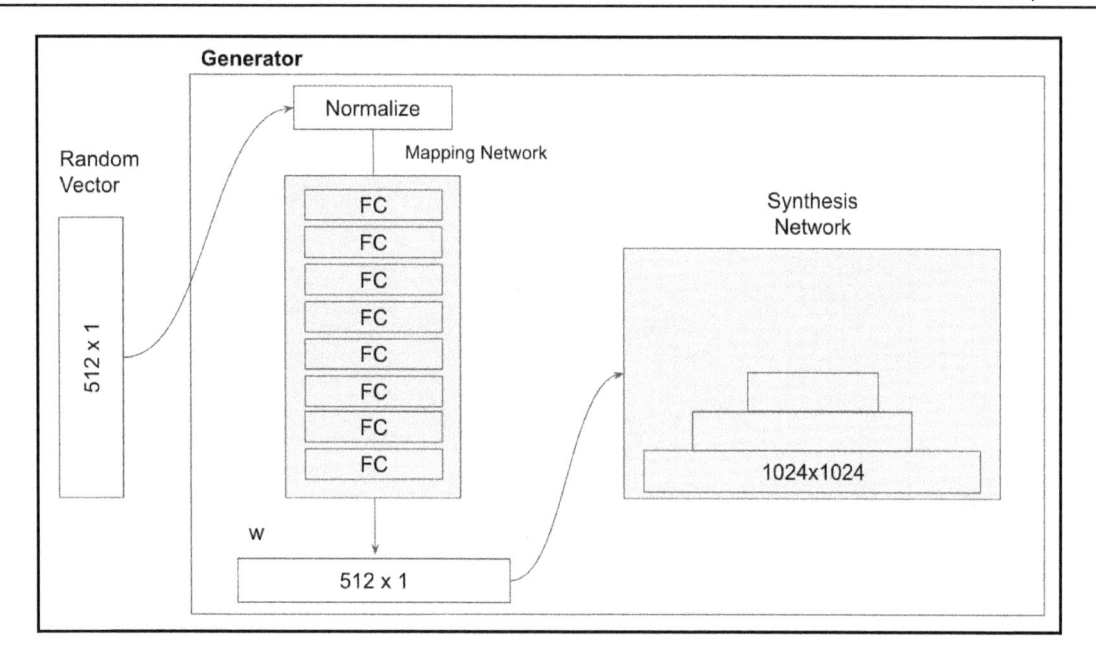

Style modules

The **Adaptive Instance Normalization** (**AdaIN**) module transfers the encoded information (that is, the output of the mapping network, w) into the generated image. The AdaIN module is added to each resolution level of the synthesis network. It defines the visual expression of the features at that level. The steps it takes are as follows:

1. Each channel of the convolutional layer output is normalized. This is to ensure that the scaling and shifting in *step 3* have the anticipated affect.
2. Another fully connected layer, A, transforms the intermediate vector w into scale and bias vectors for each channel.
3. These scale and bias vectors shift each channel of the convolution output, defining the importance of every filter in the convolution. This tuning process translates w into a visual representation.

Working with Generative Algorithms

What this means in simple terms is that it changes the mean and variance of an image's neural network layers to match that of a style image (that is, the image whose style we want to emulate), as shown in the following diagram:

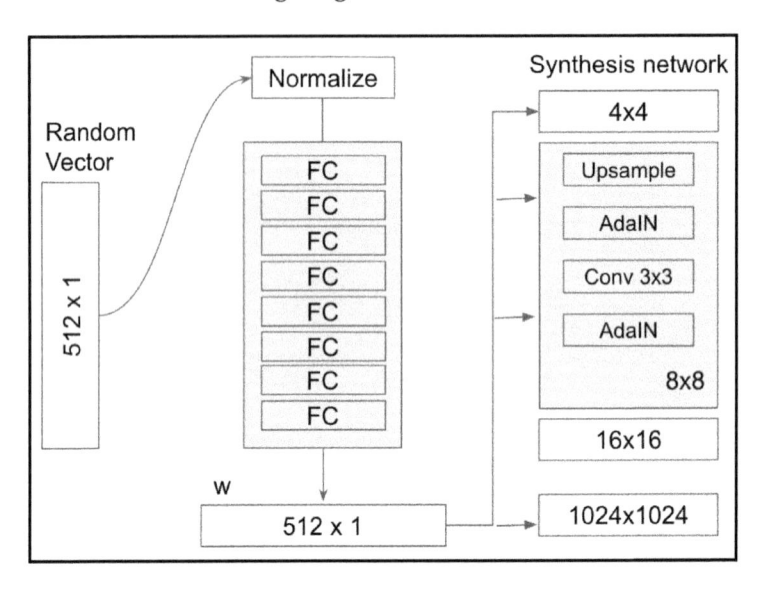

Most GANs (including ProGAN) use random input to create the initial image of the generator (that is, the input to the 4 x 4 level). However, with StyleGAN, the initial input is replaced with constant values due to the fact that the image features are controlled by w and the AdaIN module.

A synthesis network is replaced with constant input, as shown in the following diagram:

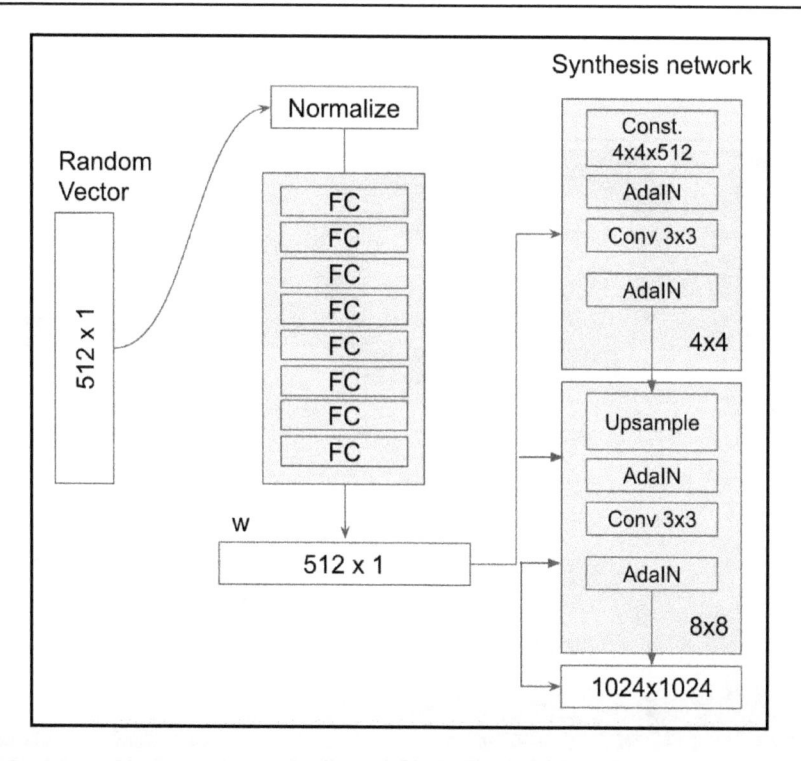

StyleGAN provides a striking example as to how GANs could completely transform how the majority of media produces its content and alter how consumers interpret the information presented to them.

StyleGAN implementation

In February 2019, NVIDIA announced that it was open sourcing a tool that generates hyper-realistic images of faces using StyleGAN. The model is trained on the Flickr Faces dataset, which contains 70,000 high-quality PNG images of human faces. The images are at 1,024 x 1,024 resolution and were first aligned and cropped. Users of the open source tool can either use the pretrained model or train their own model in order to generate images of faces.

The tool can be downloaded by cloning the GitHub repository at: `https://github.com/NVlabs/stylegan.git`.

Working with Generative Algorithms

Some examples of the realistic images generated by the tool are shown in the following photos:

The source for this image can be found at: https://github.com/NVlabs/stylegan.git

Deepfakes

Deepfake technology uses GANs to create fake realistic videos. The craze began in December 2017, where a user on Reddit named Deepfakes started fabricating fake videos of celebrities online by swapping the faces of people in two separate videos. The models were even advanced enough to lip-sync with a fake audio clip.

In order to swap the faces of the people in the video, thousands of images are collected of each person. An **autoencoder** (**AE**) is then used to reconstruct the images. From there, the video is processed frame by frame. The face is extracted from **Person A**, fed into the encoder, and then the decoder of **Person B** is used to reconstruct the picture. Essentially, when the face is swapped, the face of **Person B** is drawn in the context of **Person A**. A GAN is then used to determine whether the image is real or fake, ensuring the images generated are realistic, as follows:

Chapter 7

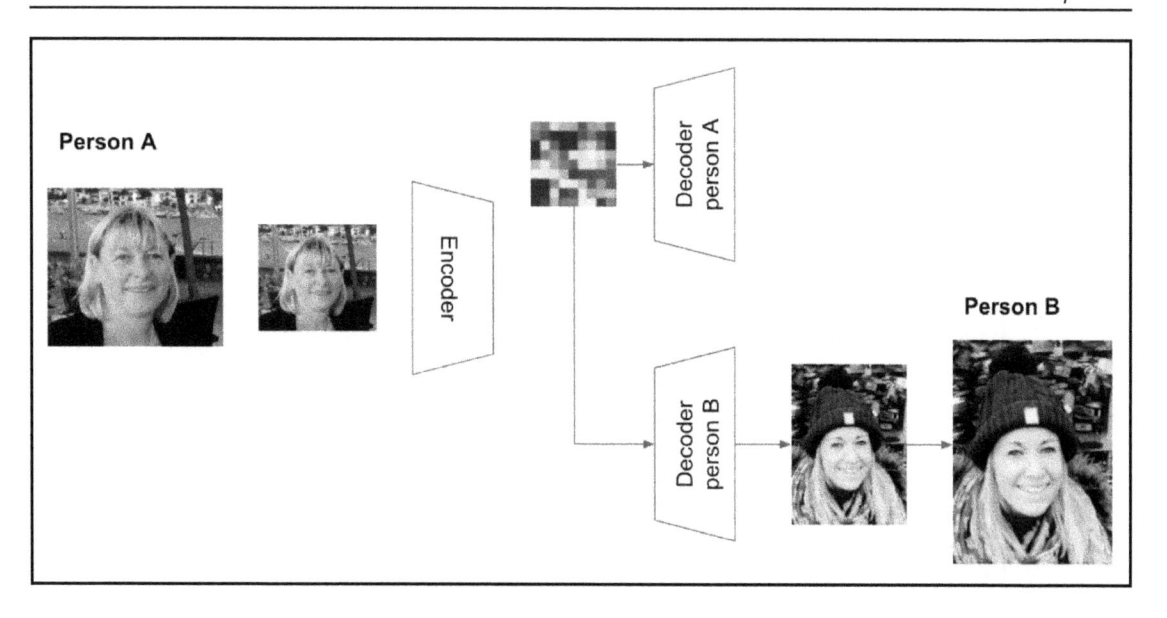

A **Long Short-Term Memory** (**LSTM**) network is used to perform the lip syncing within the video and the paper detailing how this can be done is referenced in the *Further reading* section at the end of this chapter.

RadialGAN

While the majority of well-known GANs are used for image creations, RadialGAN is designed for numerical analysis. If we consider an example where we want to evaluate how effective a new medical treatment is, we would need to combine data from a number of different hospitals in order to ensure we have enough data to make concrete conclusions. However, this poses problems such as different hospitals measuring outcomes in different ways, using laboratories that give different results in different environments, and so on. In order to address this problem, RadialGAN firstly transforms the dataset from each hospital into latent space, which allows us to hold the data from different sources in a uniform format. From here, the latent space data can be converted into the feature space of each unique dataset.

Each dataset considered by the RadialGAN has an encoder neural network. This encoder transforms the data into the same structure as the latent space. Each dataset also has a decoder, which is a GAN with a generator converting information from the latent space into a structure that is the same as the dataset. Every decoder GAN has a discriminator that verifies whether the information coming out of the latent space is aligned with the properties of the target data domain. Such a setup ensures that the domain transfer of information works in both directions, as follows:

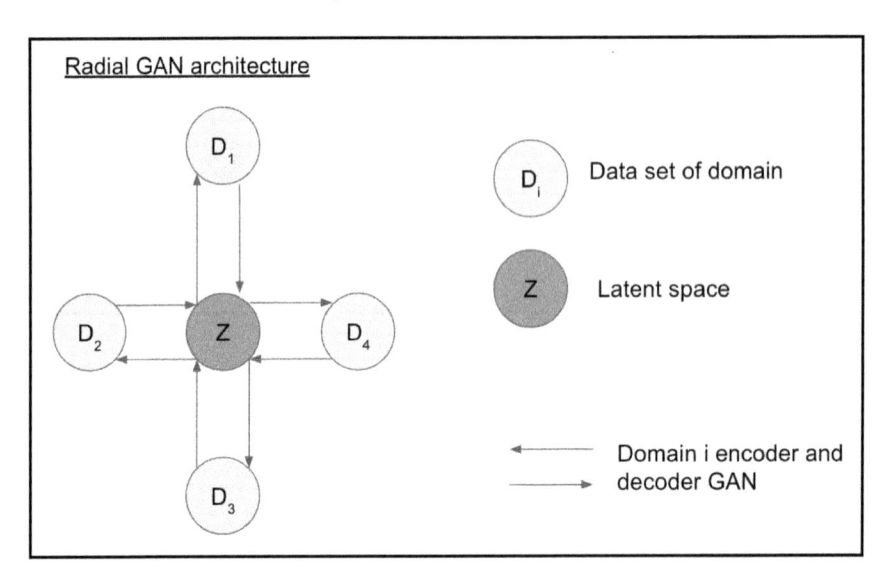

Radial GAN architecture

D_i Data set of domain

Z Latent space

Domain i encoder and decoder GAN

Once the networks are trained simultaneously, RadialGAN can be used to create the augmented dataset. Each of the other datasets are run through their encoders in order to transfer that knowledge into latent space. All of the information is then extracted from that space using the decoder. From here, the transformed information is appended to the original dataset.

The overall result is a larger dataset, constructed using information from each domain that also matches the characteristics of the domain being considered.

Summary

In this chapter, we explained the key differences between a generator and a discriminator and how these form the foundations of a GAN. We covered different variations and architectures of GANs and their applications, along with showcasing some of their results.

The GAN revolution has produced some major technological breakthroughs in recent times. Pioneering AI techniques such as GANs are rapidly changing our relationships with technology and with one another; GANs are most certainly something to keep an eye on!

In the next chapter, we will be looking at implementing AEs and their different types.

Further reading

- *Generative Adversarial Networks*, Ian J Goodfellow and others (2014): `https://arxiv.org/abs/1406.2661`
- *On Discriminative vs. Generative Classifiers: A comparison of logistic regression and naive Bayes*, Andrew Y Ng and Michael I. Jordan (2002): `https://ai.stanford.edu/~ang/papers/nips01-discriminativegenerative.pdf`
- *Unsupervised Representation Learning with Deep Convolutional Generative Adversarial Networks*, Radford et al (2016): `https://arxiv.org/pdf/1511.06434.pdf`
- *Conditional Generative Adversarial Nets*, Mehdi Mirza and Simon Osindero (2014): `https://arxiv.org/pdf/1411.1784.pdf`
- *Unrolled Generative Adversarial Networks*, Luke Metz, Ben Poole, David Pfau, Jascha Sohl-Dickstein (2016): `https://arxiv.org/abs/1611.02163`
- *Wasserstein GAN*, Martin Arjovsky, Soumith Chintala, Léon Bottou (2017): `https://arxiv.org/pdf/1701.07875.pdf`.
- *Improved Training of Wasserstein GANs*, Ishaan Gulrajani, Faruk Ahmed, Martin Arjovsky, Vincent Dumoulin, Aaron Courville (2017): `https://arxiv.org/pdf/1704.00028.pdf`
- *Unpaired Image-to-Image Translation using Cycle-Consistent Adversarial Networks*, Jun-Yan Zhu, Taesung Park, Phillip Isola Alexei A Efros (2017): `https://arxiv.org/pdf/1703.10593.pdf`
- *Image-to-Image Translation with Conditional Adversarial Networks*, Phillip Isola, Jun-Yan Zhu, Tinghui Zhou, Alexei A. Efros (2016): `https://arxiv.org/pdf/1611.07004.pdf`

- *StackGAN: Text to Photo-realistic Image Synthesis with Stacked Generative Adversarial Networks*, Han Zhang, Tao Xu, Hongsheng Li, Shaoting Zhang, Xiaogang Wang, Xiaolei Huang, Dimitris Metaxas (2016): https://arxiv.org/pdf/1612.03242.pdf
- *Large Scale GAN Training for High Fidelity Natural Image Synthesis*, Andrew Brock, Jeff Donahue, Karen Simonyan (2018): https://arxiv.org/abs/1809.11096
- *BEGAN: Boundary Equilibrium Generative Adversarial Networks*, David Berthelot, Thomas Schumm, Luke Metz (2017): https://arxiv.org/pdf/1703.10717.pdf
- *StarGAN: Unified Generative Adversarial Networks for Multi-Domain Image-to-Image Translation*, Yunjey Choi, Minje Choi, Munyoung Kim, Jung-Woo Ha, Sunghun Kim, Jaegul Choo (2017): https://arxiv.org/pdf/1711.09020.pdf
- *Progressive Growing of GANs for Improved Quality, Stability, and Variation*, Tero Karras, Timo Aila, Samuli Laine, Jaakko Lehtinen (2017): https://arxiv.org/pdf/1710.10196.pdf
- *A Style-Based Generator Architecture for Generative Adversarial Networks*: https://arxiv.org/abs/1812.04948
- *Synthesizing Obama: Learning Lip Sync from Audio*, Supasorn Suwajanakorn, Steven M. Seitz, Ira Kemelmacher-Shlizerman (2017): https://grail.cs.washington.edu/projects/AudioToObama/siggraph17_obama.pdf
- *RadialGAN: Leveraging multiple datasets to improve target-specific predictive models using Generative Adversarial Networks*, Jinsung Yoon, James Jordon, and Mihaela van der Schaar (2018): https://arxiv.org/abs/1802.06403

Implementing Autoencoders

In this chapter, we explain what **autoencoders** are and discuss different types of them. We will give an overview as to how they have been applied to some real-world problems. Coded examples of how different types of autoencoders can be implemented, using the Keras library in Python, will also be provided.

Specifically, the following topics will be covered in this chapter:

- An overview of autoencoders and their applications
- Bottleneck and loss functions
- Standard types of autoencoders and coded examples
- **Variational autoencoders (VAEs)** and coded examples

Overview of autoencoders

An autoencoder is an unsupervised learning technique. Autoencoders can model an unsupervised learning problem as a supervised one by taking an unlabeled dataset and tasking it with reconstructing the original input. In other words, the goal of the autoencoder is for the input to be as similar as possible to the output.

An **autoencoder** is composed of an **encoder** and a **decoder**, as shown in the following diagram:

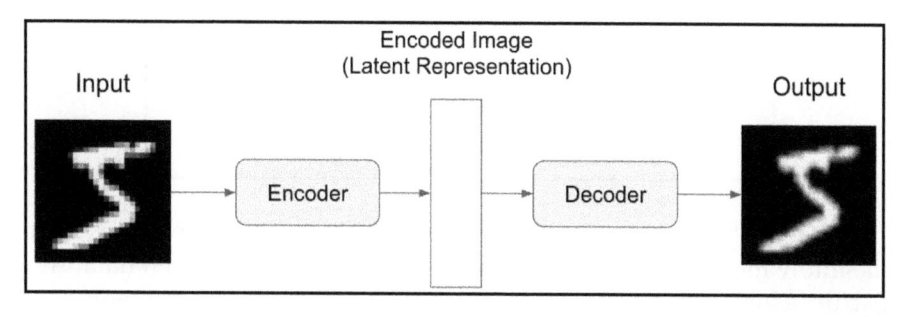

Autoencoder applications

There are many applications for autoencoders:

- Data denoising
- Dimensionality reduction for data visualization
- Image generation
- Interpolating text

Bottleneck and loss functions

Autoencoders impose a bottleneck on the network, which enforces a compressed knowledge representation of the original input. If the bottleneck were not present, the network would simply learn to memorize the input values. This would mean that the model wouldn't generalize well on unseen data.

Let's take a look at the following diagram, which depicts an autoencoder bottleneck:

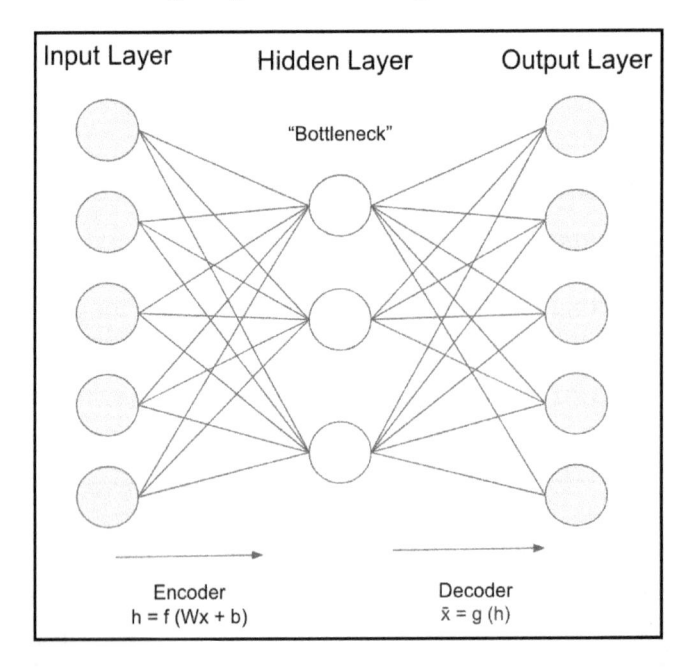

We want the model to be sensitive to the inputs so that it detects their signal, but not so much that it simply memorizes them and doesn't predict well on unseen data. As such, we need to construct a loss/cost function, which determines the optimal trade-off.

The loss function can be defined as per the following formula, where **x**$_i$ is the value at each node in the input layer and **x̄**$_i$ is the value of each node in the output layer. **L(x, x̄)** represents the reconstruction loss, the part of the function that allows it to be sensitive to the inputs. The *regularizer* helps to ensure the model doesn't overfit:

$$Loss = L(x, \bar{x}) + regularizer$$

There are some commonly used autoencoder architectures for imposing these two constraints and ensuring that there is an optimal trade-off between the two.

Standard types of autoencoder

There are various types of standard autoencoder. Here we will explain the most widely used ones and go through some coded examples in Keras.

Undercomplete autoencoders

Undercomplete autoencoder architectures can be used to constrain the number of nodes that are present in the hidden layers of the network, limiting the amount of information that can flow through it. The model can learn the most important attributes of the input data by penalizing it as per the reconstruction error. This reconstruction error is essentially the difference between the input and the reconstructed output from the encoding. The encoding learns and describes the latent attributes of the input data.

Example

In this example, we will show how you can compile an undercomplete autoencoder model in Keras by performing the following steps:

1. First, we import the relevant libraries along with the **Modified National Institute of Standards and Technology (MNIST)** dataset as follows:

    ```
    import keras
    from keras.layers import Input, Dense
    from keras.models import Model
    from keras.datasets import mnist
    import numpy as np
    import tensorflow
    (x_train, _), (x_test, _) = mnist.load_data()
    Now we scale the data so that the feature values are in a range
    ```

Implementing Autoencoders

```
between 0 and 1.
x_train = x_train.astype('float32')/255 # 255 = np.max(x_train)
x_test = x_test.astype('float32')/255
x_train = x_train.reshape(len(x_train), np.prod(x_train.shape[1:]))
x_test = x_test.reshape(len(x_test), np.prod(x_test.shape[1:]))
print(x_train.shape)
print(x_test.shape)
(60000, 784)
(10000, 784)
```

2. We assign the sizes of layers in the three-layered network: input, hidden, and output. Note that we assign the hidden layer to be smaller than the input and output layers, as it is an undercomplete model:

```
input_size = 784 # Pixel values 28*28
hidden_size = 64
output_size = 784
```

3. In the following example code, we use the `adam` optimizer and the **mean squared error** (**MSE**) as the `loss` function:

```
input_image = Input(shape=(input_size,))
# Encoder
e = Dense(hidden_size, activation='relu')(input_image)
# Decoder
d = Dense(output_size, activation='sigmoid')(e)
encoder = Model(input_image, d)
encoder.compile(optimizer='adam', loss='mse')
encoder.summary()
```

The preceding commands generate the following output:

Layer (type)	Output Shape	Param #
input_4 (InputLayer)	(None, 784)	0
dense_1 (Dense)	(None, 64)	50240
dense_2 (Dense)	(None, 784)	50960

Total params: 101,200
Trainable params: 101,200
Non-trainable params: 0

4. From here, we fit the model and train it as follows:

   ```
   autoencoder_train = encoder.fit(x_train, x_train,
   batch_size=128,epochs=10,verbose=1, validation_data=(x_test,
   x_test))
   ```

   The preceding command generates the following output:

   ```
   Train on 60000 samples, validate on 10000 samples
   Epoch 1/10
   60000/60000 [==============================] - 3s 42us/step - loss: 0.0446 - val_loss: 0.0221
   Epoch 2/10
   60000/60000 [==============================] - 1s 22us/step - loss: 0.0172 - val_loss: 0.0128
   Epoch 3/10
   60000/60000 [==============================] - 1s 22us/step - loss: 0.0109 - val_loss: 0.0087
   Epoch 4/10
   60000/60000 [==============================] - 1s 22us/step - loss: 0.0077 - val_loss: 0.0065
   Epoch 5/10
   60000/60000 [==============================] - 1s 22us/step - loss: 0.0061 - val_loss: 0.0055
   Epoch 6/10
   60000/60000 [==============================] - 1s 22us/step - loss: 0.0053 - val_loss: 0.0049
   Epoch 7/10
   60000/60000 [==============================] - 1s 22us/step - loss: 0.0048 - val_loss: 0.0045
   Epoch 8/10
   60000/60000 [==============================] - 1s 22us/step - loss: 0.0046 - val_loss: 0.0043
   Epoch 9/10
   60000/60000 [==============================] - 1s 22us/step - loss: 0.0044 - val_loss: 0.0042
   Epoch 10/10
   60000/60000 [==============================] - 1s 22us/step - loss: 0.0043 - val_loss: 0.0041
   ```

Visualizing with TensorBoard

When fitting the model, it is possible to pass the TensorBoard callback parameter so that performance metrics during training can be monitored. To do so, we can perform the following steps:

1. First, import the `TensorBoard` function as follows:

   ```
   from keras.callbacks import TensorBoard
   ```

2. From here, we can call the `TensorBoard` function from within the `fit` function. We define the log directory, in which we want the files to be saved, as follows:

   ```
   ae.fit(x_train, x_train, batch_size=128,epochs=10,verbose=1,
   validation_data=(x_test, x_test),
   callbacks=[TensorBoard(log_dir='/tmp/autoencoder_example'))])
   ```

The TensorBoard web interface can then be accessed by navigating to the link: `http://0.0.0.0:6006`.

Visualizing reconstructed images

We can view the reconstructed images the model has produced by running the following commands:

```
#Decoded images
d_images = encoder.predict(x_test)
x = 10
plt.figure(figsize=(20, 2))
for i in range(1, x):
# Display original images
ax = plt.subplot(2, x, i)
plt.imshow(x_test[i].reshape(28, 28))
ax.get_xaxis().set_visible(False)
ax.get_yaxis().set_visible(False)
# Display reconstructed images
ax = plt.subplot(2, x, i + x)
plt.imshow(d_images[i].reshape(28, 28))
ax.get_xaxis().set_visible(False)
ax.get_yaxis().set_visible(False)
plt.show()
```

The preceding commands generate the following output:

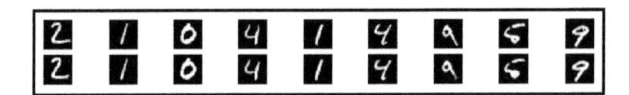

Multilayer autoencoders

A multilayer autoencoder has more than one hidden layer. Any of the hidden layers can be used as the feature representation, as shown in the following diagram:

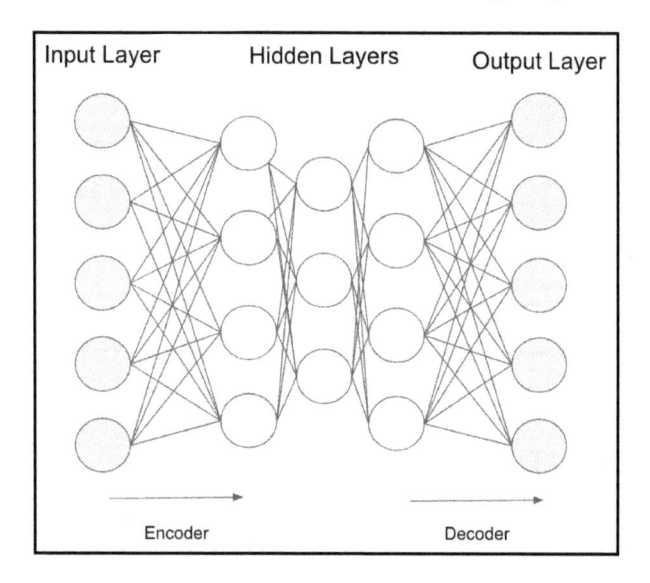

Example

In the following coded example, we define the layer sizes along with the hidden layers and compile the model:

```
input_size = 784
hidden_size = 128 # 64*3
code_size = 64
input_image = Input(shape=(input_size,))
# Encoder
hidden_1 = Dense(hidden_size, activation='relu')(input_image)
e = Dense(code_size, activation='relu')(hidden_1)
# Decoder
hidden_2 = Dense(hidden_size, activation='relu')(e)
d = Dense(input_size, activation='sigmoid')(hidden_2)
autoencoder = Model(input=input_image, output=d)
autoencoder.compile(optimizer='adam', loss='mse')
autoencoder.summary()
```

The preceding command generates the following output:

```
Layer (type)                 Output Shape              Param #
=================================================================
input_3 (InputLayer)         (None, 784)               0
_____
dense_7 (Dense)              (None, 128)               100480
_____
dense_8 (Dense)              (None, 64)                8256
_____
dense_9 (Dense)              (None, 128)               8320
_____
dense_10 (Dense)             (None, 784)               101136
=================================================================
Total params: 218,192
Trainable params: 218,192
Non-trainable params: 0
```

Convolutional autoencoders

Autoencoders can be used with convolutions instead of fully connected layers. This can be done using 3D vectors instead of 1D vectors. In the context of images, downsampling the image forces the autoencoder to learn a compressed version of it.

Example

We obtain the train and test datasets from the MNIST datasets, as we did previously:

```
(x_train, _), (x_test, _) = mnist.load_data()
# Scale the training and testing data so that they are in a range between 0 and 1
x_train = x_train.astype('float32')/255
x_test = x_test.astype('float32')/255
print(x_train.shape)
print(x_test.shape)
(60000, 28, 28)
(10000, 28, 28)
```

As the images in the dataset are greyscale, with pixel values ranging from 0 to 255 and a dimension of 28 x 28, we need to convert each image into a matrix of 28 x 28 x 1, as follows:

```
x_train = x_train.reshape(-1, 28,28, 1)
x_test = x_test.reshape(-1, 28,28, 1)
print(x_train.shape)
print(x_test.shape)
(60000, 28, 28, 1)
(10000, 28, 28, 1)
```

Now, load in the additional functions from the keras library. We will use the Conv2D and MaxPooling2D layers for the encoder and the Conv2D and Upsampling2D layers for the decoder:

```
from keras.models import Sequential
from keras.layers import Flatten, Reshape, Conv2D, MaxPooling2D, UpSampling2D
#Subsequently we can define the model as follows.
ae = Sequential()
# Layers of the encoder
ae.add(Conv2D(32, (3, 3), activation='relu', padding='same', input_shape=x_train.shape[1:]))
ae.add(MaxPooling2D((2, 2), padding='same'))
ae.add(Conv2D(64, (3, 3), activation='relu', padding='same'))
ae.add(MaxPooling2D((2, 2), padding='same'))
ae.add(Conv2D(128, (3, 3), strides=(2,2), activation='relu', padding='same'))
# Layers of the decoder
ae.add(Conv2D(128, (3, 3), activation='relu', padding='same'))
ae.add(UpSampling2D((2, 2)))
ae.add(Conv2D(8, (2, 2), activation='relu', padding='same'))
ae.add(UpSampling2D((2, 2)))
ae.add(Conv2D(64, (3, 3), activation='relu'))
ae.add(UpSampling2D((2, 2)))
ae.add(Conv2D(1, (3, 3), activation='sigmoid', padding='same'))
ae.summary()
```

Implementing Autoencoders

The preceding commands generate the following output:

```
Layer (type)                 Output Shape              Param #
=================================================================
conv2d_4 (Conv2D)            (None, 28, 28, 32)        320
_____
max_pooling2d_3 (MaxPooling2 (None, 14, 14, 32)        0
_____
conv2d_5 (Conv2D)            (None, 14, 14, 64)        18496
_____
max_pooling2d_4 (MaxPooling2 (None, 7, 7, 64)          0
_____
conv2d_6 (Conv2D)            (None, 4, 4, 128)         73856
_____
conv2d_7 (Conv2D)            (None, 4, 4, 128)         147584
_____
up_sampling2d_1 (UpSampling2 (None, 8, 8, 128)         0
_____
conv2d_8 (Conv2D)            (None, 8, 8, 8)           4104
_____
up_sampling2d_2 (UpSampling2 (None, 16, 16, 8)         0
_____
conv2d_9 (Conv2D)            (None, 14, 14, 64)        4672
_____
up_sampling2d_3 (UpSampling2 (None, 28, 28, 64)        0
_____
conv2d_10 (Conv2D)           (None, 28, 28, 1)         577
=================================================================
Total params: 249,609
Trainable params: 249,609
Non-trainable params: 0
```

From here, we can compile and fit the model as follows:

```
ae.compile(optimizer='adam', loss='binary_crossentropy')
autoencoder_train = ae.fit(x_train, x_train,
batch_size=128,epochs=10,verbose=1, validation_data=(x_test, x_test))
```

The preceding commands generate the following output:

```
Train on 60000 samples, validate on 10000 samples
Epoch 1/10
60000/60000 [==============================] - 185s 3ms/step - loss: 0.1039 - val_loss: 0.1011
Epoch 2/10
60000/60000 [==============================] - 188s 3ms/step - loss: 0.1012 - val_loss: 0.0993
Epoch 3/10
60000/60000 [==============================] - 166s 3ms/step - loss: 0.0992 - val_loss: 0.0970
Epoch 4/10
60000/60000 [==============================] - 173s 3ms/step - loss: 0.0975 - val_loss: 0.0956
Epoch 5/10
60000/60000 [==============================] - 180s 3ms/step - loss: 0.0963 - val_loss: 0.0951
Epoch 6/10
60000/60000 [==============================] - 211s 4ms/step - loss: 0.0951 - val_loss: 0.0936
Epoch 7/10
60000/60000 [==============================] - 158s 3ms/step - loss: 0.0942 - val_loss: 0.0927
Epoch 8/10
60000/60000 [==============================] - 166s 3ms/step - loss: 0.0933 - val_loss: 0.0919
Epoch 9/10
60000/60000 [==============================] - 176s 3ms/step - loss: 0.0925 - val_loss: 0.0912
Epoch 10/10
60000/60000 [==============================] - 171s 3ms/step - loss: 0.0918 - val_loss: 0.0906
```

Sparse autoencoders

Sparse autoencoders introduce a bottleneck without reducing the number of nodes in the hidden layers. The number of nodes in each hidden layer is the same as the number of nodes in the input and output layers. The loss function is reconstructed such that it penalizes activations within a layer. This means that the network is encouraged to learn by activating only a small number of neurons at a time.

The architecture of a sparse autoencoder is shown in the following diagram, where how opaque the node is corresponds to the level of activation. Different inputs to the model result in the activation of different nodes throughout the network. This allows the network to sensitize individual hidden layer nodes towards specific attributes of the data fed into it. This differs from undercomplete autoencoders, as they use the same network for every observation:

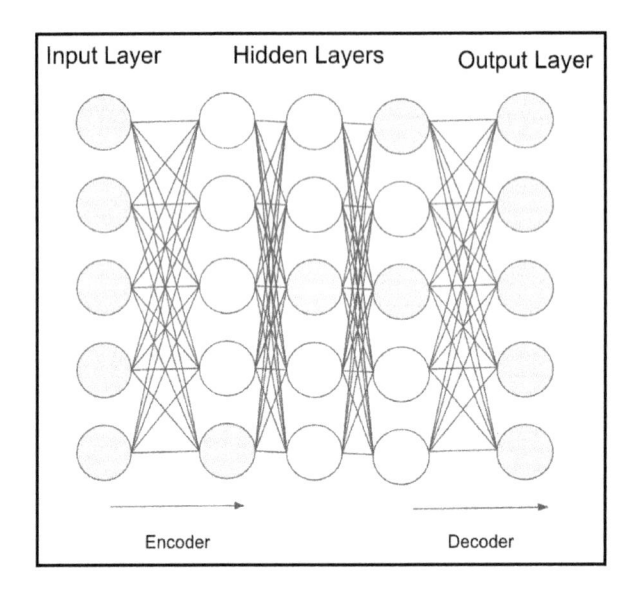

Example

It is possible to add a sparsity constraint on the latent variables by using the `activity_regularizer` function in Keras. This function limits the number of nodes that are activated in a given time. It is added to the dense layer, as follows:

```
from keras import regularizers
input_size = 784
h_size = 64
o_size = 784
x = Input(shape=(input_size,))
# Encoder
h = Dense(h_size, activation='relu',
activity_regularizer=regularizers.l1(10e-5))(x)
# Decoder
r = Dense(o_size, activation='sigmoid')(h)
autoencoder = Model(input=x, output=r)
```

Denoising autoencoders

Denoising encoders deliberately add noise to the input of the network; they essentially create a corrupted copy of the data. The denoising encoder does this to help the model learn the latent representation present in the input data, making it more generalizable:

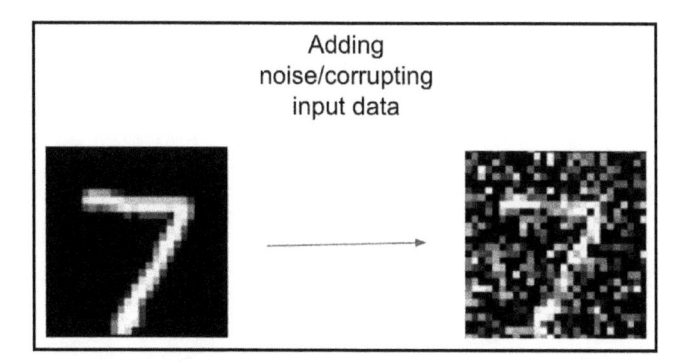

The corrupted/noisy image is then fed into the network in a similar fashion to other standard autoencoders:

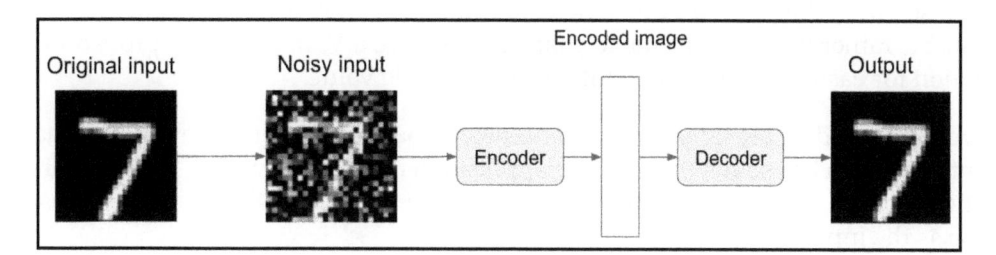

Example

We can add noise to the MNIST dataset as shown in the following example. The noise that has been added is with normal distribution, centered at 0.5 and standard deviation 0.5:

```
add_noise = np.random.normal(loc=0.5, scale=0.5, size=x_train.shape)
x_train_with_noise = x_train + add_noise
add_noise = np.random.normal(loc=0.5, scale=0.5, size=x_test.shape)
x_test_with_noise = x_test + add_noise
x_train_noisy = np.clip(x_train_with_noise, 0., 1.)
x_test_noisy = np.clip(x_test_with_noise, 0., 1.)
```

Contractive autoencoder

The aim of a **contractive autoencoder** (**CAE**) is to have a learned representation of the latent attributes of the input data that is less sensitive to a small variation in the data. In other words, we require the model to be robust against noise.

To ensure the CAE is robust, a *regularizer* (penalty term) is added to the cost function. The name CAE comes from the fact that the penalty term generates a mapping, which strongly **contracts** the data:

$$L = \|X - \hat{X}\|_2^2 + \lambda \|J_h(X)\|_F^2$$

$$\|J_h(X)\|_F^2 = \sum_{ij} \left(\frac{\partial h_j(X)}{\partial X_i}\right)^2$$

Variational Autoencoders

Variational Autoencoders (**VAEs**) differ from the standard autoencoders that we have discussed so far, in the sense that they describe an observation in latent space in a probabilistic, rather than deterministic, manner. As such, a VAE outputs a probability distribution for each latent attribute, rather than a single value.

Standard autoencoders are only really useful when you want to replicate the data that was input into it, which has somewhat limited applications in the real world. As VAEs are generative models, they can be applied to cases where you don't want to output data that is the same as the input data.

Considering this in a real-world context, when training an autoencoder model on a dataset of faces, one would hope that it would learn latent attributes such as whether the person is smiling, their skin tone, whether they are wearing glasses, and so on. Standard autoencoders represent these latent attributes as discrete values, as shown in the following diagram:

Chapter 8

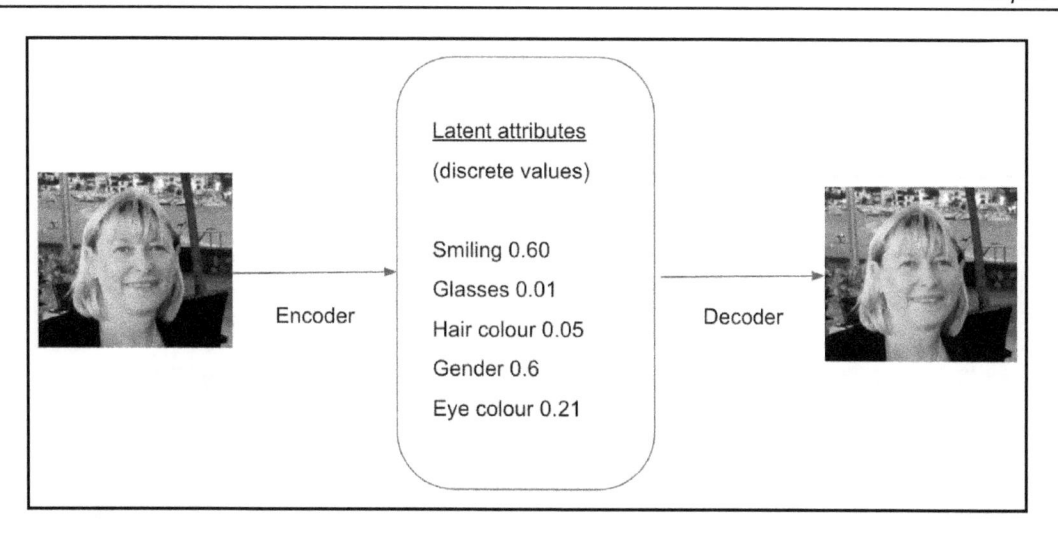

Using VAEs, we can describe these attributes in probabilistic terms, allowing each feature to be within a range of possible values, rather than a single value. The following diagram depicts how we can represent whether the person is smiling, as either a discrete value or as a probability distribution:

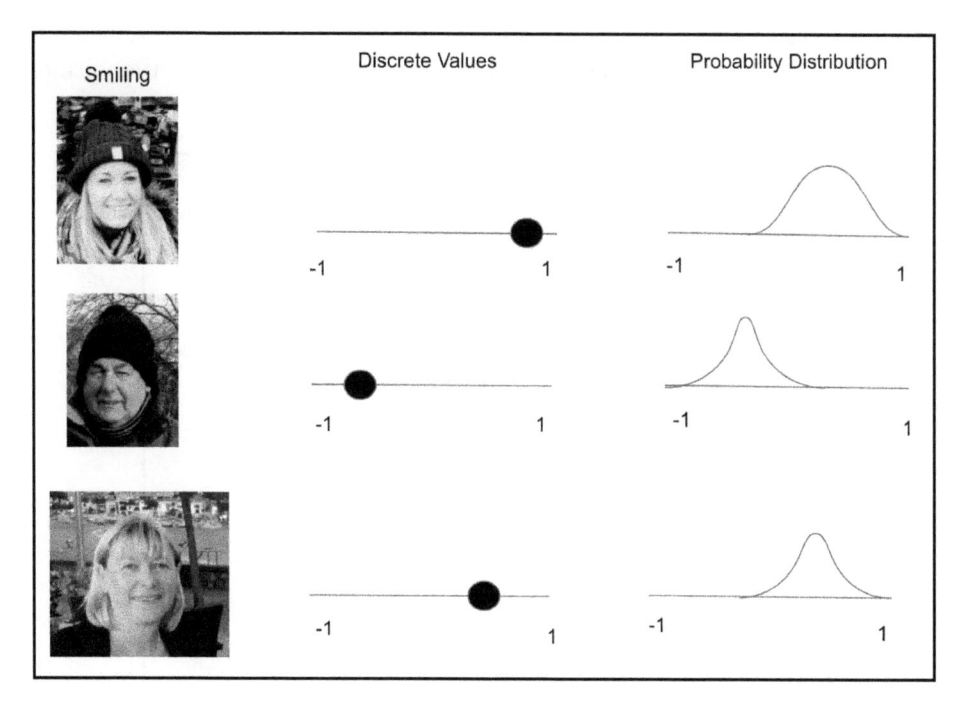

[199]

Implementing Autoencoders

For VAEs, the distribution of each latent attribute is sampled from the image to generate the vector that is used as the input for the decoder model, as shown in the following diagram:

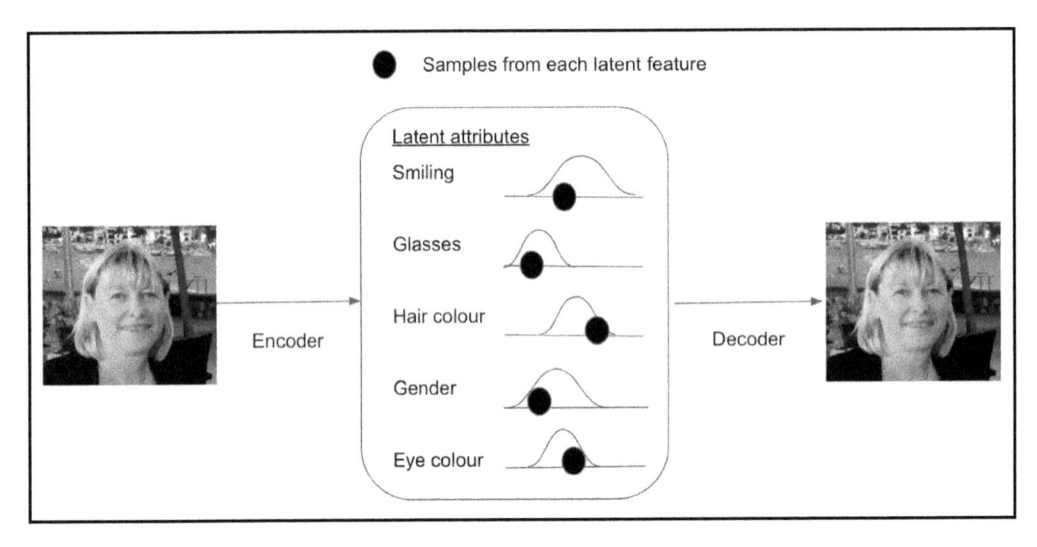

It is assumed that the distributions from each latent feature are **Gaussian**. As such, two vectors are output where one describes the mean and the other describes the variance of the distributions:

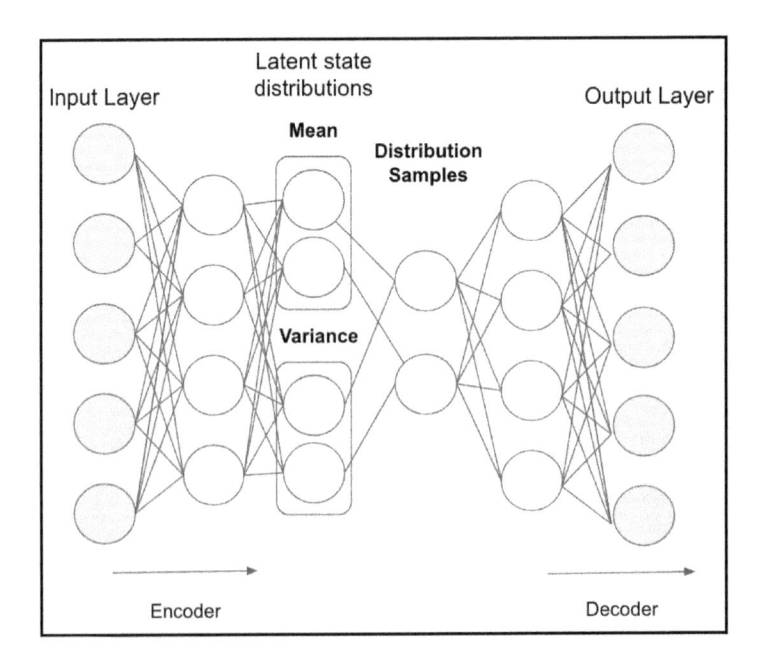

Training VAEs

When training a VAE, it is necessary to be able to calculate the relationship of each parameter in the network with respect to the overall loss. This process is called **backpropagation**.

Standard autoencoders use backpropagation in order to reconstruct the loss across the weights of the network. However, VAEs are not as straightforward to train, owing to the fact that the sampling operation is not differentiable: the gradients cannot be propagated from the reconstruction error:

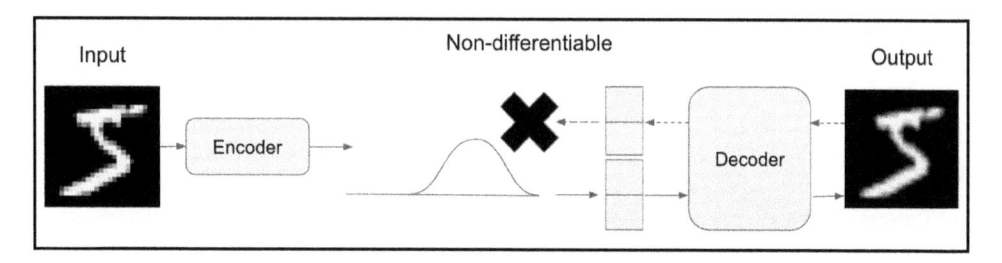

The **reparameterization trick** can be used to overcome this limitation. The idea behind the reparameterization trick is to sample ε from a unit normal distribution, then shift it by the mean μ of the latent attribute, and scale it by the latent attributes' variance σ:

$$z = \mu + \sigma\epsilon$$

Implementing Autoencoders

Performing this operation essentially removes the sampling process from the flow of gradients, as it is now outside the network. As such, the sampling process doesn't depend on anything in the network. This means that we can now optimize the parameters of the distribution, while maintaining the ability to randomly sample from it:

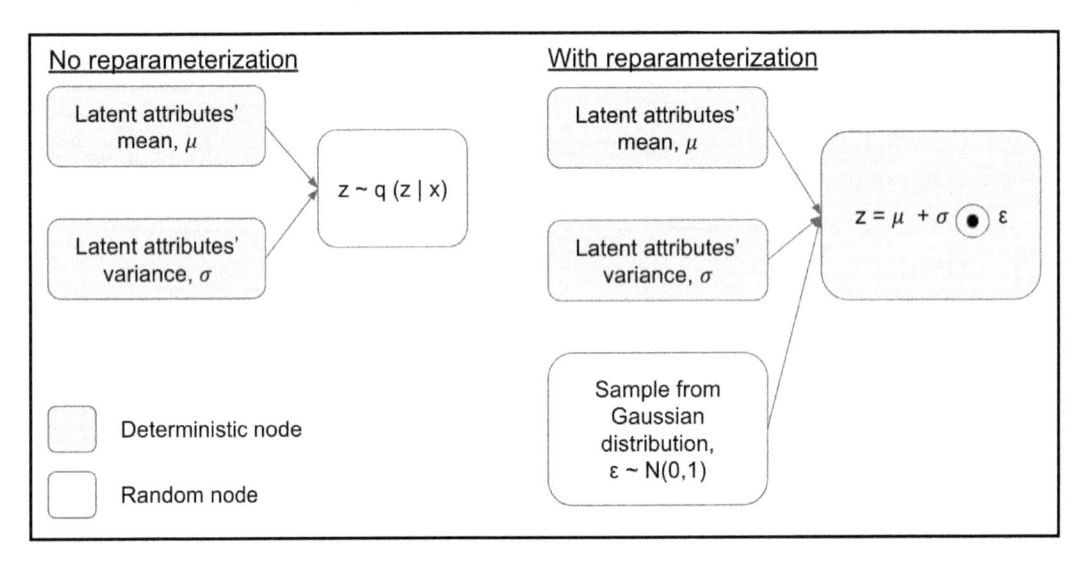

In other words, as the distribution of each attribute is Gaussian and, as per the associated properties of such a distribution, we can transform with mean μ and covariance matrix Σ as per the following formula:

$$z = \mu + \Sigma^{1/2} \epsilon$$

Here, $\epsilon \sim N(0,1)$.

Chapter 8

With the introduction of the reparameterization trick, we can now train the model via simple backpropagation:

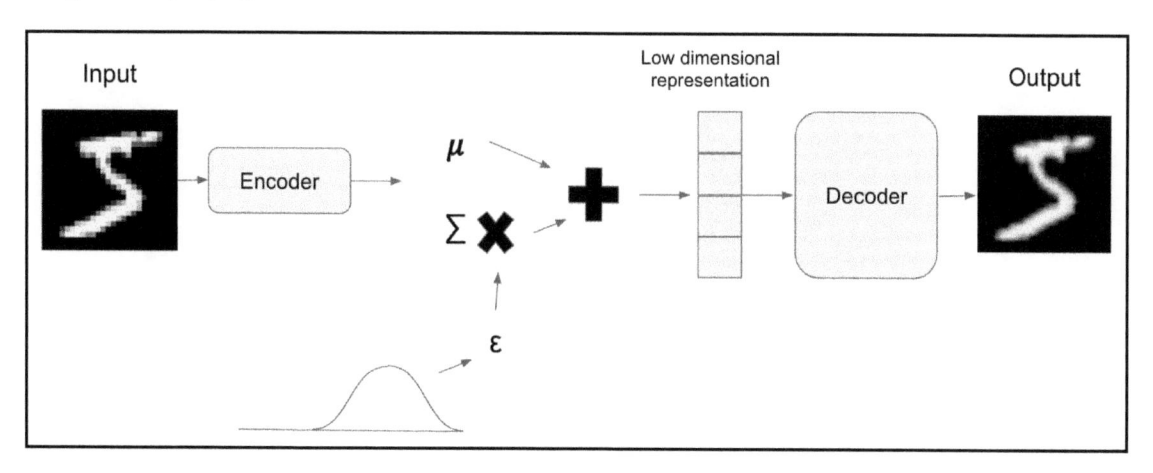

Example

This coded example shows how to build a VAE while continuing to use the Keras library and MNIST dataset, by performing the following steps:

1. First, we import the required libraries along with the MNIST dataset and scale as we have done previously:

   ```
   import numpy as np
   import matplotlib.pyplot as plt
   from scipy.stats import norm
   from keras.layers import Input, Dense, Lambda
   from keras.models import Model
   from keras import backend as K
   from keras import metrics
   from keras.datasets import mnist
   (x_train, y_train), (x_test, y_test) = mnist.load_data()
   # Scale the training and testing data so that they are in a range
   between 0 and 1
   x_train = x_train.astype('float32')/255
   x_test = x_test.astype('float32')/255
   x_train = x_train.reshape(len(x_train), np.prod(x_train.shape[1:]))
   x_test = x_test.reshape(len(x_test), np.prod(x_test.shape[1:]))
   Assign appropriate values for each of the variables.
   batch_size = 50
   input_dim = 784 # Pixel values 28*28
   latent_dim = 2 # The mean and variance
   ```

```python
hidden_dim = 256 # Required to be smaller than the input
epochs = 20
epsilon_std = 1.0
```
Now we define the encoder, mean and standard deviation of the latent variables.
```python
x = Input(shape=(input_dim,))
# Encoder
h = Dense(hidden_dim, activation='relu')(x)
# Mean of the latent variables
z_mean = Dense(latent_dim)(h)
# Standard deviation of latent variables
z_log_var = Dense(latent_dim)(h)
```
Define a function that will sample from the latent space.
```python
def sampling_function(args):
    z_mean, z_log_var = args
    epsilon = K.random_normal(shape=(K.shape(z_mean)[0], latent_dim),
    mean=0., stddev=epsilon_std)
    return z_mean + K.exp(z_log_var / 2) * epsilon
```
Define z to be a random sample from the latent normal distribution.
```python
z = Lambda(sampling_function, output_shape=(latent_dim,))([z_mean,
z_log_var])
```
Assign the three layers for the decoder; we map the sampled points from the latent space.
```python
decoder = Dense(hidden_dim, activation='relu')
decoder_mean = Dense(input_dim, activation='sigmoid')
h_decoded = decoder(z)
x_decoded_mean = decoder_mean(h_decoded)
```
Now instantiate the VAE model.
```python
vae = Model(x, x_decoded_mean)
```
Compile and fit the model.
```python
vae.add_loss(vae_loss)
vae.compile(optimizer='rmsprop')
vae.summary()
vae.fit(x_train,
shuffle=True,
epochs=epochs,
batch_size=batch_size,
validation_data=(x_test, None))
```

The preceding commands generate the following output:

```
Layer (type)                    Output Shape         Param #     Connected to
================================================================================
input_1 (InputLayer)            (None, 784)          0
_____
dense_1 (Dense)                 (None, 256)          200960      input_1[0][0]
_____
dense_2 (Dense)                 (None, 2)            514         dense_1[0][0]
_____
dense_3 (Dense)                 (None, 2)            514         dense_1[0][0]
_____
lambda_1 (Lambda)               (None, 2)            0           dense_2[0][0]
                                                                 dense_3[0][0]
_____
dense_4 (Dense)                 (None, 256)          768         lambda_1[0][0]
_____
dense_5 (Dense)                 (None, 784)          201488      dense_4[0][0]
================================================================================
Total params: 404,244
Trainable params: 404,244
Non-trainable params: 0
```

2. A key benefit of a VAE is that it can learn smooth latent state representations of the input data. Here, we build a model to project the inputs onto the latent space:

```
encoder = Model(x, z_mean)
From here we can plot the digit classes in the latent space.
x_test_e = encoder.predict(x_test, batch_size=batch_size)
plt.figure(figsize=(10, 8))
plt.scatter(x_test_e[:, 0], x_test_e[:, 1], c=y_test)
plt.colorbar()
plt.show()
```

Implementing Autoencoders

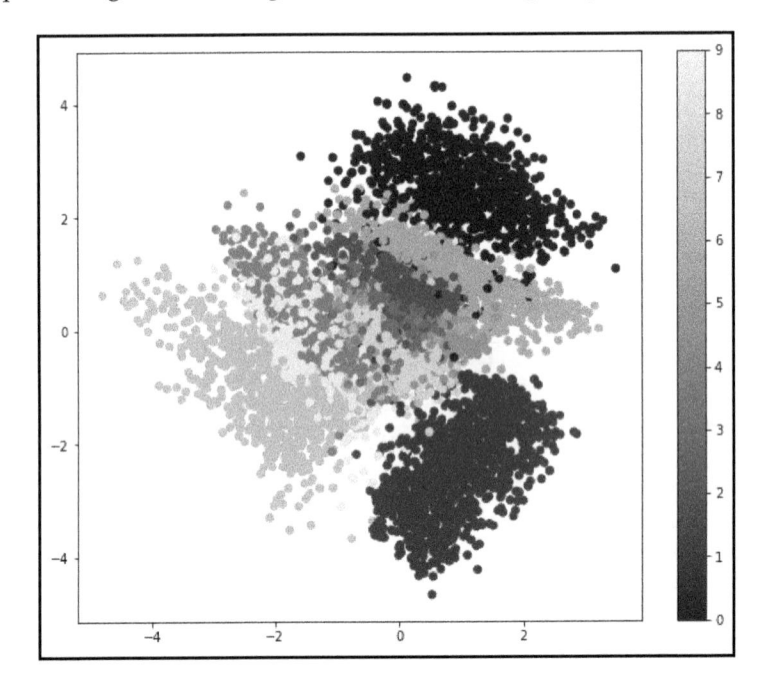

The preceding commands generate the following output:

3. Now, we build a digit generator that can sample from the learned distribution, as follows:

```
input_decoder = Input(shape=(latent_dim,))
_h_decoded = decoder(input_decoder)
_x_decoded_mean = decoder_mean(_h_decoded)
gen = Model(input_decoder, _x_decoded_mean)
In order to display a manifold of the digits we can run the below.
n = 10
size_digit = 28
figure = np.zeros((size_digit * n, size_digit * n))
grid_x = norm.ppf(np.linspace(0.05, 0.95, n))
grid_y = norm.ppf(np.linspace(0.05, 0.95, n))
for i, yi in enumerate(grid_x):
    for j, xi in enumerate(grid_y):
        z_sample = np.array([[xi, yi]])
        x_decoded = gen.predict(z_sample)
        digit = x_decoded[0].reshape(size_digit, size_digit)
        figure[i * size_digit: (i + 1) * size_digit,
               j * size_digit: (j + 1) * size_digit] = digit
plt.figure(figsize=(10, 10))
plt.imshow(figure, cmap='Greys_r')
plt.show()
```

[206]

The preceding commands generate the following output:

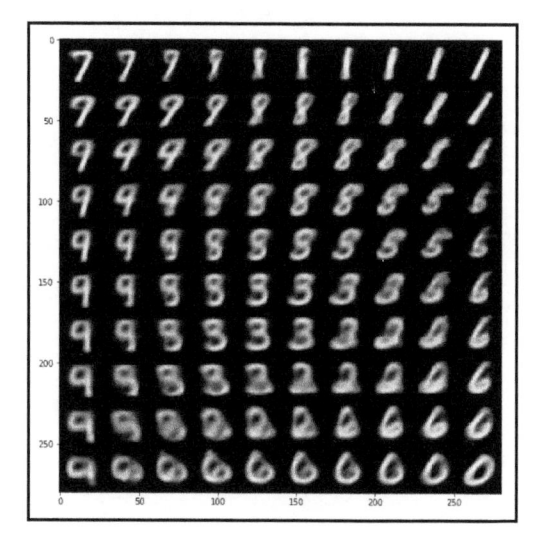

Summary

In this chapter, we have explained what autoencoders are and discussed their various types. Throughout, we have given coded examples as to how autoencoders can be applied to the MNIST dataset.

In the next chapter, we will introduce **Deep Belief Networks** (**DBNs**) along with some fundamental concepts that underpin their architecture.

Further reading

- *Tutorial on Variational Autoencoders*: https://arxiv.org/abs/1606.05908
- *CS598LAZ - Variational Autoencoders*: http://slazebni.cs.illinois.edu/spring17/lec12_vae.pdf
- *Auto-Encoding Variational Bayes*: https://arxiv.org/abs/1312.6114
- *Deep Learning Book*: https://www.deeplearningbook.org/contents/autoencoders.html

9
Deep Belief Networks

In this chapter, we will explain what **Deep Belief Networks** (**DBNs**) are and how they have been applied to some real-world problems. We will initially introduce some fundamental concepts that need to be understood first, before diving into the details of DBNs. We will give examples as to how these models can be implemented in Python and make predictions on some commonly used datasets.

The following are the topics covered in this chapter:

- Overview of DBNs
- DBN architecture
- Training DBNs
- Fine-tuning
- Datasets and libraries

Overview of DBNs

DBNs are a class of unsupervised probabilistic/graphical deep learning algorithms. The goal of a DBN is to classify data into different categories. They are composed of multiple layers of stochastic latent variables, which can be referred to as feature detectors or hidden units. It is these hidden units that capture correlations present in the data.

DBNs were introduced in 2006 by Geoffrey Hinton and have since been widely used in the following areas:

- Image recognition, generation, and clustering
- Speech recognition
- Video sequences
- Motion capture data

Before trying to fully understand a DBN, there are two fundamental notions to be considered and understood:

- **Bayesian Belief Networks (BBNs)**
- **Restricted Boltzmann machines (RBMs)**

BBNs

BNNs are probabilistic graphical models that can be used to describe the conditional dependencies between random variables. They can be used to help determine what caused a certain outcome or the probabilities of different effects, given an action. They can also be used to make future predictions.

In the previous example, we considered the conditional probabilities of a person smiling when it is sunny. Through previously observed outcomes (that is, our prior belief), the probability of a person smiling and it being sunny is 31/50; it represents a joint probability of the two outcomes occurring at the same time. All of the four joint probability outcomes sum to 1. The overall probability of an event occurring is referred to as the marginal probability. For example, the marginal probability of it being sunny is 34/50, as shown in the following table:

	Sunny	Not sunny	
Smiling	31/50	8/50	39/50
Not smiling	3/50	8/50	11/50
	34/50	16/50	50/50

The relationships of these probabilities can be represented as a BBN where a node represents a hypothesis/random process that takes at least two possible values. As such, Bayesian networks make certain assumptions about the probabilistic dependencies between the events they model. For example, the sunny node represents the state whether the person is smiling or not, as shown in the following diagram:

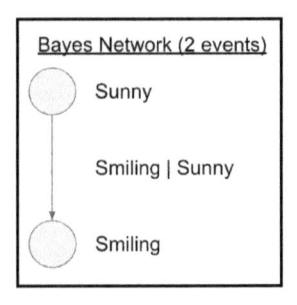

Let's now also consider the relationship between whether there is a rainbow and the person is smiling, as shown in the following table:

	Rainbow	No rainbow	
Smiling	36/50	6/50	42/50
Not smiling	2/50	6/50	8/50
	38/50	12/50	50/50

We can represent all of these three events (**Smiling**, **Sunny**, and **Rainbow**) in a single BBN. The core concept is that a node is created for each set of complementary and mutually exclusive events, and arrows are placed between those that directly depend on one another:

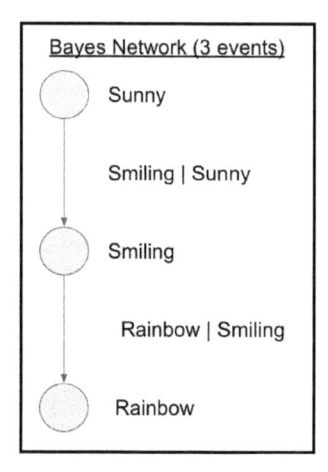

Bayes Network (3 events)

Sunny

Smiling | Sunny

Smiling

Rainbow | Smiling

Rainbow

There are two ways in which information can be propagated in the BBN: predictive and retrospective.

Predictive propagation

During predictive propagation, information is passed in the direction of the arrows. An example of making a prediction from the preceding is that, if the probability of it being sunny is high, then the probability of a person smiling is also high.

Retrospective propagation

If we are to follow the arrows in the opposite direction, we can explain the observations via retrospective propagation. An example of this is that, if the person is smiling, it is because it is sunny.

RBMs

RBM is an algorithm that has been widely used for tasks such as collaborative filtering, feature extraction, topic modeling, and dimensionality reduction. RBMs are able to learn patterns in a dataset in an unsupervised fashion.

For example, if you watch a movie and say whether you liked it or not, we could use an RBM to help us to determine the reason why you made this decision.

RBMs belong to a family of models called **Energy-Based Models** (**EBMs**). They embrace the notion of energy as a metric to measure the quality of the model. Their goal is to minimize energy defined by the following formula, which depends on the configurations of visible/input states, hidden states, weights, and biases. In other words, during the training of the RBM, we aim to find the parameters for given values so that the energy reaches its minimum:

$$E(v, h) = -\sum_i a_i v_i - \sum_j b_j h_j - \sum_{i,j} v_j h_j w_{ij}$$

RBMs are two-layer networks that are the fundamental building blocks of a DBN. The first layer of an RBM is a visible/input layer of neurons and the second is the hidden layer of neurons. Similar to BBNs, the neurons/nodes are where the calculations take place:

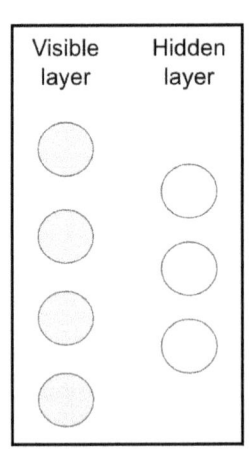

In simple terms, the RBM takes the inputs from the visible layer and translates them into a set of numbers in order to represent them. The numbers are then translated back to reconstruct the inputs through several forward and backward passes during training. The **restriction** in the RBM is such that nodes in the same layer are not connected.

Each node in the **Visible layer** takes a low-level feature from the training dataset. For example, in image classification, each node would receive one pixel value for each pixel in an image:

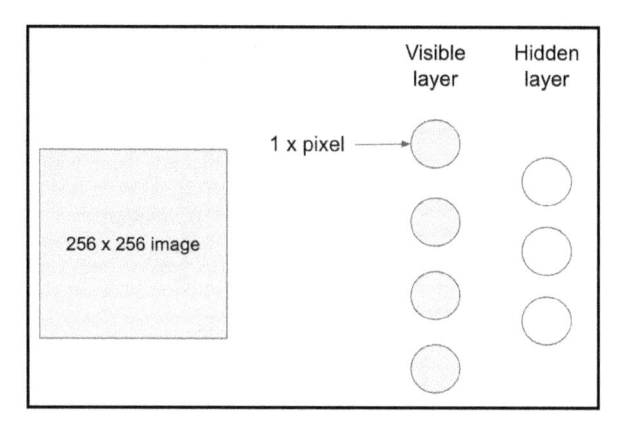

Let's follow this one pixel value through the network. The input **x** is multiplied by the weight from the hidden layer and a bias is then added. This is then fed into an activation function which produces the output. This output is essentially the strength of the signal passing through it, given the input **x**:

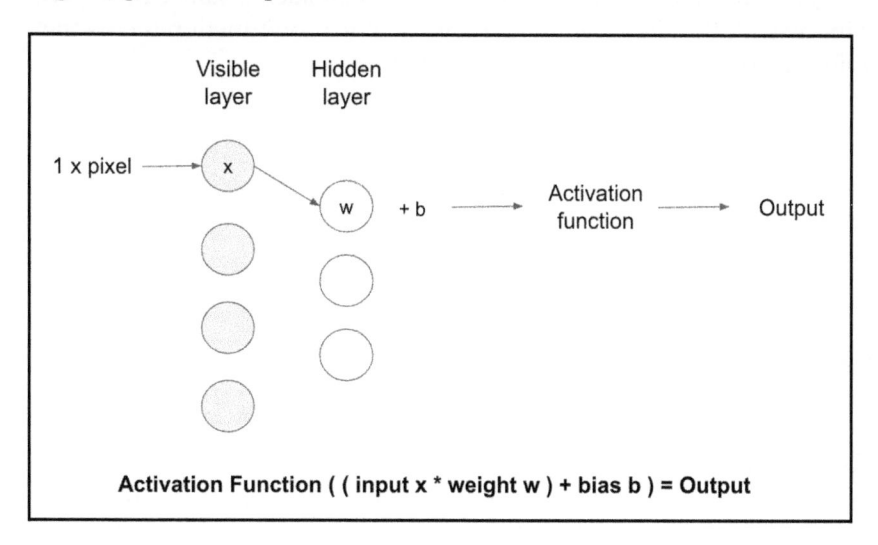

At each node in the hidden layer, **x** from each pixel value is multiplied by a separate weight. The products are then summed and a bias is added. The output of this is then passed through an activation function, producing the output at that single node, as shown in the following diagram:

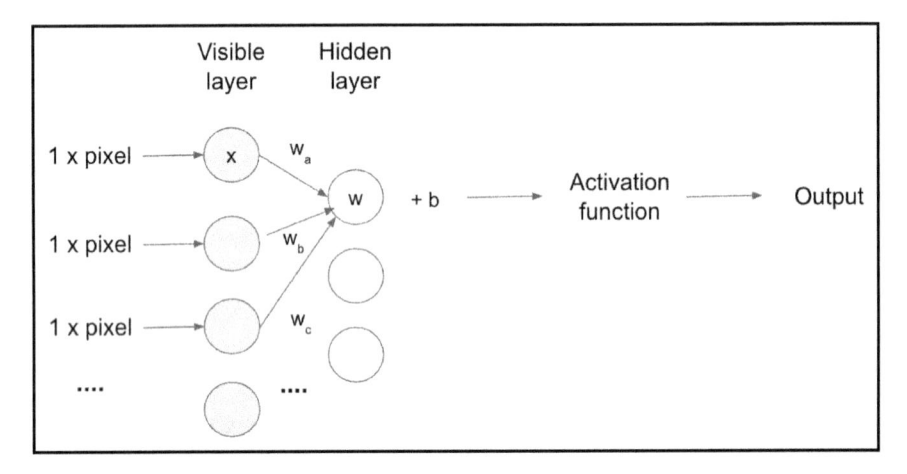

At each point in time, the RBM is in a certain state, which refers to the values of the neurons in the visible, v, and hidden, h, layers. The probability of such a state can be given by the following joint distribution function where Z is the partition function that is the summation over all possible pairs of visible and hidden vectors:

$$p(\mathbf{v}, \mathbf{h}) = \frac{1}{Z} e^{-E(\mathbf{v},\mathbf{h})}$$

$$Z = \sum_{v,h} e^{-E(\mathbf{v},\mathbf{h})}$$

RBM training

There are following, two main steps an RBM carries out during training:

1. **Gibbs sampling**: The first step in the training process uses Gibbs sampling, which repeats the following process k times. Probability of hidden vector given the input vector; prediction of the hidden values. Probability of the input vector given the hidden vector; prediction of the input values. From this, we obtain another input vector, which was recreated from the original input values.

2. **Contrastive divergence**: RBMs adjust their weights through contrastive divergence. During this process, weights for visible nodes are randomly generated and used to generate hidden nodes. The hidden nodes then use the same weights to reconstruct visible nodes. The weights used to reconstruct the visible nodes are the same throughout. However, the generated nodes are not the same, because they aren't connected to each other.

Once an RBM has been trained, it is essentially able to express the following two things:

- The interrelationship between the features of the input data
- Which features are the most important when identifying patterns

Example – RBM recommender system

In the context of movies, we can use RBMs to uncover a set of latent factors that represent their genre and consequently determine which genre of movie a person likes; for example, we could ask someone to tell us which movies they have watched and whether they liked them or not, and represent them as binary inputs (1 or 0) to the RBM. For those movies they haven't seen or haven't told us about, we need to assign a value of -1 so that the network can identify those during training and ignore their associated weights.

Let's consider an example where a user likes **Mrs Doubtfire**, **The Hangover**, and **Bridesmaids**; does not like **Scream** or **Psycho**, and has not yet seen **The Hobbit**, given these inputs, the RBM may identify three hidden factors, **Comedy**, **Horror**, and **Fantasy**, which correspond to the genres of movies shown in the following diagram:

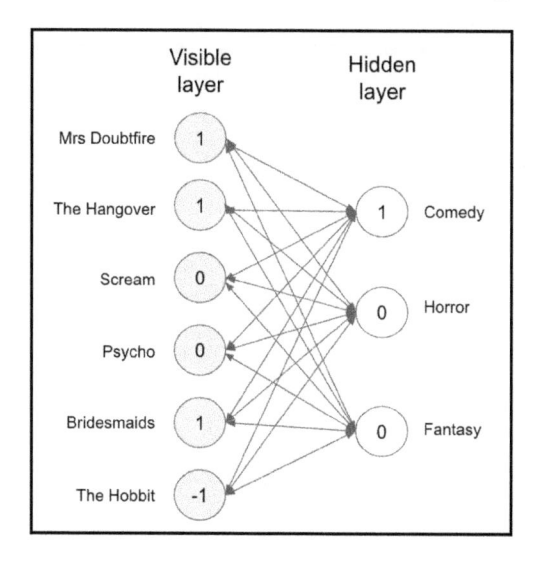

Deep Belief Networks

For each hidden neuron, the RBM assigns a probability of the hidden neuron given the input neuron. The final binary values of the neurons are obtained by sampling from the Bernoulli distribution.

In the preceding example, the only hidden neuron that represents the genre comedy becomes active. As such, given the movie ratings input into the RBM, it predicts that the user likes comedy films the most.

In order for the trained RBM to make predictions on movies the user has not yet seen based on their preference, the RBM uses the probability of the visible neurons, given the hidden neurons. It samples from the Bernoulli distribution to find out which one of the visible neurons then becomes active.

Example – RBM recommender system using code

Continuing in the context of movies, we will now give an example as to how we can build a RBM recommender system using the TensorFlow library. The goal of the example is to train a model to determine whether a user will like a movie or not.

In this example, we will use the MovieLens dataset (https://grouplens.org/datasets/movielens/) with 1 million ratings, which was created by the GroupLens Research Group at the University of Minnesota, by performing the following steps:

1. Firstly, we download the datasets. This can be done through Terminal commands, as follows:

   ```
   wget -O moviedataset.zip http://files.grouplens.org/datasets/movielens/ml-1m.zip
   unzip -o moviedataset.zip -d ./data
   unzip -o moviedataset.zip -d ./data
   ```

2. Now, we import the libraries that we will use, as follows:

   ```
   import pandas as pd
   import numpy as np
   import tensorflow as tf
   import matplotlib.pyplot as plt
   %matplotlib inline
   ```

3. Then, we import the data, as follows:

   ```
   movies_df = pd.read_csv('data/ml-1m/movies.dat', sep = '::', header = None)
   movies_df.columns = ['movie_id', 'title', 'genres']
   movies_df['List Index'] = movies_df.index
   ```

Chapter 9

```
ratings_df = pd.read_csv('data/ml-1m/ratings.dat', sep = '::',
header = None)
ratings_df.columns = ['user_id', 'movie_id', 'rating', 'timestamp']
```

4. We now merge the movies and ratings datasets and drop unnecessary columns:

```
merged_df= movies_df.merge(ratings_df, on='movie_id')
merged_df = merged_df.drop(['timestamp', 'title', 'genres'],
axis=1)
merged_df.head(2)
```

The preceding commands generate the following output:

movie_id	List Index	user_id	rating
1	0	1	5
1	0	6	4

5. Now, we group the user IDs by executing the following commands:

```
usergroup = merged_df.groupby('user_id')
usergroup.first().head()
```

The preceding commands generate the following output:

user_id	movie_id	List Index	rating
1	1	0	5
2	21	20	1
3	104	102	4
4	260	257	5
5	6	5	2

6. Then, we create a list of lists, where each list in the training data will be the ratings given to all of the movies by a user normalized into the interval [0,1]; they are divided by 5, as it needs to be normalized before it can be fed into the neural network:

```
training_users = 1000
training_data = []
for userID, curUser in usergroup:
    temp = [0]*len(movies_df)
```

Deep Belief Networks

```
for num, movie in curUser.iterrows():
    temp[movie['List Index']] = movie['rating']/5.0
training_data.append(temp)
if training_users == 0:
    break
training_users -= 1
```

7. Now, we assign values for the number of hidden units, h, and number of visible units, v. We choose the number of hidden units and set the number of visible units to be the length of the input dataset. The weight matrix will be created using the size of these hidden and visible units:

```
h = 20
v = len(movies_df)
```

8. Now, we assign `tf.placeholder` to be an appropriate size. It is essentially a literal placeholder into which we will feed values during training:

```
# This is the number of unique movies
vb = tf.placeholder(tf.float32, [v])
# This is the number of features we are going to learn in the
hidden unit
hb = tf.placeholder(tf.float32, [h])
# This is the placeholder for the weights
W = tf.placeholder(tf.float32, [v, h])
```

9. Then, we obtain our output for the hidden layer. This is our processing phase and the commencement of Gibb's sampling. We use a **Rectified Linear Unit (ReLU)** as our activation function. It is possible to use other activation functions such as the hyperbolic tangent function of the sigmoid function, but they are computationally more expensive to computer:

```
v0 = tf.placeholder(tf.float32, [None, v])
# Visible layer activation
_h0 = tf.nn.sigmoid(tf.matmul(v0, W) + hb)
# Gibb's Sampling
hidden0 = tf.nn.relu(tf.sign(_h0 -
tf.random_uniform(tf.shape(_h0))))
```

10. Now, we define the reconstruction phase; we recreate the input from the hidden layer activations, as follows:

```
# Hidden layer activation; reconstruction
_v1 = tf.nn.sigmoid(tf.matmul(hidden0, tf.transpose(W)) + vb)
visible1 = tf.nn.relu(tf.sign(_v1 -
tf.random_uniform(tf.shape(_v1))))
h1 = tf.nn.sigmoid(tf.matmul(visible1, W) + hb)
```

11. We set the learning rate to alpha. We also initiate positive and negative gradients via matrix multiplication. We also define the code that will update the weights matrix and biases using the contrastive divergence algorithm. This approximates the log-likelihood gradient, given the data and persons gradient ascent on the approximations:

    ```
    alpha = 0.6
    w_pos_grad = tf.matmul(tf.transpose(v0), hidden0)
    w_neg_grad = tf.matmul(tf.transpose(visible1), h1)
    # Calculate the contrastive divergence
    CD = (w_pos_grad - w_neg_grad) / tf.to_float(tf.shape(v0)[0])
    # Methods to update weights and biases
    update_w = W + alpha * CD
    update_vb = vb + alpha * tf.reduce_mean(v0 - visible1, 0)
    update_hb = hb + alpha * tf.reduce_mean(hidden0 - h1, 0)
    ```

12. The following code creates weights and bias matrices for computation in each iteration of training. The weights are initialized with random values from a normal distribution with a small standard deviation:

    ```
    # Current weight
    cur_w = np.random.normal(loc=0, scale=0.01, size=[v, h])
    # Visible unit biases at current state
    cur_vb = np.zeros([v], np.float32)
    # Hidden unit biases at current state
    cur_hb = np.zeros([h], np.float32)
    # Previous weight of network
    previous_w = np.zeros([v, h], np.float32)
    # Visible unit biases (previous)
    previous_vb = np.zeros([v], np.float32)
    # Hidden unit biases (previous)
    previous_hb = np.zeros([h], np.float32)
    err = v0 - visible1
    err_sum = tf.reduce_mean(err*err)
    #We set the error function to be the mean absolute error.
    err = v0 - visible1
    err_sum = tf.reduce_mean(err*err)
    ```

13. Now, we initialize a session in TensorFlow with the appropriate configuration if running on GPU, as shown in the following commands:

    ```
    config = tf.ConfigProto()
    config.gpu_options.allow_growth = True
    sess = tf.Session(config=config)
    sess.run(tf.global_variables_initializer())
    ```

Deep Belief Networks

14. From here, we train the model as per the following code:

    ```
    epochs = 15
    batch_size = 100
    errors = []
    for i in range(epochs):
        for start, end in zip( range(0, len(training_data), batch_size),
        range(batch_size, len(training_data), batch_size)):
            batch = training_data[start:end]
            cur_w = sess.run(update_w, feed_dict={v0: batch, W: previous_w, vb:
            previous_vb, hb: previous_hb})
            cur_vb = sess.run(update_vb, feed_dict={v0: batch, W: previous_w,
            vb: previous_vb, hb: previous_hb})
            cur_nb = sess.run(update_hb, feed_dict={v0: batch, W: previous_w,
            vb: previous_vb, hb: previous_hb})
            previous_w = cur_w
            previous_vb = cur_vb
            previous_hb = cur_nb
        errors.append(sess.run(err_sum, feed_dict={v0: training_data, W:
        cur_w, vb: cur_vb, hb: cur_nb}))
    ```

15. Now, we plot the error across epochs during training, as follows:

    ```
    plt.plot(errors)
    plt.ylabel('Error')
    plt.xlabel('Epoch')
    plt.show()
    ```

    The preceding commands generate the following diagram:

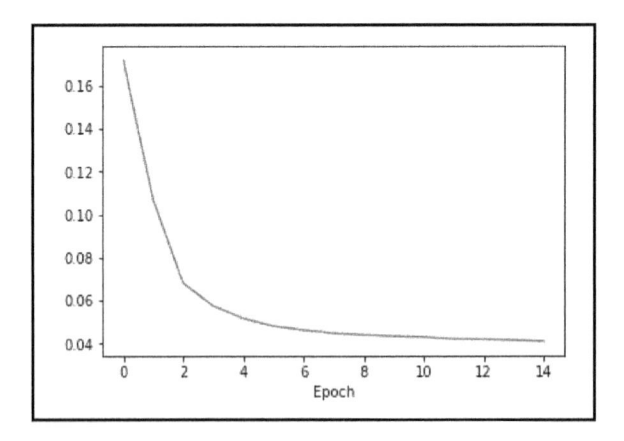

Chapter 9

The graph also helps us to determine how many epochs we should run the training for. It shows that, after six epochs, the improved performance rate drops and hence we should consider stopping the training at this stage.

DBN architecture

A DBN is a multilayer belief network where each layer is an RBM stacked against one another. Apart from the first and final layers of the DBN, each layer serves as both a hidden layer to the nodes before it, and as the input layer to the nodes that come after it:

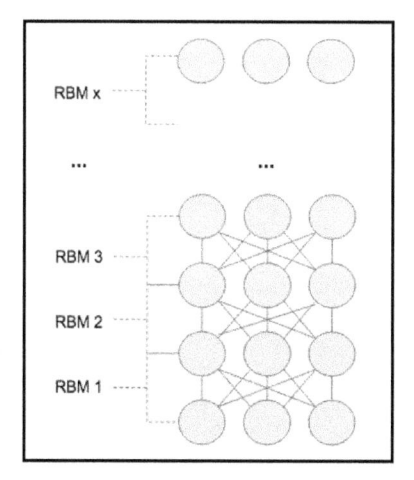

Two layers in the DBN are connected by a matrix of weights. The top two layers of a DBN are undirected, which gives a symmetric connection between them, forming an associative memory. The lower two layers have directed connections from the layers above. The presence of direction converts associative memory into observed variables:

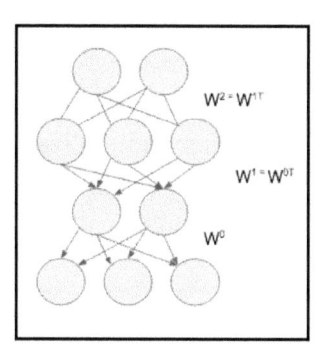

The two most significant properties of DBNs are as follows:

- A DBN learns top-down, generative weights via an efficient, layer by layer procedure. These weights determine how the variables in one layer depend on the layer above.
- Once training is complete, the values of the hidden variables in each layer can be inferred by a single bottom up pass. The pass begins with a visible data vector in the lower layer and uses its generative weights in the opposite direction.

The probability of a joint configuration network over both visible and hidden layers depends on the joint configuration network's energy, compared with the energy of all other joint configuration networks.

Once the pre-training phase of the DBN is complete by the RBM stack, a feedforward network can then be used for the fine-tune phase in order to create a classifier, or simply help to cluster unlabeled data in an unsupervised learning scenario:

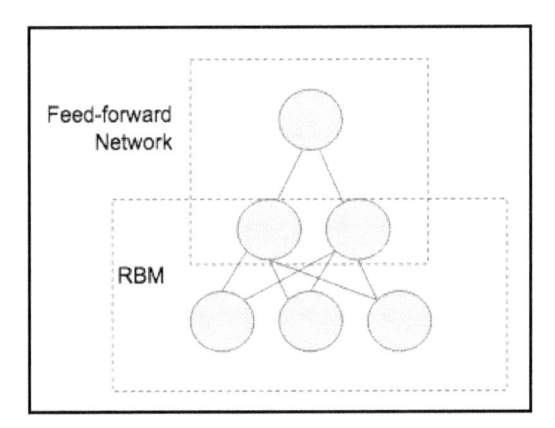

Training DBNs

DBNs are trained using a greedy algorithm where one layer is trained at a time; the RBMs are learned sequentially. A key concept surrounding this greedy approach is that it allows each model in the sequence to receive a different representation of the input data.

There are two phases to be considered during the training of a DBN, a positive phase and a negative phase:

- **Positive phase**: The first layer is trained with the data from the training dataset whilst all of the other layers are frozen. All of the individual activation probabilities for the first hidden layer are derived. This is referred to as the positive phase:

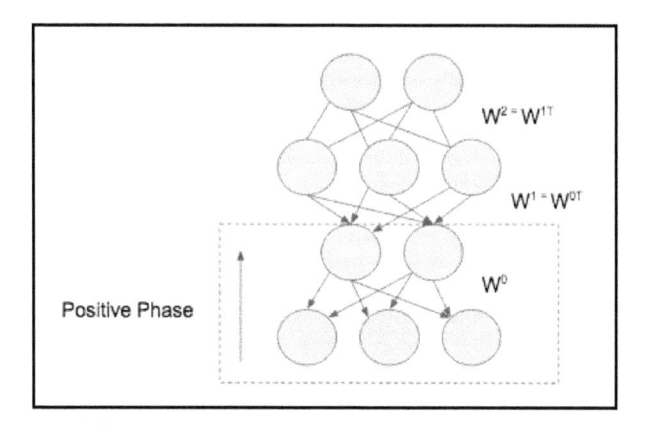

- **Negative phase**: During the negative phase the visible units are reconstructed in a similar fashion to the positive phase. From here, all of the associated weights are updated:

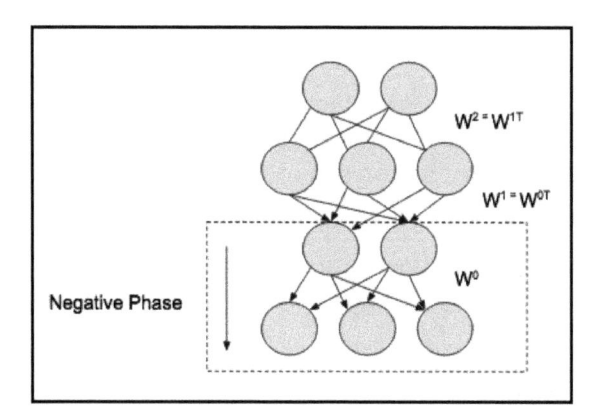

From here, the activations of the previously trained features are treated as visible units in order to learn the features of those in the second layer.

The weights in this second RBM are the transpose of the weights in the first RBM. As with the first RBM, the contrastive divergence method is used with Gibbs sampling. The positive and negative phases are calculated and the associated weights are then updated. We iterate over this process until the threshold values are obtained:

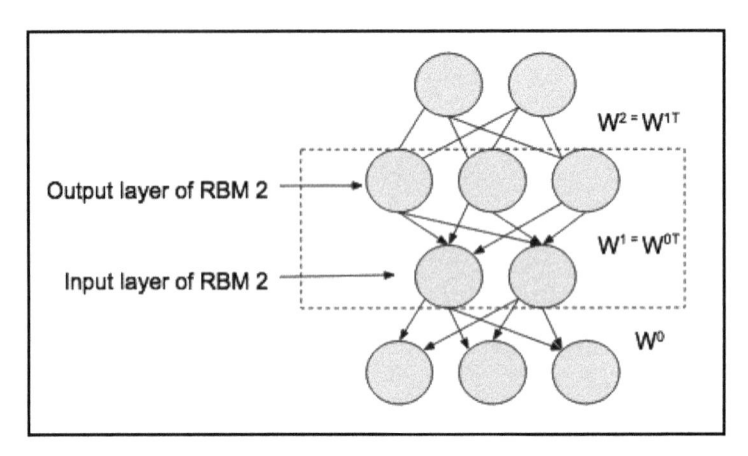

Each of the subsequent layers takes the output of the previous one as an input to produce an output. The output at each layer is essentially a new representation of the data with a simpler distribution. The whole DBN is trained when the learning for the final hidden layer is complete.

Fine-tuning

The objective of fine-tuning is to improve the accuracy of the model, better discriminating between classes. It aims to find the optimal values of the weights between layers. Fine-tuning slightly tweaks the original features in order to obtain more precise boundaries of the classes.

A small labelled dataset is used for fine-tuning, as this helps the model to associate patterns and features to the datasets. Back propagation is a method used to fine-tune and helps the model to generalize better.

Once we have identified some reasonable feature detectors, backward propagation only needs to perform a local search.

Fine-tuning can be applied as a stochastic bottom-up pass and adjust the top-down weights. Once the top is reached, recursion is applied to the top layer. In order to fine-tune further, we can do a stochastic top-down pass and adjust the bottom-up weights.

Datasets and libraries

Now that we have covered DBNs from a theoretical perspective, we take a look at some examples of code using the TensorFlow library along with the TensorFlow DBN Git repository (https://github.com/albertbup/deep-belief-network/). The repository allows you to develop simple, fast, Python implementations of DBN, which is based on binary RBMs.

We will consider the following two commonly used datasets in the machine learning community, in order to do so:

- **MNIST dataset**: For this dataset, you can refer to `Chapter 3`, *Convolutional Neural Networks for Image Processing*. This is a dataset of images, each of which displays a number from 0-9. Each image is 28 pixels in height and 28 pixels in width. It is available in the `sklearn` library but can be downloaded from the following web page, http://yann.lecun.com/exdb/mnist/:

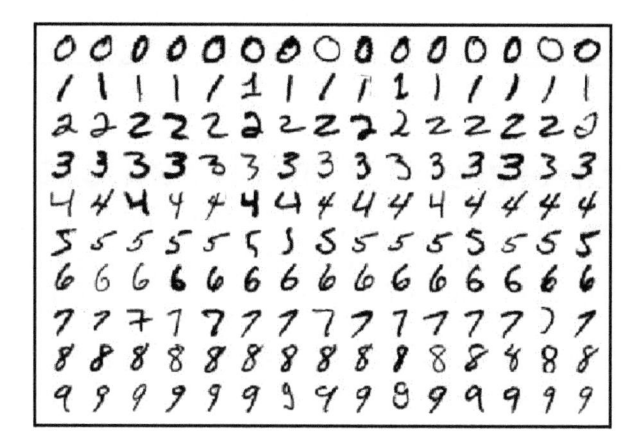

Deep Belief Networks

- **Boston house prices dataset**: It contains information about different houses in Boston. It is available within the `sklearn` library but can be downloaded from the following web page, https://www.cs.toronto.edu/~delve/data/boston/bostonDetail.html:

```
Boston house prices dataset
---------------------------

**Data Set Characteristics:**

    :Number of Instances: 506

    :Number of Attributes: 12 numeric/categorical predictive. Median Value (attribute 13) is usually the target.

    :Attribute Information (in order):
        - CRIM     per capita crime rate by town
        - ZN       proportion of residential land zoned for lots over 25,000 sq.ft.
        - INDUS    proportion of non-retail business acres per town
        - CHAS     Charles River dummy variable (= 1 if tract bounds river; 0 otherwise)
        - NOX      nitric oxides concentration (parts per 10 million)
        - RM       average number of rooms per dwelling
        - AGE      proportion of owner-occupied units built prior to 1940
        - DIS      weighted distances to five Boston employment centres
        - RAD      index of accessibility to radial highways
        - TAX      full-value property-tax rate per $10,000
        - PTRATIO  pupil-teacher ratio by town
        - LSTAT    % lower status of the population
        - MEDV     Median value of owner-occupied homes in $1000's

    :Missing Attribute Values: None

    :Creator: Harrison, D. and Rubinfeld, D.L.

This is a copy of UCI ML housing dataset.
https://archive.ics.uci.edu/ml/machine-learning-databases/housing/
```

Example – supervised DBN classification

In this example code, we implement a supervised DBN classification model. We use the TensorFlow DBN GitHub repository and use the MNIST dataset in order to train a model that will classify the images as numbers from 0-9. Let's perform the following steps:

1. Firstly, we import the relevant libraries, as follows:

    ```
    import numpy as np
    import pandas as pd
    from dbn.tensorflow import SupervisedDBNClassification
    from sklearn.model_selection import train_test_split
    from sklearn.metrics.classification import accuracy_score
    from sklearn.preprocessing import StandardScaler
    ```

2. We then import the MNIST dataset, as follows:

    ```
    data = pd.read_csv("train.csv")
    ```

3. We assign the feature variables (X), which are essentially the pixel values of the images, as follows:

   ```
   X = np.array(data.drop(["label"], axis=1))
   ```

4. We assign the target variables (Y), which are the numbers 0-9, as follows:

   ```
   Y = np.array(data["label"])
   array([1, 0, 1, ..., 7, 6, 9])
   ```

5. We then use the `StandardScaler` function from the `sklearn` library in order to normalize the pixel values in X, and then split the dataset into train and test sets, as follows:

   ```
   ss = StandardScaler()
   X = ss.fit_transform(X)
   X_train, X_test, Y_train, Y_test = train_test_split(X, Y, test_size=0.2, random_state=0)
   ```

6. Next, we initialize the `SupervisedDBNClassifier` classifier and fit it to the training dataset, as follows:

   ```
   classifier = SupervisedDBNClassification(hidden_layers_structure=[256, 256], learning_rate_rbm=0.05, learning_rate=0.1, n_epochs_rbm=10, n_iter_backprop=100, batch_size=32, activation_function='relu', dropout_p=0.2)
   classifier.fit(X_train, Y_train)
   ```

7. From here, we can make predictions on the test data and review the performance accuracy of the model:

   ```
   Y_pred = classifier.predict(X_test)
   accuracy = accuracy_score(Y_test, Y_pred)
   ```

Example – supervised DBN regression

In this example, we will take the Boston house prices dataset in order to train a model that will predict the prices of houses using the features in the dataset. Perform the following steps:

1. Firstly, we import the relevant libraries and assign our feature and target values, X and Y. We then split these into train and test datasets as done previously:

   ```
   from sklearn.datasets import load_boston
   from sklearn.model_selection import train_test_split
   ```

```
from sklearn.metrics.regression import r2_score, mean_squared_error
from sklearn.preprocessing import MinMaxScaler
from dbn.tensorflow import SupervisedDBNRegression
# Load the Boston dataset
boston = load_boston()
# Define x and y variables
x, y = boston.data, boston.target
# Split dataset between train and test
x_train, x_test, y_train, y_test = train_test_split(x, y,
test_size=0.3, random_state=100)
```

2. We use the `MinMaxScaler` function of the `sklearn` library in order to rescale feature values to be in the range [0,1] as follows:

```
min_max_scaler = MinMaxScaler()
x_train = min_max_scaler.fit_transform(x_train)
x_test = min_max_scaler.transform(x_test)
```

3. Next, we initiate the `SupervisedDBNRegression` classifier and fit the model to our dataset, as follows:

```
regressor = SupervisedDBNRegression(hidden_layers_structure=[100],
learning_rate_rbm=0.01, learning_rate=0.01, n_epochs_rbm=20,
n_iter_backprop=100, batch_size=20, activation_function='relu')
regressor.fit(x_train, y_train)
```

4. From here, we can make predictions on the test dataset and review the performance of the model:

```
y_pred = regressor.predict(X_test)
mean_squared_error(y_test, y_pred)
```

Example – unsupervised DBN classification

In this example, we show how to build a classification pipeline with an unsupervised DBN feature extractor along with a logistic regression classifier using the MNIST dataset.

In addition to the libraries previously imported, also import `Pipeline` of the `sklearn` library and the `UnsupervisedDBN` function, along with the MNIST dataset:

```
from sklearn.pipeline import Pipeline
from sklearn import linear_model
from dbn.models import UnsupervisedDBN
data = pd.read_csv('train.csv')
X = np.array(data.drop(['label'], axis=1))
Y = np.array(data['label'])
```

```
X_train, X_test, Y_train, Y_test = train_test_split(X, Y, test_size=0.2,
random_state=0)
```

Now, we initiate the models and combine them into a pipeline, as follows:

```
logistic = linear_model.LogisticRegression()
dbn = SupervisedDBNClassification(hidden_layers_structure=[256, 256],
learning_rate_rbm=0.05, learning_rate=0.1, n_epochs_rbm=10,
n_iter_backprop=50, batch_size=32, optimization_algorithm='sgd',
activation_function='relu', dropout_p=0.1)
classifier = Pipeline(steps=[('dbn', dbn), ('logistic', logistic)])
history = classifier.fit(x_train, y_train)
```

Summary

In this chapter, we introduced belief networks along with RBMs and explained how these can be developed into a DBN. We gave examples as to how both supervised and unsupervised DBNs can be implemented in TensorFlow, in order to make predictions on a dataset.

Moving on from this chapter, this book will dive into some more unsupervised learning approaches in the form of Monte Carlo methods and reinforcement learning.

Further reading

- *A Fast Learning Algorithm for Deep Belief Nets*: http://www.cs.toronto.edu/~fritz/absps/ncfast.pdf
- *Training restricted Boltzmann machines: An Introduction*: https://www.sciencedirect.com/science/article/abs/pii/S0031320313002495
- *Deep Boltzmann Machines*: http://proceedings.mlr.press/v5/salakhutdinov09a/salakhutdinov09a.pdf
- *A Practical Guide to Training Restricted Boltzmann Machines*: https://www.cs.toronto.edu/~hinton/absps/guideTR.pdf
- *Deep Belief Networks*: https://link.springer.com/chapter/10.1007/978-3-319-06938-8_8

10
Reinforcement Learning

So far, we have explored many different ways of learning from observed data. Even generative algorithms are, after all, based on a dataset that is used to create a very generic representation of the data that has been used to train them.

Now we are going to examine a completely different learning paradigm, which doesn't need any training dataset or output label: **reinforcement learning** (**RL**). RL operates using a different paradigm; the main difference is that, with RL, we want to explore different solutions and, in a certain way, it's the algorithm itself that creates its own dataset.

These learning paradigms appear to be more similar to general human intelligence. This is because most of our learning does not come from explicit learning and clear labels, but by trial and error or generalization.

In this chapter, we will present an overview of the main RL algorithms and we will demonstrate an example of its implementation in Python.

The following topics are covered in this chapter:

- Basic definitions
- Introduction to Q-learning
- Playing with OpenAI Gym
- The frozen lake problem

Basic definitions

Recently, RL has been gaining more and more popularity. Notably, many of its breakthroughs have come from improvements from supervised methods such as deep learning.

At the moment, most RL algorithms are used in virtual environments such as video games. Luckily, there are companies, such as OpenAI, that have created and released learning environments where it's easy to test the algorithm in different environments.

It's possible to download this learning environment, called Gym, from OpenAI's website.

Additionally, there are real-world applications on RL, and some of them are incredibly impactful. For example, DeepMind, after being used to optimize Google's data centers, was able to reduce the energy consumption and overall energy bill of Google's data centers by 10% and 40%.

A major problem in these algorithms is generalizing the learning. Ultimately, we want to solve real-world problems, but the most efficient way of exploring RL algorithms is by applying it to video games.

There are two main ways to make sure that the algorithm will be successfully applied to real-world issues:

- **Focusing the simulation**: In this way, we want to make sure that the environment we are running is generic enough so that we will maintain similar results when switching to the real-world application. This is viable only for very specific applications, as the cost of reproducing accurately complex environments increases with their complexity.
- **Focusing the algorithms**: If we follow this path, we will want to make sure that the algorithm is generic enough to be successfully applied to the real-world application. This approach is easier to implement for complex problems compared to the previous method as it's possible to test the algorithm in more virtual environments to see how it performs in different scenarios.

Before we look at our problems, we should make sure that we have the basic definitions in place:

- **Agent**: The agent is whatever the algorithm has control over and receives feedback from. If we think about robotics, clearly the agent is the robot that needs to perform a certain action. In the case of video games (for example, *Pong*), the agent is only the pad of the algorithm controls:

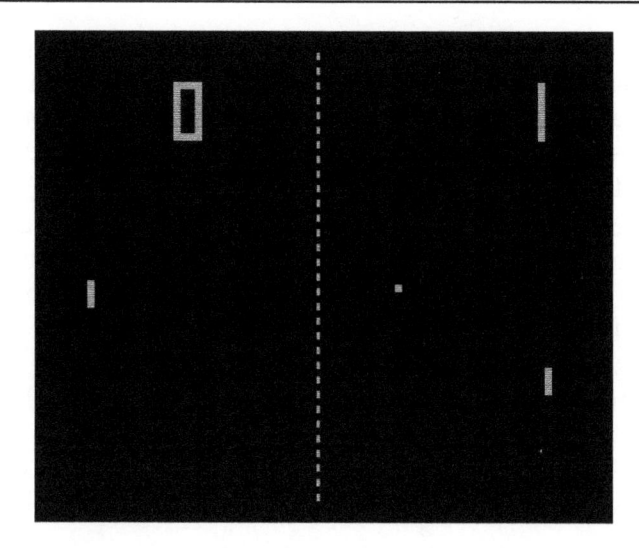

- **Environment**: The environment is, essentially, everything that is not the agent, and the one thing that the algorithms can't control directly. This is a very broad definition and, sometimes, it's quite difficult to define the environment in practice. To prove this, let's go back to the previous example, *Pong*; this game uses a very simple environment, but we still have a few options in terms of what to consider as the environment. For example, should we consider every pixel on the screen as a part of our environment? What about the score and the dotted line in the middle? More complex examples, such as a robot, require a lot more thinking, as we want to find the most complete and simple representation to guide our algorithm to the best solution. How we define it will determine how complex the algorithms we will use are; therefore, it's one of the most important problems to solve.
- **Goal and feedback**: The goal refers to what our algorithm wants to achieve, and the feedback is what is provided to the algorithm to guide it in the right direction. One of the most important differentiators of RL from other methods is that RL does not optimize to the next action but to the cumulative sum of all rewards. Together, with the definition of the environment, this is the most critical step in defining our problem. For the game of *Pong*, the goal seems quite clear: we want to win the game, but there are multiple ways in which this can be achieved. Let's assume, for example, that we think our agent should be rewarded when it does not allow the opponent to score a point. We could provide some positive feedback after any second it has passed, but, in this case, the agent will try to neither win nor lose the game, as that will limit its reward. Instead, it will try to keep the game running as long as possible by avoiding scoring or receiving points.

- **State**: The state is how we represent the current situation of the environment. In video games, a popular representation is to have the screen in raw pixel values, as if it was an image. This allows us to use some common computer vision techniques–in particular, deep learning. For a robot, the state could be represented by joint angles and velocities.
- **Action space**: This refers to all the possible action our agent can take. It's usually environment-specific and it can be discrete or continuous. This distinction is quite important as some algorithms are specific to either a continuous or a discrete action space.
- **Policy**: This refers to a set of rules that the agent has learned so that it can decide which action to take in order to maximize the total reward. Policies are usually denoted with π. We have two different types of policies: deterministic and stochastic. A deterministic policy, as the name suggests, is a well-defined mapping from space to action, and it is denoted using the following formula:

$$\pi : S \to A$$

A stochastic policy will sample from a distribution that uses the state as a priority in order to decide what action to take. We can denote these policies as follows:

$$\pi(a|s)$$

Stochastic policies are what **deep neural networks** (**DNNs**) are used for. They have the advantage of sampling the action and computing the likelihood of particular actions. With sampling, we are exploring alternatives that are not maximizing our goals with the current assumptions, which is one of the main advantages of RL. By computing the maximum likelihood, we are maximizing our gains, which is another key aspect of RL.

Introducing Q-learning

There are many different types of RL algorithms; the main distinction is between the model-based and model-free RL algorithms. What we model about the environment is shown in the following diagram:

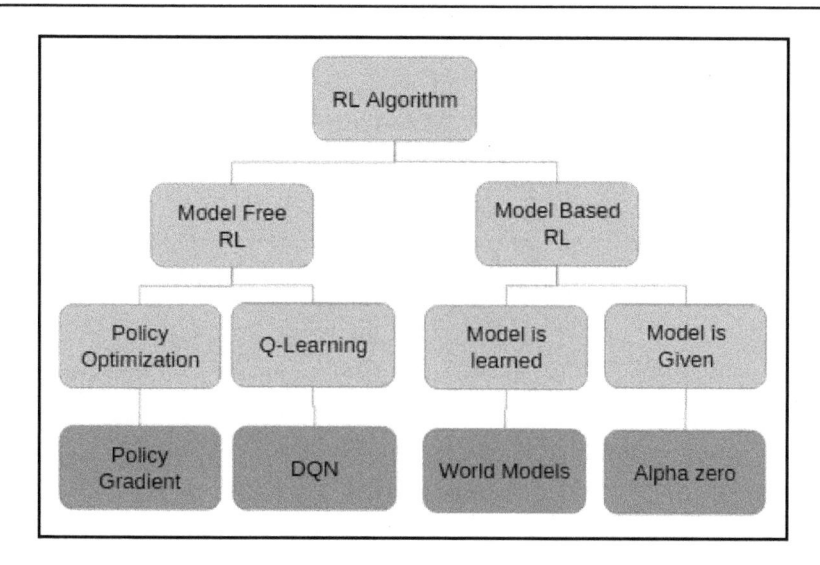

Some simple examples of RL algorithms

Model-based RL, as the name suggests, already starts with an idea of the world. This allows the agent to plan and think ahead. One of the problems with this approach is that, usually, the true model of the environment is not available and the model has to learn it by experience. An example of this is AlphaZero, from DeepMind, which was trained by self-play.

On the other hand, we have model-free methods, which, of course, don't use a model. One of the main advantages of this method is the sample efficiency and the fact that (currently) these models are easier to work with and improve.

In this chapter, we will focus on model-free methods.

Learning objectives

The second main differentiator of RL is the learning goal. Based on the type of problem and its complexity, we might want to learn different things. Therefore, the objectives could be as follows:

- Policy optimization
- Action value functions
- Value functions
- Environment models

Policy optimization

In this case, we want to find a good policy. In order to accomplish that, we need to represent the policy by parameterizing it. In this case, we can represent the policy, π, as follows:

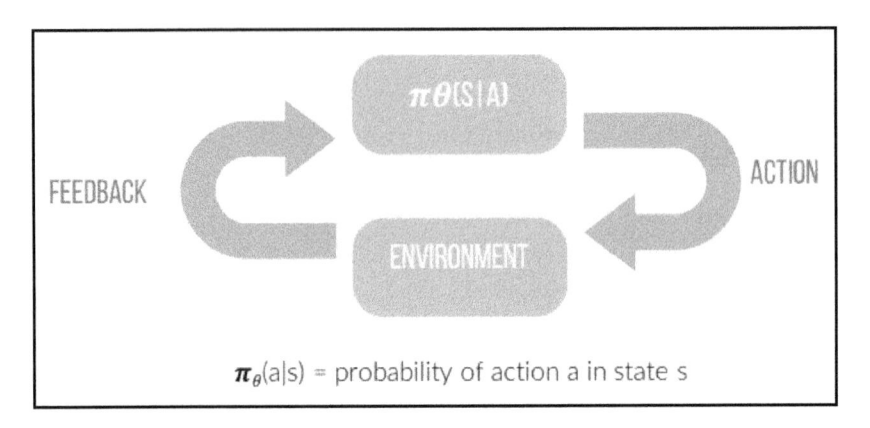

$$\pi_\theta(a|s) = \text{probability of action } a \text{ in state } s$$

Here, θ is the parameter that our algorithm needs to optimize.

Usually, these algorithms are also on-policy, meaning that the policy is directly updated while acting on it. We also need an estimation of the policy goodness, and that is obtained using the value function, V, under the policy, π.

These methods have received a lot of attention recently, as there have been a number of breakthroughs that have pushed the limits of RL research.

Some examples of policy optimization methods are the actor-critic models, such as A2C and A3C and **Proximal Policy Operation (PPO)**.

Methods of Q-learning

This family of methods focuses on learning the **Q matrix**, $Q(s,a)$, which is an approximation of the optimal action-value function, $Q_\theta(s,a)$. Usually, these algorithms perform an off-policy optimization, meaning that each update can be collected at any data point during the training period. The policy is fixed and is used to choose the next action that's aimed at maximizing the reward.

An example of Q-learning is a **Deep Q Network (DQN)**.

Playing with OpenAI Gym

As we mentioned previously, OpenAI is one of the main research companies that is working on RL. They released a set of environments to test different algorithms under one interface. You can find out more information about this at https://gym.openai.com/.

Installing it on macOS or Linux it's quite straightforward; you can type in the following command:

```
pip install gym
```

At the time of writing this book, it's more complicated to install on Windows. To do so, you can perform the following steps:

1. Install VcXsrv Windows X Server from vcXsrv.
2. Run bash.
3. Install all the dependencies listed at https://github.com/openai/gym/#installing-everything by using the following command:

   ```
   pip install gym
   ```

4. After rebooting, invoke VcXsrv.
5. Run the following command:

   ```
   export DISPLAY=:0
   ```

Now, it should be possible to run a very simple algorithm, which is just repeating the same action, to test our installation:

1. First of all, we need to import the gym library by executing the following command:

   ```
   import gym
   ```

2. Then, we need to specify the environment. We picked the Cart-Pole environment (CartPole-v0), but there are several others; some of them are also from old atari arcade games, for example, the beloved *Space Invaders* (SpaceInvaders-v0):

   ```
   env = gym.make('CartPole-v0')
   ```

Reinforcement Learning

3. To test `SpaceInvaders`, you will need the Atari dependencies, which can be installed using the following command:

```
pip install -e 'gym[atari]'
env = gym.make('SpaceInvaders-v0')
```

Now, we can see the basics of the Gym. We can start the game by calling the reset method on the environment we picked.

In this example, we decided to study 20 different episodes. At the beginning of each one, we need to reset the environment, which will bring everything to the start:

```
for i_episode in range(20):
    observation = env.reset()
```

We picked 100 as the maximum time horizon that we want to study. For the Cart-Pole problem, it's enough to determine a win if the agent can survive for this long:

```
for t in range(100):
```

At the beginning of each time step, we want to update the state of the environment. We should be able to visualize the following diagram:

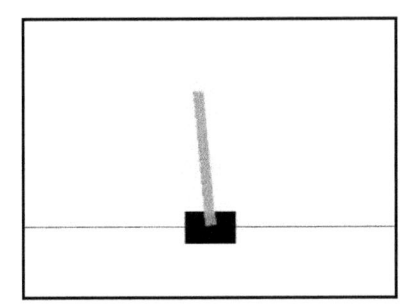

Let's take a look at the following code:

```
CartPole-V0 at the start
env.render()
```

Here, we decided to simply always pick the same action; in our case, 1 tells the agent to go right:

```
action = 1
```

[238]

Then, we perform the action. To do that, we can use the `step` method of the environment and pass the chosen action as an argument:

```
observation, reward, done, info = env.step(action)
```

The environment will return the following four pieces of information:

- **Observation**: The current state of the world
- **Reward**: The feedback from the environment
- **Done**: The Boolean value communicating whether the episode ended
- **Info**: Debugging information

Once the preceding information is returned, execute the following commands:

```
print("Episode finished after {} timesteps".format(t+1))
Break
```

To terminate the program, you can call the `close()` function, as follows:

```
env.close()
```

The frozen lake problem

One of the environments that's available is the frozen lake one. The goal of this environment is quite simple: we want to cross a frozen lake divided into sward blocks, but there are some holes (**H**) that we need to avoid. We can walk on top of the frozen parts (**F**) without a problem and move in a maximum of four different directions: up, down, left, and right:

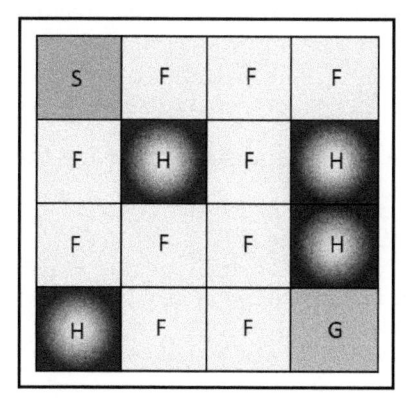

A visualization of the frozen lake problem

The Q-learning algorithm needs the following parameters:

1. Step size: s $\alpha \in (0, 1]$
2. Small $\varepsilon > 0$

Then, the algorithm works as follows:

1. Initialize $Q(s,a)$ for all $s \in S+$ and $a \in A(s)$ arbitrarily, except that $Q(terminal,) = 0$.
2. Loop for each episode.
3. Initialize S.
4. Choose A from S using the policy derived from Q (for example, ε-greedy).
5. Loop for each step of the episode, as follows:
    1. Choose A' from S' using the policy derived from Q (for example, ε-greedy).
       Take action A and observe R, S':
       $Q(S, A) \leftarrow Q(S, A) + \alpha[R + \gamma \max Q(S', a) - Q(S, A)]$
    2. Update the state and actions, $S \leftarrow S'$ $A \leftarrow A'$; , until S is terminal.

For the implementation in TensorFlow, we will need to import all the required libraries:

```
import gym
import numpy as np
import random
import tensorflow as tf
import matplotlib.pyplot as plt
plt.rcParams['figure.figsize'] = (16,8)

%matplotlib inline
```

Now, we can load the environment of choice; here, we decided to use the first version of the frozen lake environment:

```
env = gym.make('FrozenLake-v0')
```

We can then check the possible actions and states by using the following code:

```
n_actions = env.action_space.n
n_states = env.observation_space.n
# Actions are left, up, right, down
print(f'Number of actions {n_actions}')
# States are the 16 fields
print(f'Number of possible states {n_states}')
```

The preceding commands generates the following output:

```
Number of actions 4
Number of possible states 16
```

Let's now visualize the current state of the environment:

```
SFFF
FHFH
FFFH
HFFG
```

Here, we can see that we start at the top-left corner; we can also check what happens when we interact with it:

```
env.reset()
env.step(1)
env.step(2)
(0, 0.0, False, {'prob': 0.3333333333333333})

env.render()
   (Right)
SFFF
FHFH
FFFH
HFFG
```

We will now use TensorFlow version 2, which is more integrated with `keras`; its usages are as follows:

- It clears the default graph stack and resets the global default graph
- It is useful during the testing phase while we experiment in Jupyter Notebook

Now, let's take a look at the following command:

```
# Clears the default graph stack and resets the global default graph.
# Useful during the testing phase while I experiment in jupyter notebook.
tf.reset_default_graph()
```

Let's create a placeholder for the inputs, as follows:

```
# Creating a placeholder for the inputs
inputs = tf.placeholder(shape=[1,n_states],dtype=tf.float32)
```

[241]

Reinforcement Learning

Here, we are creating the initial weight as a small, randomized matrix. In this simple example, we will use only one set of weights:

```
# Creating the initial weights as a small randomized matrix
# In this simple example we will use only one set of weights
mean = 0
std = 0.01
init_weights = tf.random_uniform([n_states, n_actions], mean, std)
```

TensorFlow uses lazy evaluation, meaning that it computes the values only when necessary. Because of this, if we want to check whether we can visualize our weights, we need to wrap them in a session and explicitly evaluate our `tensor`:

```
# Visualizing the initial weights
with tf.Session() as sess_test:
    print(init_weights.eval())
```

The preceding commands generate the following output:

```
[[0.00095421 0.00098864 0.00698167 0.00750466]
 [0.00570747 0.00089916 0.00711703 0.00038618]
 [0.00076457 0.00454047 0.00860003 0.00577745]
 [0.00455219 0.00055421 0.00049394 0.00343634]
 [0.00286473 0.00446176 0.00975701 0.00300927]
 [0.00323193 0.00409729 0.0022279  0.00965145]
 [0.00770885 0.00027495 0.00470571 0.00601063]
 [0.00518226 0.00761208 0.00074768 0.00878333]
 [0.00118302 0.00627028 0.00792606 0.0069023 ]
 [0.00330688 0.00721038 0.00506496 0.00677231]
 [0.00541128 0.00174315 0.00387131 0.00637214]
 [0.00548014 0.00976339 0.00628941 0.00262038]
 [0.00733525 0.00279449 0.00077582 0.00691394]
 [0.00079324 0.00387187 0.0059192  0.00177472]
 [0.00299844 0.00402844 0.0062203  0.0023068 ]
 [0.00816794 0.00160594 0.00133737 0.0026781 ]]
```

We will then create a very simple architecture by hitting only one set of weights. It's possible to replace this architecture with more complex networks:

```
weights = tf.Variable(init_weights)

# Matrix product of two arrays
q_out = tf.matmul(inputs, weights)
predict = tf.argmax(q_out, 1)
```

To update the weights, as we saw in the previous chapters, we need to calculate the loss and use it to calculate the update to provide to the network.

We calculate the loss by taking the difference of the sum of the squares between the target and predicted Q values:

```
# We calculate the loss
# by taking the sum of squares difference between the target and prediction
Q values.
next_q = tf.placeholder(shape=[1, n_actions],dtype=tf.float32)
loss = tf.reduce_sum(tf.square(next_q - q_out))
trainer = tf.train.GradientDescentOptimizer(learning_rate=0.1)
update_model = trainer.minimize(loss)
```

What we want to approximate is a matrix that, considering states and actions, will calculate the future as the Q-function. Each state-action will be associated with the prediction of all the future rewards that the pair will provide to the agent, considering all future actions:

$$Q = \begin{matrix} & \begin{matrix} 0 & 1 & 2 & 3 & 4 & 5 \end{matrix} \\ \begin{matrix} 0 \\ 1 \\ 2 \\ 3 \\ 4 \\ 5 \end{matrix} & \begin{bmatrix} 0 & 0 & 0 & 0 & 400 & 0 \\ 0 & 0 & 0 & 320 & 0 & 500 \\ 0 & 0 & 0 & 320 & 0 & 0 \\ 0 & 400 & 256 & 0 & 400 & 0 \\ 320 & 0 & 0 & 320 & 0 & 500 \\ 0 & 400 & 0 & 0 & 400 & 500 \end{bmatrix} \end{matrix}$$

ACTIONS / STATES

In the highlighted Q-matrix, we can see our options if we are in state S1. This matrix will guide our agent in taking the action that maximizes the sum of the total rewards, based on its current knowledge. The matrix will be updated after every reward:

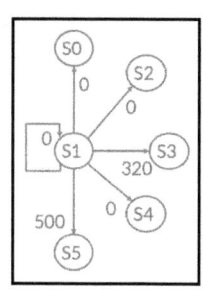

Reinforcement Learning

Given a state, the Q-matrix will tell us the sum of all future rewards that we can get if we pick a certain action.

To explore other alternatives, we will use the **epsilon-greedy** algorithm, which, given a state, takes the action that will provide the highest reward, except for a small amount of time (determined by the value of epsilon).

To implement this, we will need to use the network we created before and compute a random variable to include the stochastic element. This stochasticity is fundamental in RL as it gives the agent the ability to explore different solutions:

```
def epsilon_greedy(predict, q_out, s, epsilon):
    a, q_matrix = sess.run([predict, q_out],
                            feed_dict={inputs: np.identity(n_states)
                            [s:s + 1]})
    if np.random.rand(1) < epsilon:
        a[0] = env.action_space.sample()
    return a, q_matrix
```

We will need a few parameters for our algorithms:

- Gamma, which is the weight episode, is as follows:

    ```
    y = .99
    ```

- Epsilon, which determines how often we will pick a random action:

    ```
    epsilon = 0.3
    ```

We want to include a discount factor to decrease our epsilon as our agent learns:

```
epsilon_decay = 0.999
```

Here, we decide to learn for 1,000 episodes, and consider it a failure if we don't solve the problem within 20 steps:

```
num_episodes = 1000
max_steps = 20
```

We will store the history of the learning path in some vectors:

```
#create lists to contain total rewards and steps per episode
step_list = []
reward_list = []
```

Like we did previously, we need to start a session and reinitialize the graph by running the initialization procedure we defined earlier using `init`:

```
with tf.Session() as sess:
sess.run(init)
for i in range(num_episodes):
```

We then need to reset the environment to start from scratch; we will need to do this at the end of every episode:

```
#Reset environment and get first new observation
s = env.reset()
total_reward = 0
done = False
```

For each time step in the episode, we need to decide the action and find the updated `q_matrix` given the current status and the expected rewards. To achieve this, we will be using the epsilon-greedy function that we created earlier:

```
for step in range(max_steps):
# Choose an action using epsilon greedy using the Q-network
a, q_matrix = epsilon_greedy(predict, q_out, s, epsilon)
```

After this, we interact with the environment that can check the next step. The environment will return the next state but also the reward we got regarding whether the episode is over or not. In this case, we have a reward only when we reach the goal:

```
# Receive new state and reward from environment
s_prime, reward, done, _ = env.step(a[0])
```

Then, we can use the network again to estimate the q function.

Calculate *Q* using the network, as follows:

```
q_prime = sess.run(q_out, feed_dict={inputs:
np.identity(16)[s_prime:s_prime + 1]})
```

Obtain `max_q_prime` and set our target value for the chosen action:

```
max_q_prime = np.max(q_prime)
target_q = q_matrix
```

Reinforcement Learning

To calculate the update, we need to take the reward into consideration; additionally, we need to consider the following command:

```
target_q[0, a[0]] = reward + y * max_q_prime
```

Then, we will train our network using the target and predicted Q values, as follows:

```
_, w_prime = sess.run([update_model, weights], feed_dict={
inputs: np.identity(n_states)[s:s + 1], next_q: target_q
})
```

Now, we can update the reward and the state:

```
total_reward = total_reward + reward
s = s_prime
```

We also want to reduce the probability of choosing a random action with time, as our agent is supposed to get more and more knowledgeable. To accomplish this, we will carry out a very simple strategy, that is, at every step, we will use a very small discount factor. We could also apply this discount at the end of each episode.

As we train, the model reduces epsilon to reduce the random actions:

```
epsilon = epsilon * epsilon_decay
if done == True:
break
step_list.append(step)
reward_list.append(total_reward)
```

To check the performance, we can plot the number of steps that an episode lasts for and the number of rewards that our agent can get for each episode.

By checking the rewards that our agent is getting, we can see that the network begins to consistently reach the goal around the 300 episode mark:

```
fig = plt.figure()
plt.plot(reward_list)
fig.suptitle('Reward per episode', fontsize=20)
plt.xlabel('Episode number', fontsize=18)
plt.ylabel('Reward', fontsize=16)
plt.show()
```

The preceding commands generate the following output:

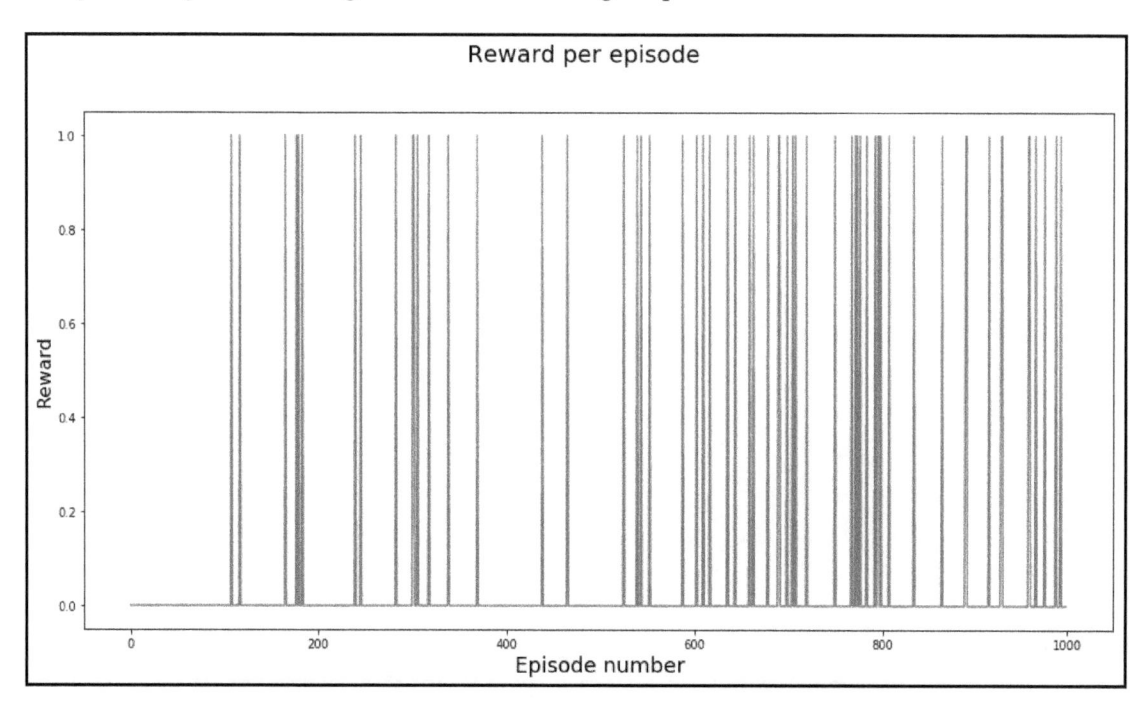

![Reward per episode plot showing sparse vertical lines indicating rewards achieved across episodes 0 to 1000, with increasing density after episode 400.]

The agent is learning to get the rewards better and better with each episode.

By checking the number of steps that the agent is able to do per episode, we can see that it increases with each episode. In particular, after the 400 episode mark, we can see that the agent becomes quite good at avoiding the holes and is able to survive for the maximum number of steps:

```
fig = plt.figure()
plt.plot(step_list)
fig.suptitle('Number of steps completed per episode', fontsize=20)
plt.xlabel('Episode number', fontsize=18)
plt.ylabel('Number of steps', fontsize=16)
```

[247]

The preceding commands generate the following output:

Number of steps completed per episode

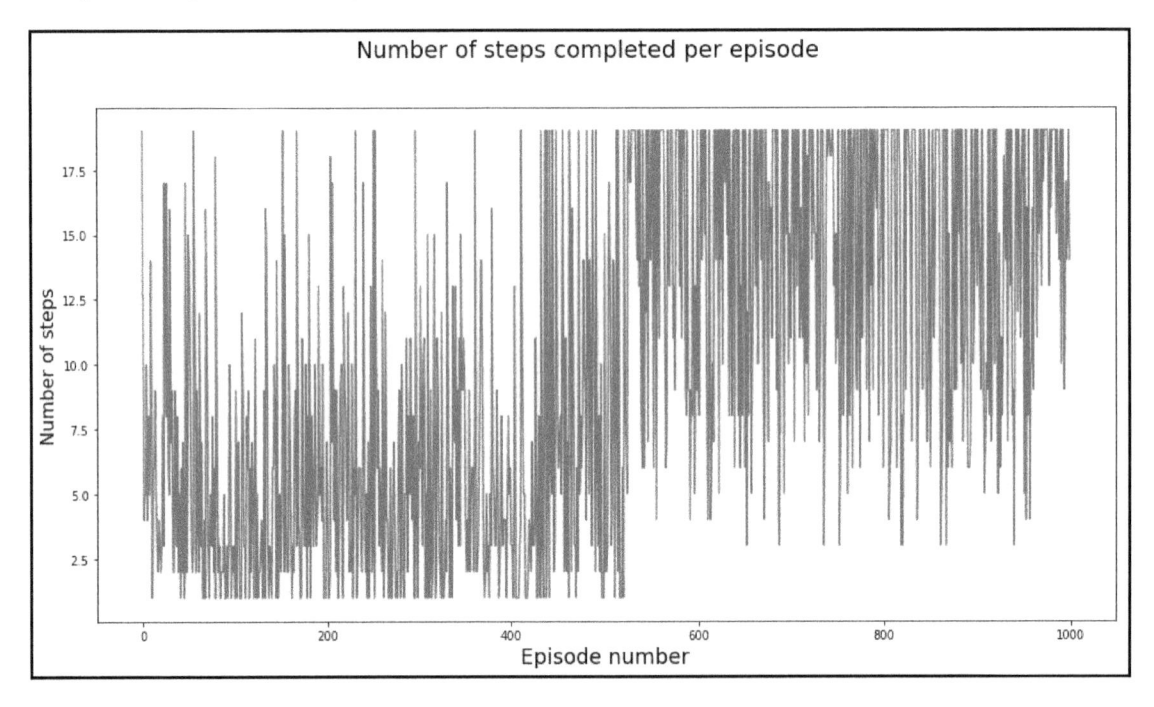

The agent is becoming better and better at avoiding the holes.

With a better network, our agent would be able to learn things much better and faster.

Summary

In this chapter, we explored the nomenclature and main concepts of RL. We also learned how to use OpenAI Gym to test our RL algorithms.

Additionally, we examined how to use TensorFlow to create a simple network to solve a simple task.

DNNs are now used in RL to solve more complex tasks that can be easily tested in Gym.

The next chapter is a summary of what we have learned in this book; reading it will be a refresher of all the concepts that we have covered so far.

11
Whats Next?

We now reach the end of our journey in deep learning. We touched on many different topics, starting from the fundamentals of machine learning and ending with more modern and advanced topics, such as GANs and Deep reinforcement learning.

In this book, we have tried to always give a concrete example after laying down the theory, and we hope that this approach has benefited the reader's learning experience.

The following topics covered in this chapter:

- Summarizing the book
- Future of machine learning
- Artificial general intelligence

Summarizing the book

We started with supervised learning approaches and focused on how to create classification models. In particular, we saw how it's possible to do the following:

- Use a perceptron for a linearly separable problem (Chapter 2, *Neural Network Fundamentals*)
- Use **feedforward neural networks** (**FFNNs**) for non-linearly separable tasks (Chapter 3, *Convolutional Neural Networks for Image Processing*)
- Use embeddings to extract useful information from text (Chapter 4, *Exploiting Text Embedding*)
- Use **Convolutional Neural Networks** (**CNNs**) for tasks whose inputs have a spatial relationship (Chapter 5, *Working with RNNs*)

Whats Next?

- Use pre-trained (Neural Network) (NN) as a feature extractor (Chapter 6, *Reusing Neural Networks with Transfer Learning*)
- Use generative models to reproduce the creativity process (Chapter 7, *Working with Generative Algorithms*, Chapter 8, *Implementing Autoencoders*, and Chapter 9, *Deep Belief Networks*)
- Use **reinforcement learning** (**RL**) to explore different solutions (Chapter 10, *Reinforcement Learning*)

Let's take a look at the following diagram, which illustrates this:

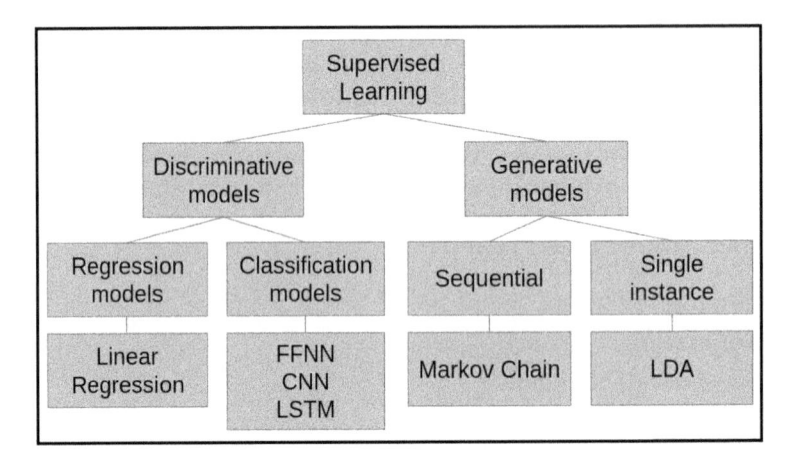

A simple classification of the supervised learning methods

Some of these methods are quite old, while some of them are quite new and are very promising for the future of machine learning and **artificial intelligence** (**AI**). And in particular, GANs are an innovation because, for the first time, the loss function is learned and not given. The other topic we would like to highlight is Deep RL, in particular Actor Critic models, which follow a similar concept as Adversarial Networks, that is, dividing the tasks to estimate the reward function into one network, and the policy into the other network.

Future of machine learning

Machine learning has the potential to improve almost every field of our society. Anywhere where learning, optimization, and decision-making are involved, there is a chance for machine learning to improve the current state of that particular field. With more recent technologies, such as GANs, more and more fields are going to opt for machine learning.

Chapter 11

Some of the most promising research applications can be found in the following fields:

- Drug discovery
- Healthcare
- Self-driving cars
- Translation
- Legal
- Art:

A picture modified using transfer learning using a style from Asterix

Generative methods, such as GANs, are now being explored in drug discovery, potentially making the process much cheaper than it was earlier. In healthcare, deep learning methods are now able to automate a lot of visual diagnostic tasks, for example, radiologists' tasks.

By analyzing the examples explained in the book, it's possible to notice that there are a few main factors that have contributed to the sudden explosion of AI:

- New and innovative algorithms that have achieved unprecedented performance
- Higher data quality
- New and more powerful hardware to process the data

Surprisingly, the last two are the most important factors for the quick development of the field, and for attracting a large amount of investment from major companies. It's a constant cycle of improvements; investment in data increases investment in hardware and research. Better results lead to more investment.

AI has already been through many boom and bust cycles. When there is a lot of hype, like now, there is always a justifiable concern. The field seems to have been in a bull run since early 2010, passing through different hypes, from big data to streaming, from data science to AI. Now the word AI is everywhere, and it's often improperly used in many products and services just for marketing purposes.

This is almost offensive to the people who are actually using these techniques and progressing the field, but most importantly, it is confusing the general public and misinforming them, increasing the risk of another hype and bust cycle.

Artificial general intelligence

Artificial general intelligence (**AGI**) is the ability of a machine to successfully perform any given intellectual task that humans can perform.

If we buy in to the theory that animals, and therefore humans as well, are biological machines, there is no reason to believe an artificial machine could not surpass our computational capabilities relatively soon. Our species' intellectual growth to develop requires much longer than the growth that is required from a machine. It seems just a question of time for machines to catch up and overtake us.

At the moment, we seem pretty far away from AGI, preferring a type of intelligence that is specific to each single task it's required to solve. The most promising field for AGI seems to be RL, where we are now seeing algorithms that can solve different tasks (such as successfully solving different video games) without requiring human intervention. It's worth noting that improvements in RL techniques were not sufficient in themselves to achieve this breakthrough. Deep learning methods helped enormously, and probably the future requires more and more collaboration between machine learning subfields. For example, stronger unsupervised learning techniques could also help RL get closer to AGI.

There are several questions that will arise if we ever achieve an AI that is equal to, or even better than, human intelligence. At this level, the discussion is not technical anymore, but philosophical and ethical. Everyone should be included in this discussion, as it's something that can potentially change human life and society like no other technological discovery.

Ethics in AI

The fact that machines can make decisions independently has raised quite a few issues. Some of them are justified; some of them seem a bit far-fetched. We will limit our discussion for this book to the topics we feel are most important:

- Interpretability
- Automation and its effect on society
- AI safety
- AI ethics
- Accountability

Interpretability

There is a lot of research at the moment on how to make machine learning more interpretable. In many fields, being able to interpret and perfectly understand all decisions made by a machine is mandatory. Usually, it's the case because these decisions require some sort of ethics or will have an important impact on someone's life. A classic example is mortgages, where the decision must be easy to understand and explainable to make sure people are not denied a loan because of reasons out of their control. These problems can arise from using the wrong input data and considering variables such as gender or country of origin for the algorithm. Other times, the problem lies in an unfair society that created a biased dataset. Machine learning in this case might amplify these differences by blindly perpetuating the injustices in society.

On the other hand, certain decisions are even now impossible to explain, because the systems can be very complex and can influence each other in ways that a human would not understand. And that can be an extremely good thing, as we are able to explore solutions that otherwise we would never be able to achieve. RL is now used in video games by human players to discover new strategies to win the game.

Automation

One of the main fears that the media propagates is the automation that the AI will be able to achieve, which might make most of us unemployed, if not all of us.

If we look historically, most important innovations have had a big impact in the job market in the short term, but in the long term people rebalance, and overall there is a positive impact on society.

It's also true that even the industrial revolution required human operators to operate the machines, but AI has the potential to eliminate any human intervention.

In the future society, if resources stop being a problem, the world will not need to work as it does currently because it will not need money to function. Money is just the most widely acceptable resource allocator, which in this case will cease to exist. Governments might not be necessary anymore, because AI should be able to organize society as well.

On the other hand, this change can't happen straight away; therefore, there must be a transition period that might be quite delicate. Large corporations that can leverage large datasets and AI research will receive all the benefits, while common people will pay the price.

Also, governments will not need a large number of people to defend its interests. Therefore, the democratic paradigm might be challenged before the need for governments ceases to exist.

AI safety

Another big topic for debate is AI safety. A common fear is that machines will rise against their human enslavers and exterminate our species. A different concern is that AI will lose control and terminate us in the quest to optimize our society.

My personal opinion is that it's good to have an open debate on these topics, and involve not only technical people but the whole of society; at least those that are concerned and curious.

At this point in time, this scenario seems quite far off, not only because it will require a huge technological jump, but also because AI is used mostly in tools that optimize specific functions.

A much more concrete risk is weaponized AI. With AI, it is possible to create better and more autonomous weapons, which will require less manpower and money to operate, and which might be more effective. An example is drone strikes. In this case, we always have a human operator that takes the final decision, but it's easy to imagine that the whole process could be automated.

AI ethics

The more decisions AI will be able to take, the more dilemmas it will face. If we take self-driving cars as an example, sometimes the car will be asked to take a decision that will determine the life or death of human beings. There may be cases in which it will have to choose to save one person, such as the driver, over another person, such as the driver of another car coming from the opposite direction.

Some humans in that instant will either take conscious or not different decision, based on their belief and their altruism, but how a machine should take that decision is an open topic of discussion.

Accountability

By the end of this book, it should not come as a surprise that AI also makes mistakes. The more responsibilities machines have, the more serious mistakes they will commit. In that case, who will be accountable? The company that created the algorithm, or the person that owns the tool that was running the algorithm? And what if the algorithm was fooled by an adversarial attack?

Conclusions

We are still at the very beginning of an exciting journey. AI is an emerging field in which a lot has yet to be discovered and proven mathematically. Just by looking back to 2010, which is nine years ago at the time of writing, the landscape is totally different. At that time, data science and machine learning were just foggy terms for a few researchers, and most people were extremely skeptical about machines taking autonomous decisions. Now, mathematics and a data-driven culture are considered almost universally to be the basis of any respectable business, from large to small.

Lastly, I just want to say that it's incredibly exciting to be part of this revolution, which will surely be regarded by our descendants as one of the most important moments in human history. I hope we have conveyed the main concepts and ideas behind some of the most important algorithms, but also our passion for this fascinating field.

Thanks.

Other Books You May Enjoy

If you enjoyed this book, you may be interested in these other books by Packt:

Neural Network Projects with Python
James Loy

ISBN: 978-1-78913-890-0

- Learn various neural network architectures and its advancements in AI
- Master deep learning in Python by building and training neural network
- Master neural networks for regression and classification
- Discover convolutional neural networks for image recognition
- Learn sentiment analysis on textual data using Long Short-Term Memory
- Build and train a highly accurate facial recognition security system

Other Books You May Enjoy

Neural Networks with Keras

Niloy Purkait

ISBN: 978-1-78953-608-9

- Understand the fundamental nature and workflow of predictive data modeling
- Explore how different types of visual and linguistic signals are processed by neural networks
- Dive into the mathematical and statistical ideas behind how networks learn from data
- Design and implement various neural networks such as CNNs, LSTMs, and GANs
- Use different architectures to tackle cognitive tasks and embed intelligence in systems
- Learn how to generate synthetic data and use augmentation strategies to improve your models
- Stay on top of the latest academic and commercial developments in the field of AI

Leave a review - let other readers know what you think

Please share your thoughts on this book with others by leaving a review on the site that you bought it from. If you purchased the book from Amazon, please leave us an honest review on this book's Amazon page. This is vital so that other potential readers can see and use your unbiased opinion to make purchasing decisions, we can understand what our customers think about our products, and our authors can see your feedback on the title that they have worked with Packt to create. It will only take a few minutes of your time, but is valuable to other potential customers, our authors, and Packt. Thank you!

Index

A
action space 234
activation functions
  about 49
  Rectified Linear Unit (ReLU) 51, 52
  softmax 50
  tanh 50, 51
Adaptive Instance Normalization (AdaIN) 177
agent 232
alpha 160
Anaconda 16
Area Under the Curve (AUC) 60
artificial general intelligence (AGI) 252
Artificial Intelligence (AI)
  about 9
  accountability 255
  automation 253
  ethics 253, 255
  history 10, 11
  interpretability 253
  safety 254
Artificial Neural Networks (ANNs) 33
autoencoders
  about 13, 180
  applications 186
  bottleneck 186
  contractive autoencoder (CAE) 198
  convolutional autoencoders 192
  decoder 185
  denoising autoencoders 197
  encoder 185
  loss function 187
  multilayer autoencoders 191
  overview 185
  sparse autoencoders 195
  types 187
  undercomplete autooencoders 187

B
backpropagation 46, 47, 48, 201
Bayesian Belief Networks (BBNs)
  about 210, 211
  predictive propagation 211
  retrospective propagation 211
BigGAN model
  about 174
  robustness 175
  scalability 174
  stability 175
Boston house prices dataset 226

C
callbacks 29
categories 18
chain rule 53, 54, 55
classification 18
classification metrics
  about 26
  binary accuracy 26
  categorical accuracy 27
  ROC AUC 27
  sparse categorical accuracy 27
  sparse top k categorical accuracy 27
  top k categorical accuracy 27
clustering 13
CNNs, in Keras
  about 79
  data, loading 79, 80
  model, creating 80, 81
conditional GANs 158
containerization 17
continuous bag-of-words (CBOW) 97, 98
continuous skip-gram 98

contractive autoencoder (CAE) 198
contrastive divergence 215
convolutional autoencoders
  about 192
  example 192, 194, 195
Convolutional Neural Networks (CNNs)
  about 69, 70, 114, 158, 249
  convolutional layers 71, 73, 74
  different lag 120
  dropout layers 77
  input layers 70, 71
  loss functions 120, 121
  network configuration 81, 82, 83
  network, optimizing 90, 91, 92
  normalization layers 77
  output layers 78
  pooling layers 75
  same lag 120
  theory 116
cross-validation 28
Cycle-Consistent Adversarial Networks (CycleGANs)
  about 168
  reference 170

D

data cleaning 19
decoder 185
Deep Belief Networks (DBNs)
  about 209
  applications 209
  architecture 221, 222
  Bayesian Belief Networks (BBNs) 210
  negative phase 223
  overview 209
  positive phase 223
  properties 222
  Restricted Boltzmann machines (RBMs) 212
  training 222, 224
Deep Convolutional Generative Adversarial Network (DCGAN)
  about 158
  architecture 160
  coded example 161, 162, 163, 164
deep learning

feature engineering, performing 22
Deep Neural Networks (DNNs) 11, 234
Deep Q Network (DQN) 236
deep residual learning 144
Deepfake 180
denoising autoencoders
  about 197
  example 197
detector stage 74
discriminative algorithms
  versus generative algorithms 150
discriminative classifiers
  examples 151
discriminative model 150
Docker 17
dying state 160
Dynamic Computational Graph (DCG) 129

E

edge-maps 166
embedding layer
  creating 100, 101, 103
encoder 185
Energy-Based Models (EBMs) 212
environment
  about 233
  setting up 14
epsilon-greedy algorithm 244
experience replay 157

F

Facial Expression Recognition (FER) 2013 dataset 84
feature engineering
  about 20, 21
  in Keras 23, 24
  performing 22
feature extraction 139
feature extractors
  networks, reusing as 137
feature scaling 22
feedback 233
feedforward neural network (FFNN)
  about 44, 45, 46, 70, 116, 249
  in Python 57, 59, 60

FFNN Keras implementation 61, 62
fine-tuning 224
forget layer 123
frozen lake problem 239, 240, 241, 242, 243,
    244, 245, 246, 247, 248

G

Gated Recurrent Units (GRUs) 125
Gaussian 200
Generative Adversarial Networks (GANs)
    about 13, 149, 151, 152, 153
    challenges 155, 156
    conditional GANs 158
    Cycle-Consistent Adversarial Networks
        (CycleGANs) 168
    Deep Convolutional Generative Adversarial
        Network (DCGAN) 158
    Pix2Pix GAN 166
    Progressive Growing of GAN (ProGAN) 170
    StackGAN 167
    StarGAN 172
    timelines 157
    training 154
    variations 157
generative algorithms
    about 149
    versus discriminative algorithms 150
generative classifiers
    examples 151
generative model 149, 150
Gibbs sampling 214
GloVe model
    text classification 111
    using 107, 108, 109
GloVe
    about 104
    global matrix factorization 104
goal 233
Graphic Processing Unit (GPU) 11, 42, 129

H

Hidden Markov Models (HMMs) 151
Hyperspace Analogue to Language (HAL) 105

I

image classification 23
Independent Component Analysis (ICA) 13
inductive learning 13
Internet of Things (IoT) 11

J

Jensen-Shannon divergence 157

K

Keras implementation
    about 52
    chain rule 53, 54, 55
    XOR problem 55
Keras
    about 14, 41
    feature engineering 23
    for expression recognition 84, 86, 87, 88, 89
    perceptron, implementing 42, 43
    word embeddings 99

L

Latent Semantic Analysis (LSA) 105
latent variable model 104
Leaky ReLU
    versus ReLU 160
learning rate 48
lemmatization 94
Long Short-Term Memory (LSTM)
    about 121, 122, 181
    architecture 122, 123, 124, 125
    Forget Gate 122
    in Keras 125, 127, 128
    Input Gate 122
    Output Gate 122
    time series prediction 130, 131, 133

M

Machine Learning (ML)
    about 11
    for NLP 94
    future 250, 251, 252
    overview 11
    reinforcement learning (RL) 13

semi-supervised learning 13
supervised learning 12
unsupervised learning 12
matrix factorization 104
max pooling 75
metrics
  about 26
  classification metrics 26
  regression metrics 26
Microsoft Cognitive Toolkit 14
minibatch discrimination 157
miniconda 16
MinMax scaling 22
MNIST dataset 152, 225
model
  evaluating 27
Modified National Institute of Standards and Technology (MNIST) dataset 79
Multi-task learning (MTL)
  about 136
  advantages 138
  hard parameter sharing 137
  implementing 137, 138
  soft parameter sharing 138
multilayer autoencoders
  about 191
  example 191
Multilayer Neural Networks 45
multinomial 18

N

n-grams 22
Natural Language Processing (NLP) 22, 129
Natural Language Toolkit (NLTK) 94
networks
  reusing, as feature extractors 137
Neural Networks (NNs) 14, 33, 113, 136
NLP
  about 94
  methods 94
  rule-based methods 94, 95
  sub-fields 94
numerical transformations 23

O

object-oriented programming (OOP) 57
OpenAI Gym
  working with 237, 238, 239
OpenAI
  reference 11

P

Part-of-Speech (PoS) tagging 95, 130
PatchGAN 166
perceptron convergence theorem 38
Perceptron Learning Rule 39
perceptron
  about 33, 34
  implementing 35, 37, 38, 40, 41
  implementing, in Keras 42, 43
Pix2Pix GAN 166
policy 234
pooling layers, CNNs
  max pooling 75
  stride 75
  zero padding 76
pre-trained models 104
Principal Component Analysis (PCA) 13
Progressive Growing of GAN (ProGAN)
  about 170, 171
  reference 172
Proximal Policy Operation (PPO) 236
Python 14
PyTorch
  basics 129
  transfer learning (TL), implementing in 139, 142, 144, 145

Q

Q matrix 236
Q-learning
  about 234, 235
  learning objectives 235
  methods 236
  policy optimization 236

R

R language 14
RadialGAN 181
random forest 25
RBM recommender system (coded)
  example 216, 217, 219, 220, 221
RBM recommender system (theoretical)
  example 215, 216
receptive field 70
Rectified Linear Unit (ReLU) 46, 51, 52, 74, 160, 218
Recurrent Neural Networks (RNNs)
  about 113, 114, 115
  many-to-many 119
  one-to-many 119
  one-to-one 119
  types 117, 118
Region-CNN (R-CNN) 78
regression metrics
  about 26
  Cosine Proximity 26
  Mean Absolute Error 26
  Mean Absolute Percentage Error 26
  Mean Squared Error 26
regression
  about 18
  linear regression 18
  logistic regression 18
reinforcement learning (RL) 13, 231, 234, 250
ReLU
  versus Leaky ReLU 160
reparameterization trick 201
Restricted Boltzmann Machines (RBMs)
  about 212, 213, 214
  contrastive divergence 215
  Gibbs sampling 214
  training 214
root mean square error (RMSE) 46

S

scale method 22
Scale-Invariant Feature Transform (SIFT) 20
semi-supervised learning 13
sequence vectors 99

sigmoid function 50
softmax function 50
sparse autoencoders
  about 195
  example 196
StackGAN 167, 168
StarGAN
  about 172
  discriminator objectives 173
  generator functions 174
  reference 174
state 234
Stochastic Gradient Descent (SGD) 43
stride 75
StyleGAN
  about 175
  implementing 179
  style modules 177
supervised DBN classification
  example 226, 227
supervised DBN regression
  example 227
supervised learning
  about 12
  algorithms 24, 25
  binary classification 18
  data cleaning 19
  metrics 26
  model, evaluating 27
  multiclass classification 18
  multilabel classification 18
  predicting phase 12
  scoring phase 12
  training phase 12
  types 18
  with Python 18
Support vector machines (SVMs) 151

T

tanh function 50, 51
TensorBoard
  about 29, 62
  on XOR problem 63, 64, 65
TensorFlow
  datasets 225

libraries 225
text 94
text classification
　with GloVe 111
time series prediction 130, 133
Toronto Face dataset 152
training set 19
transductive learning 13
transfer learning (TL)
　about 26, 135, 136
　implementing, in PyTorch 139, 142, 144, 145
transformations
　PowerTransformer 23
　QuantileTransformer 23
Turing machine 10

U

undercomplete autooencoders
　about 187
　example 187, 188, 189
　reconstructed images, visualizing 190
　visualization, with TensorBoard 189
Universal Approximation Theorem 22
unsupervised DBN classification
　example 228
unsupervised learning 12

V

VAEs
　about 198
　example 203, 205, 206, 207
　training 201, 202
　using 199, 200
virtual environments 15, 16

W

Wasserstein GANs (WGANs) 157
word embeddings
　about 95, 96
　applications 96
　in Keras 99
　types 96
Word2vec 96

X

XOR problem 55

Y

You Only Look Once (YOLO) 78

Z

zero padding 76

Lightning Source UK Ltd.
Milton Keynes UK
UKHW051919171119
353714UK00010B/279/P